Praise for *Transparent Design in Higher Education Teaching and Leadership*

"The Association of American Colleges & Universities has advocated for higher levels of transparency as a key principle of twenty-first-century general education design. This book provides practical examples on how to turn that vision into practice at institutions and across systems. The Transparency Framework represents a strategy that has the potential to transform siloed student success efforts to scalable and sustainable models for ᴄ⸱⸱ ᵎⁱ equity."—*Tia Brown McNair; Vice President, Offiᵣᵣ ᵣᵣ Student Success; Association of American Colleges &*

"How I wish I had had this book a half century ag career as a college professor. I would have known ₚₐᵣₑₙₜᵎ with my underprepared, first-generation, motivated, ᵣ ₋ₙₜgent, and creative students, in ways that would have made both them and me more successful much sooner and much more intentionally."—*John N. Gardner, Chair and Chief Executive Officer, John N. Gardner Institute for Excellence in Undergraduate Education*

"With the overarching goal of assessment being directly tied to the improvement of student learning, this book reinforces the general idea of the more information a student has about themselves, the way they learn, and the subject being studied, the more successful they will be in achieving academic success. The editors present a process (the Transparency Framework) that includes the who, what, when, where, and why of what students are expected to learn and how a faculty member can help ensure they do. Their research shows that the model is adaptable to every class size and institutional type. While not the proverbial silver bullet, it comes as close in its practical implementation of research-based theories on student learning as I've ever seen."—*Belle Wheelan, President, Southern Association of Colleges and Schools, Commission on Colleges*

"*Transparent Design in Higher Education Teaching and Leadership* brings together evidence and examples of one of the most elegant and transformative ideas I have encountered: revising assignments to clearly include the purpose, task, and criteria fosters student success and contributes to closing achievement gaps. This practical yet visionary volume offers a unique set of resources of special value to educational developers—faculty and staff working to improve higher education from centers for teaching and learning and similar units. With cases that are adaptable to a wide range of institutional settings and goals, this book should be one of the first resources educational developers turn to when designing programs, evaluating impact, and collaborating with institutional leaders."—*Cassandra Volpe Horii*; *Founding Director, Caltech Center for Teaching, Learning, and Outreach; Professional and Organizational Development Network President, 2018–2019*

"Who knew we could enrich and deepen learning by clearly explaining to students what they should focus on and why it matters! This book takes the mystery out of improving learning and teaching by appropriating a powerful idea hiding in plain sight to concentrate student and instructor effort on understandable, purposeful educational tasks adaptable to any classroom, lab, or studio."—*George D. Kuh*; *Chancellor's Professor Emeritus of Higher Education, Indiana University; Founding Director, National Survey of Student Engagement; Cofounder, National Institute on Learning Outcomes Assessment*

TRANSPARENT DESIGN IN HIGHER
EDUCATION TEACHING AND LEADERSHIP

NEW PEDAGOGIES AND PRACTICES FOR TEACHING IN HIGHER EDUCATION SERIES

Series Editor: James Rhem

SoTL in Action
Illuminating Critical Moments of Practice
Edited by Nancy L. Chick

Blended Learning
Across the Disciplines, Across the Academy
Edited by Francine S. Glazer

Clickers in the Classroom
Using Classroom Response Systems to Increase Student Learning
Edited by David S. Goldstein and Peter D. Wallis

Cooperative Learning in Higher Education
Across the Disciplines, Across the Academy
Edited by Barbara Millis

Just-in-Time Teaching
Across the Disciplines, Across the Academy
Edited by Scott Simkins and Mark Maier

Team Teaching
Across the Disciplines, Across the Academy
Edited by Kathryn M. Plank

Using Reflection and Metacognition to Improve Student Learning
Across the Disciplines, Across the Academy
Edited by Matthew Kaplan, Naomi Silver, Danielle LaVaque-Manty, and Deborah Meizlish

TRANSPARENT DESIGN IN HIGHER EDUCATION TEACHING AND LEADERSHIP

A Guide to Implementing the Transparency Framework Institution-Wide to Improve Learning and Retention

Edited by

Mary-Ann Winkelmes, Allison Boye, and Suzanne Tapp

Foreword by Peter Felten and Ashley Finley

STERLING, VIRGINIA

Published by Stylus Publishing, LLC.
22883 Quicksilver Drive
Sterling, Virginia 20166-2019

Library of Congress Cataloging-in-Publication Data

Names: Winkelmes, Mary-Ann, 1964- editor. | Boye, Allison, 1977- editor. | Tapp, Suzanne, 1966- editor.
Title: Transparent design in higher education teaching and learning : a guide to implementing the transparency framework institution-wide to improve learning and retention / edited by Mary-Ann Winkelmes, Allison Boye, and Suzanne Tapp ; foreword by Peter Felten and Ashley Finley.
Description: First edition. | Sterling, Va. : Stylus Publishing, 2019. | Includes index. | Includes bibliographical references.
Identifiers: LCCN 2018043726 (print) | LCCN 2018055456 (ebook) | ISBN 9781620368244 (Library networkable e-edition) | ISBN 9781620368251 (Consumer e-edition) | ISBN 9781620368237 (pbk. : alk. paper) | ISBN 9781620368220 (cloth : alk. paper)
Subjects: LCSH: Education, Higher--Aims and objectives--United States. | College teaching--United States. | Teacher-student relationships--United States. | Communication in education--United States. | Educational leadership--United States. | College dropouts--United States--Prevention.
Classification: LCC LA227.4 (ebook) | LCC LA227.4 .T736 2019 (print) | DDC 378.1/25--dc23
LC record available at https://lccn.loc.gov/2018043726

13-digit ISBN: 978-1-62036-822-0 (cloth)
13-digit ISBN: 978-1-62036-823-7 (paperback)
13-digit ISBN: 978-1-62036-824-4 (library networkable e-edition)
13-digit ISBN: 978-1-62036-825-1 (consumer e-edition)

Printed in the United States of America

All first editions printed on acid-free paper
that meets the American National Standards Institute
Z39-48 Standard.

Bulk Purchases
Quantity discounts are available for use in workshops and for staff development.
Call 1-800-232-0223

First Edition, 2019

CONTENTS

FOREWORD

Great ideas are often sparked by the simplest of questions. More than 20 years ago, Mary-Ann Winkelmes asked colleagues: "If you could change one thing about your teaching that would best improve your students' learning experiences, what would that single change be?" This book, and the Transparency in Learning and Teaching (TILT) initiative more broadly, are the fruit of that single seed.

Winkelmes's question is powerful in part because it focuses our critical attention on the small yet significant steps we can make—and sustain—to improve learning for all of our students. A movement advocating small enhancements in teaching has gained considerable traction of late, thanks to books including Lang's (2016) *Small Teaching* and Chambliss and Takacs's (2014) *How College Works*. TILT resonates with that chorus, but it also echoes a broader reform movement that focuses on "positive deviance" (e.g., Gawande, 2007) that takes an assets-based, community-oriented approach to improvement. TILT encourages faculty to build on the existing strengths of their assignments, and to do so by collaborating in a wide range of settings—from formal faculty development workshops and informal learning communities to campus-wide initiatives and multi-institutional partnerships.

This book describes and illustrates what is possible when we are as transparent as possible with the purposes, tasks, and criteria of the work we assign our students. This book also describes and illustrates what is possible when we do this work together with our colleagues—and also with our students—to improve not only individual assignments but also entire courses, curricula, and institutions.

Being transparent might seem simple, but it's both vexing and essential. As disciplinary experts, we have so internalized the knowledge, language, and expectations of our fields that we often don't realize when we are being unnecessarily unclear. We know *why* we assign specific work to our students, but do we explain our purposes to students in ways that they understand and value? We know *what* we want them to do, but do we explain those tasks to students so that they know what they need to do to succeed? And we know *how* to evaluate the quality of that work, but do we help students know how they can monitor and improve their own performance?

Asking these questions is *not* a call for simplifying our assignments and spoon-feeding our students. Instead, it is a call for unlocking our disciplinary and pedagogical codes so that all of our students understand our expectations and aspirations for their work. By being transparent, we can *raise* our standards with the confidence that the work students do will reveal the quality of their learning rather than their capacity to sort out our implicit assumptions.

Though much time has passed since the earliest seeds of the TILT framework were planted, the presentation of findings and lessons learned in this book are particularly timely for everyone involved in teaching, faculty development, and assessment in higher education. The students arriving today on college campuses—whether two- or four-year, public or private—are more diverse than ever. The traditionally aged students in higher education today increasingly are coming from historically underrepresented minority groups, and they are the first in their families to attend college (National Center for Educational Statistics, 2017). At the same time, greater numbers of older (i.e., nontraditional) adults are seeking a postsecondary credential (National Center for Educational Statistics, 2017). Additionally, approximately one-third of college students will transfer at least once, making movement among postsecondary institutions an expected norm (Lederman, 2017). Today's college students are also reporting increasingly higher levels of anxiety and stress (American College Health Association, 2017). Our students are changing, so our pedagogies and institutions must adapt to uphold our standards while we meet their evolving needs.

In this dynamic environment, the TILT framework is a valuable tool for fostering equity of outcomes for students' success. TILT enables faculty to actively engage students from a spectrum of backgrounds in challenging and meaningful academic work. TILT is also a flexible tool for faculty developers to use in consultations, workshops, and (with this book) reading groups. Transparent assignments cultivate deep learning from all students, and also boost all students' sense of belonging in higher education. TILT is precisely the type of asset-based approach called for in the book *Becoming a Student-Ready College* (McNair, Albertine, Cooper, McDonald, & Major, 2016). Such an orientation rests on the assumption that each student possesses strengths and capabilities to learn, and that faculty and institutions should design courses and curriculum to tap into each student's potential.

One of the distinct benefits of TILT is that it focuses the conversation around equity and student success at the most granular and fundamental levels of faculty action. Like amino acids to protein molecules, assignments are the building blocks of every course. Changing the way faculty develop and design these building blocks can fundamentally reset the way that students achieve intended outcomes. We often talk about the need to help students find the meaning in our assignments and learning outcomes. Yet the key to students' discovery often involves helping faculty to articulate and clarify these connections first. The TILT framework enables faculty to make plain the purposes, tasks, and criteria of assignment design, while also encouraging critical reflection on the role of pedagogical practices to support students' demonstrated learning.

No matter how effective a single assignment is, a student's success in college hinges on more than one assignment or even a single course. Most campuses have adopted broad learning outcomes that speak to a range of intellectual, practical, and civic capacities that students should acquire by the time they *leave* college. Each assignment, therefore, is not only a building block for another assignment aligned with the same outcome in the same course but also a building block for the entire curriculum. This level of scaffolding across assignments *and* outcomes throughout the curriculum is often completely invisible to students and often befuddling to faculty who are trying on their own to help students reach those outcomes. In faculty development programming, and in departmental and institutional planning, the TILT framework provides a means to clarify and make visible learning outcomes for both students and faculty.

As part of assessment processes today, courses are often tracked and connected with program-specific and institutional-level outcomes through curriculum maps. Equally useful for tracking and measuring outcomes, particularly for students, are *assignment maps* that might underlie curriculum maps as a way of showing exactly where outcomes are being targeted within each course, as well as across the academic program. The TILT framework provides the essential foundation for creating such a map. Imagine a campus in which such an assignment map is the guiding star for students, faculty, faculty developers, and academic administrators. This would provide everyone at the institution—including the students themselves—a road map composed of each transparently designed assignment to follow students' progressive demonstration of their twenty-first-century skills and abilities.

No one book can fully respond to the question that began this foreword and launched the TILT initiative. Learning is too complex and too mercurial for silver bullets or a single framework. But *Transparent Design in Higher Education Teaching and Leadership* brings us significantly closer to an answer.

Peter Felten
Center for Engaged Learning
Elon University

Ashley Finley
Office of the President
Association of American Colleges & Universities

References

American College Health Association (ACHA)/National College Health Assessment. (2017). *Undergraduate student reference group: Executive summary*, p. 13. Available from https://www.acha.org/documents/ncha/NCHA-II_FALL_2017_REFERENCE_GROUP_EXECUTIVE_SUMMARY.pdf

Chambliss, D., & Takacs, C. (2014). *How college works*. Cambridge, MA: Harvard University Press.

Gawande, A. (2007). *Better: A surgeon's notes on performance*. New York, NY: Picador.

Lang, J. (2016). *Small teaching: Everyday lessons from the science of learning*. San Francisco, CA: Jossey-Bass.

Lederman, D. (2017, September 14). The Bermuda Triangle of credit transfer. *Inside Higher Ed*. Available from https://www.insidehighered.com/news/2017/09/14/reports-highlight-woes-faced-one-third-all-college-students-who-transfer

McNair, T., Albertine, S., Cooper, M., McDonald, N., & Major, T. (2016). *Becoming a student-ready college: A new culture of leadership for student success*. San Francisco, CA: Jossey-Bass.

National Center for Educational Statistics (NCES). (2017). *2017 fast facts*. Available from https://nces.ed.gov/fastfacts/display.asp?id=372

PREFACE

I like to think I coined the phrase *embedded assessment*. I probably didn't. Surely, someone else put those words together earlier in the conversation about the improvement of teaching at the college and university level. But the idea of embedded assessment has had such a powerful hold on my mind and my eager desire to assist the improvement of college teaching that I've clung to it and advocated it in multiple ways in *The National Teaching & Learning FORUM*. To my mind—although it hasn't embraced *my* phrase—Mary-Ann Winkelmes's important work with the Transparency Project fulfills the ambition for college teaching I thought the phrase conveyed.

As Winkelmes announces at the outset, the foundation of the project for more than a decade has been

> the belief that the most important change any teacher could make was a small adjustment (or "tilt") rather than a massive revision—to offer students an honest look at the teacher's rationale for what students are required to do, with the goal of boosting all students' self-awareness of their learning processes. (p. 3, this volume)

Transparency means letting students in on what they're being asked to do and why they're being asked to do it—in other words, what they can expect to learn from doing it. The skills development in making these questions open ones that faculty and students are exploring together seems to me the essence of the self-awareness I've called embedded assessment and that we also talk about as *metacognition*.

The genius and great utility of what Winkelmes and her colleagues have found and proven over the last decade is that it takes but a small change to begin to see substantial rewards in increased student learning, especially for historically underserved student populations. In a month-long residence on Winkelmes's campus at the University of Nevada, Las Vegas, in 2014, I witnessed transparent revisions to assignments and entire syllabi in practice. The heartening thing to me was that these changes did not have the quality of things faculty did *to* students or, in a way, even *for* students. They were things faculty began that infused vital energy into a teaching/learning dynamic between themselves and their students. It brought them closer together, made them partners in the grand enterprise of learning. Who wouldn't want to teach in such an environment?

And what if the transparency ethic began to be applied more widely? What if it escaped the classroom and became the working norm in higher education from the presidential decisions at the top on down through the ranks of deans, vice presidents, and others leading and administering the endeavor? What might the effect of this simple purpose-task-criteria paradigm be? It may seem like a new idea, a new twist on best practices, but I think it is actually a very old idea, the idea that openness and clear, straight talk will almost always lead to better ends than more complicated pathways. In a way, transparency is Ockham's razor.

And so, having witnessed the enormous positive impact of this approach, it's an honor to bring the Transparency Project before more readers.

James Rhem
Executive Editor
The National Teaching & Learning FORUM

ACKNOWLEDGMENTS

This collection could not have come together without the many voices and contributions of our colleagues. We extend our heartfelt thanks to the Harvard University faculty seminar participants at the Derek Bok Center for Teaching and Learning, who helped catalyze the idea of transparent instruction, and the early testers from a faculty seminar at the University of Chicago's Center for Teaching Excellence, who constructed the first Transparency in Learning and Teaching in Higher Education (TILT Higher Ed) Survey; to the National Institute on Learning Outcomes Assessment colleagues who offered support and encouragement in the early stages and collaboration thereafter; to the Association of American Colleges & Universities colleagues who supported the project as part of the Liberal Education and America's Promise initiative and who collaborated on the 2015–2016 national study at minority-serving institutions; to the multitude of faculty members from institutions across the United States who were willing to jump right in and try out the Transparency Framework in their classrooms and ask their students what difference it made, and who then shared their experiences with us; to the TILT research team members who analyzed data and refined the study, especially Matt Bernacki, Jeffrey Butler, Celeste Calkins, Kathy Oleson, Dan Richard, and Carolyn Weiss; to the Applied Analysis colleagues, especially Jeremy Aguero, who keep the TILT database running; to the faculty developers and Professional and Organizational Development (POD) colleagues who got excited about TILT and decided to include it in programming at their own centers for teaching and learning (CTLs) and who collaborated to share their practices and resources with others; to the John N. Gardner Institute colleagues who advocate transparent instruction in gateway courses; to the administrators at the University of Illinois, Urbana-Champaign, where TILT was first housed, and the University of Nevada, Las Vegas, its second home, and Brandeis University, its home now; and to those across the United States who supported the idea for their own campuses; and, of course, to the tens of thousands of students who willingly shared their views about their learning experiences with the hope that they would inform better teaching practices. Their expertise and reflections about their learning have already helped thousands of college and university teachers to improve teaching and learning. We hope they will help many more through the examples, lessons, and practices this collection offers.

We would also like to thank Peter Felten and Ashley Finley for their foreword that highlights the important contributions this book makes in a broad, higher education context. We are grateful to our colleagues John Gardner, Cassandra Horii, George Kuh, Tia McNair, and Belle Wheelan, who provided notes for the back cover. We appreciate James Rhem's unflagging confidence in this work throughout the TILT project's growth and the writing of this book. Finally, we are deeply grateful to our spouses Dan Hamilton, David Faulkner, and Byron Tapp, for their encouragement of this project.

INTRODUCTION

The Story of TILT and Its Emerging Uses in Higher Education

Mary-Ann Winkelmes

The primary goal of the Transparency in Learning and Teaching in Higher Education (TILT Higher Ed) initiative is as urgent as it is simple: to make learning processes explicit and equitably accessible for all students. Transparent teaching and learning methods focus on the subject matter (the what) of a course as much as the why and the how—why teachers choose to manipulate students' learning experiences as they do, how students acquire and master the course's important lessons, and how the skills and knowledge they gain will continue to be relevant for students. Transparent instruction involves faculty/student discussion about several important aspects of academic work *before* students undertake that work: (a) the purpose of the work, including the knowledge that will be gained from completing it, the skills to be practiced and acquired, and how students might use those skills and that knowledge in their lives beyond college; (b) the tasks involved; and (c) the expected criteria and multiple examples of what those criteria look like in practice in the form of real-world work samples in the specific academic discipline. TILT Higher Ed began two decades ago with the belief that the most important change any teacher could make was a small adjustment (or "tilt") rather than a massive revision—to offer students an honest look at the teacher's rationale for what students are required to do, with the goal of boosting all students' self-awareness of their learning processes. Since that time, transparent instruction has demonstrably increased several important predictors of college student success: academic confidence, sense of belonging in college, metacognitive self-awareness of skill development, and persistence (Winkelmes et al., 2016; Winkelmes, Calkins, & Yu, forthcoming). Importantly, those gains are enduring and equitable, and although they are statistically significant for all students we've studied, underserved students experience the greatest benefits. This chapter shares the path that TILT Higher Ed has traveled from the identification of transparency as an intentional, inclusive teaching strategy to its implementation as a high-impact and equitable teaching practice, to its use as a framework for collaboration and strategic planning by faculty developers and teaching and learning centers, to its application by higher education leaders in cross-institutional and national initiatives focused on faculty development and student success. The chapter also reviews current research on how transparent instruction benefits student success equitably.

Following are several reasons for the growing popularity of transparent instruction across the United States and internationally:

1. Transparent instruction usually requires a small change to teaching practice, and it offers substantial gains for students. Just two transparently designed assignments in an academic term can offer significant benefits for student learning. To make an assignment more transparent (accessible, relevant) for students is relatively easy, consistent with most teachers' goals for student learning, and takes little time.

2. Transparent instruction is an equitable teaching practice and an instrument of social justice that can help to close college achievement gaps. Historically underserved students benefit to a greater degree from transparent instruction, although the gains are statistically significant for all students we have studied.

3. The benefits that students receive from transparent instruction persist for at least two years and perhaps longer.

4. By implementing transparent instruction faculty can contribute directly to institutional and national student success goals that have felt disconnected from their daily work. Student success initiatives often involve nonteaching administrators and staff in implementing financial assistance, tutoring, or advising programs, or targeted financial assistance. Faculty can increase the effectiveness of student success efforts directly by incorporating just one or two transparently designed exercises or assignments in their work with students.

5. The three-part Transparency Framework (purpose-task-criteria) can strengthen and support planning by higher education leaders of innovative projects that support the success of students and faculty.

These characteristics of transparent assignment design make it a powerful tool in combating inequity in students' educational experiences. Underserved students (underrepresented African American, Hispanic, Native American, and Pacific Islander students; students whose family incomes are in the bottom quartile; and first-generation college students comprise the majority of incoming college students in the United States, and they are about half as likely to complete a college degree in four years as their White and Asian classmates who are not first-generation students and whose family incomes are above the bottom quartile (Ishitani, 2006; Tough, 2014; U.S. Department of Education, 2014). This unjust situation for new-majority students presents an equity crisis in higher education. Even high-achieving high school students can struggle in college, largely because they have no prior exposure to thinking and working like an expert in an academic discipline (Colomb & Williams, 1993; National Research Council, 2000). How might a new-majority college student approach her first chemistry lab report or art history paper if she has never seen what a successful chemistry lab report or art history paper looks like? High school training might have prepared her to use reliable evidence to support her hypotheses or ideas. But how would she determine an effective way to use a chemical reaction or a fifteenth-century painting as evidence? Without access to family members or friends or advisers who know what that sort of academic work looks like, or without the expertise or available time to consult other resources for the needed information, this student will flounder. Encountering a gatekeeper teaching approach in her first year will further threaten her success. Gatekeeper teaching practices deliver subject matter only, withholding information about how to understand and apply it, in order to advance those students already skilled at learning how to learn the material while discouraging and even failing those students without access to "how to" information. Such an approach to teaching is no longer sustainable for the new-majority college student in the United States. Transparent instructional practices provide our chemistry and art history student and all her classmates with the "how to" information they need to succeed as they begin their academic work. Transparent assignments engage students with teachers in discussing the purposes, tasks, and criteria for the work before students begin, locating all students as close as possible to the same starting line.

The Beginnings of TILT Higher Ed

To help set the stage for understanding transparency, its foundational concepts, and the context of this book, it is worth considering the history of the TILT project and the current research stemming from it. My work on transparent teaching and learning has its roots in a teaching seminar I offered at Harvard University's Bok Center for Teaching and Learning in 1996–1997. Faculty and instructors in the seminar discussed ways to share with students the rationale behind our teaching choices, using metaphors like the Wizard of Oz pulling back a curtain to reveal hidden manipulations or seeing how the sausage was made. But these metaphors held negative connotations of undesirable disguised components that our teaching plans didn't contain.

Transparency was the best word we could find to describe how we wanted students to understand our teaching plans. We wanted to remove any mystery they felt about their learning experiences in our courses.

The TILT project began in 2008 when I asked a group of faculty in a teaching seminar at the University of Chicago's Center for Teaching and Learning, "If you could change one thing about your teaching that would best improve your students' learning experiences, what would that single change be?" The group said they would need more information before they could offer a satisfying answer: were the students aware of the skills they were developing in the course, was the course increasing their confidence to continue in the discipline, were they becoming better judges of the reliability of new information in the field, did the course help them to discuss ideas with others and welcome alternative views? Their list of questions grew to become the very first TILT Higher Ed Survey.

Intended as a tool to provide faculty the information they needed to inform changes to teaching practice, the TILT Survey soon grew from a small pilot project to a much larger one. Data from over 15,000 students surveyed had the power to do even more than inform individual teachers' improvements. Patterns emerged that suggested which teaching changes could benefit various students across disciplines, geographic regions, and types of postsecondary institutions. We explored a variety of teaching strategies, listed in Figure I.1.

Research and Evidence on the Impact of Transparent Instruction

Transparent assignment design seemed a good choice to study on a large scale because initial testing showed it was almost equally helpful across disciplines and for students at all levels of expertise (Winkelmes, 2013). It is a small and relatively simple change that many faculty accept as consistent with their teaching goals, it can be aimed at introductory courses across the disciplines, and it can be tested with an objective measure of success available in the form of student retention rates just one term or one year later.

A national study with the Association of American Colleges & Universities (AAC&U) funded by TG Philanthropy in 2014–2015 demonstrated that transparent instruction about problem-centered assignments has significant, equitable benefits for students; a separate University of Nevada, Las Vegas, study indicated those benefits are long-term. The AAC&U study identified transparent instruction as an easily adoptable teaching method that produces learning benefits already linked with student success (Winkelmes et al., 2016). Applying transparency to assignments demonstrably increased several important success predictors for students: confidence, belonging,

Figure I.1. Transparent teaching methods.

Transparent teaching methods[a] help students understand *how* and *why* they are learning course content in particular ways by focusing on the purposes, tasks, and criteria for their academic work. This list of contexts for transparent instruction is adapted frequently as instructors identify further ways to use the purpose-task-critera framework to provide information to students about learning and teaching practices.

Discuss assignments' learning goals and design rationale before students begin each assignment
- Chart on one page the skills students will practice in each assignment.
- Begin each assignment by defining the learning benefits to students (skills practiced, content knowledge gained, the tasks to be completed, the criteria for success).
- See Transparent Assignment Templates: for faculty; for students [Figures I.2 and I.3].
- See examples of less transparent and more transparent assignments.
- Provide criteria for success in advance and offer multiple examples. Invite students to indicate how criteria apply to examples and discuss.

Invite students to participate in class planning, agenda construction
- Give students an advanced agenda (two or three main topics) one or two days before class and ask them to identify related subtopics, examples, or applications they wish to learn about.
- Review the agenda at the outset of each class meeting, including students' subtopics.
- Explicitly evaluate progress toward fulfilling the agenda at conclusion of each class meeting.
- In large courses, a class committee gathers and contributes students' subtopics to agendas.
- Inform students about ideas and questions to be discussed in upcoming class meetings.

Gauge students' understanding during class via peer work on questions that require students to apply concepts you've taught
- Create scenarios/applications to test understanding of key concepts during class.
- Allow discussion in pairs, instructor's feedback, and more discussion.
- Provide explicit assessment of students' understanding, with further explanation if needed, before moving on to teach the next concept.

Explicitly connect "how people learn" data with course activities when students struggle at difficult transition points
- Offer research-based explanations about concepts or tasks that students often struggle to master in your discipline.

Engage students in applying the grading criteria that you'll use on their work
- Share criteria for success and examples of good work, then invite students to apply these criteria to drafts of a peer's work and to their own work.

(Continues)

Figure I.1. (*Continued*)

Debrief graded tests and assignments in class

- Help students identify patterns in their returned, graded work: what kinds of test questions were missed; what types of weaknesses characterize the assigned work?
- Ask students to review any changes or revisions they made and whether these resulted in improvements or not.
- Ask students to record the process steps they used to prepare for the exam or complete the assignment and to analyze which parts of the process were efficient, effective, inefficient, or ineffective.
- Offer running commentary on class discussions to indicate what modes of thought or disciplinary methods are in use.
- Explicitly identify what types of questioning/thinking and what skills of the discipline your students are using in each class meeting.
- Invite students to describe the steps in their thought process for addressing/ solving a problem.
- Engage students in evaluating which types of thinking are most effective for addressing the issues in each class discussion.

---

a. Examples of these strategies are found online at TILTHigherEd.org under "TILT Higher Ed Examples and Resources" (Winkelmes et al., n.d.).

Note. Reproduced with permission of Mary-Ann Winkelmes.

and metacognitive awareness of skill development. The benefits for students were statistically significant, with even larger gains for first-generation, low-income, and underrepresented college students. The faculty teams from each school later published studies and reflections on the benefits for themselves and their students at their respective institutions, and AAC&U colleagues published on lessons learned and the impact on students' work samples scored using an AAC&U Valid Assessment of Learning in Undergraduate Education (VALUE) rubric for problem-solving (McNair, 2016).

Tia McNair and Ashley Finley at the AAC&U were my coinvestigators in the national study. We intentionally selected a group of seven minority-serving institutions (MSIs) that were broadly representative of U.S. institutions of higher education, so that people viewing the results would see a collaborator in the group with whom they could identify. The schools ranged in size from small to very large; in geographical distribution across the United States; in locations in urban and rural settings, including both public and private institutions; in type, including two-year, four-year, and research universities; and in type of MSI including Native American–serving and Hispanic-serving institutions as well as historically Black colleges and universities.

The project included 1,180 students and 35 faculty. Each instructor taught 2 simultaneous sections of the same course and agreed to teach 1 as a control group and the other as an intervention group in which they would revise 2 take-home assignments to make them more transparent (accessible, relevant, problem-centered). We required only 2 transparently designed assignments

Figure I.2. Transparent Assignment Framework for faculty.

Transparent Assignment Template

This template can be used as a guide for developing, explaining, and discussing class activities and out-of-class assignments. Making these aspects of each course activity or assignment explicitly clear to students has demonstrably enhanced students' learning in a national study.[a]

Assignment Name
Due date:

PURPOSE: *Define the learning objectives, in language and terms that help students recognize how this assignment will benefit their learning. Indicate how these are connected with institutional learning outcomes, and how the specific knowledge and skills involved in this assignment will be important in students' lives beyond the contexts of this assignment, this course, and this college.*

<u>Skills:</u> The purpose of this assignment is to help you practice the following skills that are essential to your success in this course/in school/in this field/in professional life beyond school:

> *Terms from Bloom's <u>Taxonomy of Educational Objectives</u> may help you explain these skills in language students will understand. Listed from cognitively simple to most complex, these skills are:*

- understanding basic disciplinary knowledge and methods/tools
- applying basic disciplinary knowledge/tools to problem-solving in a similar but unfamiliar context
- analyzing
- synthesizing
- judging/evaluating and selecting best solutions
- creating/inventing a new interpretation, product, theory

<u>Knowledge:</u> This assignment will also help you to become familiar with the following important content knowledge in this discipline:

- . . .
- . . .

TASK: *Define what activities the student should do/perfom. "Question cues" from this chart might be helpful: www.asainstitute.org/conference2013/handouts/20-Bloom-Question-Cues-Chart.pdf. List any steps or guidelines, or a recommended sequence for the students' efforts. Specify any extraneous mistakes to be avoided. If there are sound pedagogical reasons for withholding information about how to do the assignment, protect students' confidence and sense of belonging in college with a purpose statement something like this: "The purpose of this assignment is for you to struggle and feel confused while you invent and test your own approach for addressing the problem."*

(Continues)

Figure I.2. (*Continued*)

> **CRITERIA FOR SUCCESS:**
> *Define the characteristics of the finished product. Provide multiple examples of what these characteristics look like in real-world practice, to encourage students' creativity and reduce their incentive to copy any one example too closely. Engage students in analyzing multiple examples of real-world work before the students begin their own work on the assignment. Discuss how excellent work differs from adequate work. This enables students to evaluate the quality of their own efforts while they are working, and to judge the success of their completed work. It is often useful to provide or compile with students a checklist of characteristics of successful work. Students can also use the checklist to provide feedback on peers' coursework. Indicate whether this task/product will be graded and/or how it factors into the student's overall grade for the course. Later, asking students to reflect and comment on their completed, graded work allows them to focus on changes to their learning strategies that might improve their future work.*

© 2013 Mary-Ann Winkelmes. *a*. See Winkelmes (2013); Winkelmes et al. (2016).
Note. Reproduced with permission of Mary-Ann Winkelmes.

because we wanted to see how small a change could produce significant benefits for students' learning. We avoided a rigid protocol for the revisions, recognizing that future instructors reading our study would be most likely to try transparent instruction if we measured what happened when faculty implemented transparent instruction at their own discretion in a way consistent with their teaching practice. We offered the Transparency Framework (Figure I.2) to faculty to guide their implementation of transparent instruction, along with a workshop in which they collaborated to offer feedback on drafts of the revised, more transparent assignments. Finally, we offered the participants a checklist for designing transparent assignments (see Figure 2.3) and a follow-up webinar session to support their work to revise a second assignment.

At the beginning of the term, we gathered students' views (using an online TILT Higher Ed presurvey) about their academic confidence and their mastery of a group of skills that many colleges and universities include among their institutional learning outcomes, and that employers prioritize (Hart, 2013, 2015). This survey established baseline equivalence at the beginning of term between the students who received the transparent treatment and those who did not in regard to their academic confidence and their self-described skill mastery (Winkelmes et al., 2016, Figure 5). At the end of the term, students who received more transparency (based on nine questions from the online TILT Higher Ed End-of-Term Survey that triangulated around the three concepts of purpose, task, and criteria) reported significantly larger gains in three areas that are important predictors of student success: (a) academic confidence, (b) sense of belonging, and (c) awareness of their mastery of the skills that employers value most when hiring (TILT Survey, 2015–2016). Important studies have already connected academic confidence and sense of belonging with students' greater persistence and higher grades (Aronson, Fried, & Good, 2002; Paunesku et al., 2015; Walton & Cohen, 2011). Scholars have identified metacognition as an essential learning skill (National Research Council, 2000; Wang, Haertel, & Walberg, 1994), and recent national surveys identify the skills that employers value most when hiring new employees (Hart Research Associates, 2013, 2015). Although the benefits for all students in the aggregate who received more transparency were statistically significant, the benefits for first-generation, low-income, and underrepresented students were greater, with a medium-to-large magnitude of effect.

Students who receive transparent instruction experience long-term benefits, according to a separate study at UNLV (Winkelmes, Calkins, & Yu, forthcoming). Further, those long-term gains appear to be greater for first-generation and low-income students of all ethnicities, just as the short-term gains were greater for underserved students in the AAC&U study. At UNLV, a majority of undergraduate students belong to the "underserved" cohort of either ethnically underrepresented or first-generation (in their family to attend college) or low-income students, or a combination of these (UNLV Data Warehouse, 2018). *U.S. News* ranked UNLV in first place for campus ethnic diversity at national universities in 2017 (*U.S. News and World Report*, 2017). The UNLV study tracked annual retention (re-enrollment in college) rates for a group of 870 UNLV undergraduate students who received transparent instruction in at least 1 course when they were first-time, full-time, first-year students in the fall term of 2015. One year later, those students were retained (still enrolled as full-time students at UNLV) at a rate 15.52% higher than the rest of their cohort. Two years later, those students who had received transparent instruction when they were first-time, full-time, first-year students persisted as full-time students at UNLV at a rate 13.92% greater than the rest of their cohort. Some underserved students benefited to a greater degree. For example, the mean retention gains for the group of 361 low-income students who received transparent instruction in their first year were 19.74% greater than low-income students in the rest of their cohort after 1 year and 19.52% greater than low-income students in the rest of their cohort after 2 years (Winkelmes et al., forthcoming). As a result of these findings, new faculty at UNLV receive information about transparent assignment design, all new UNLV students receive a student version of the Transparent Assignment Template from the university registrar, and the university's minimum requirements for syllabi specify that syllabi include a statement encouraging students to seek transparent instruction, with a link to the online Transparent Assignment Framework for Students (Figure I.3) (UNLV, Office of the Vice President and Provost, 2017).

The social justice appeal of transparent instruction has helped to increase its popularity. Transparent instruction is an inclusive, equitable teaching

Figure I.3. Transparent Assignment Framework for students.

The Unwritten Rules:

Decode Your Assignments and Decipher What's Expected of You

Did you know?

- UNLV researchers demonstrated in a national study that transparency around academic assignments enhances students' success at statistically significant levels, with even greater gains for historically underserved students (Winkelmes et al., 2016).
- When faculty make the purpose, tasks, and criteria of an academic assignment clear before students begin to work on it, students are more likely to experience greater academic success with that assignment, developing the knowledge, disposition, and skills necessary to succeed both at school and in life (in comparison to when students experience less clarity around purpose, tasks, and criteria for their academic work (Winkelmes et al., 2016).
- For UNLV students, benefits also included a significantly higher rate of retention (returning to college each fall term) up to two years after experiencing transparent instruction (Gianoutsos & Winkelmes, 2016; Winkelmes et al., forthcoming 2018).
- An inclusive learning environment benefits all students and offers more equitable learning opportunities for underserved students. Research on student learning links college students' academic confidence and sense of belonging with higher GPAs, persistence, and retention rates (Walton and Cohen, 2011).
- College students increased their test scores when supported by a system that advocated the belief that intelligence is not fixed but rather malleable. A year later, these students were 80% less likely to drop out of college (Aronson et al, 2002).

WHAT STUDENTS CAN DO:

Before you begin working on an assignment or class activity, ask the instructor to help you understand the following. (Bring this document to help frame the conversation.)

Purpose
- Skills you'll practice by doing this assignment
- Content knowledge you'll gain from doing this assignment
- How you can use these in your life beyond the context of this course, in and beyond college

Task
- What to do
- How to do it (Are there recommended steps? What roadblocks/mistakes should you avoid?)

Criteria
- **Checklist** (Are you on the right track? How to know you're doing what's expected?)
- **Multiple real-world examples of successful work, discussed in class** (What's good/better/best about these examples? Use the checklist to identify the successful parts.)

Note. Reproduced with permission of Mary-Ann Winkelmes.

practice that's relatively easy for faculty to adopt because it is consistent with their goals for high-quality learning by an increasingly diverse population of students. The Transparency Framework is intentionally adaptable to a broad spectrum of teaching and learning styles. Because even a small amount of transparent instruction is beneficial for students, teachers can begin with small adjustments to their existing practice and materials and witness benefits for their students almost immediately. Teachers have observed a cumulative effect of higher quality student work when they create additional transparent assignments, class activities, and teaching materials over time. Instructors working individually as well as those working in teams or groups have witnessed that transparent instruction not only increases student success but also benefits faculty by reducing student procrastination and last-minute requests for help, faculty grading time, and later questions or challenges about grades (Copeland, Winkelmes, & Gunawan, 2018; Howard, Winkelmes, & Shegog, 2019; Winkelmes et al., 2015).

For any institution seeking to right the inequities in college students' educational experiences, focusing transparent instruction on assignments in introductory courses can help to increase underserved students' success, especially in their first year of college (when the greatest numbers drop out).

Overview of Chapters

Part One of this book focuses on the fundamentals of transparent design. Chapters 1 and 2 discuss why and how transparent instruction works and suggest strategies for instructors who wish to adopt it. Chapter 3 offers insights from the faculty perspective, directly from instructors who implemented the Transparency Framework in their own classrooms. The chapters that follow describe additional strategies for applying the Transparency Framework to promote equitable instruction and transparent leadership in higher education contexts beyond assignments.

Part Two focuses specifically on the work of educational developers. Chapter 4 outlines the variety of ways that centers for teaching and learning (CTLs) have adopted the framework, and chapters 5, 6, and 7 offer additional details on applications for CTLs, which include organizing discipline-based or cross-disciplinary teams of instructors in applying and sharing best practices, framing individual consultations, focusing new programming efforts, integrating data collection into scholarship of teaching and learning (SoTL) projects, and guiding curricular revision. The framework can also elevate faculty reflections about teaching (see chapters 3 and 10).

Part Three of this book focuses on even broader implementation of transparency across higher education. Faculty developers have used the purpose-task-criteria framework to unite multiple campus collaborators around a common language and shared strategic plan (chapter 8). The framework can also help to connect the daily work of faculty with the learning goals that departments, programs, and institutions hope to demonstrate, even when those goals are defined in broad terms—for example, across a state system of community and technical colleges (chapter 9). Following the models of the AAC&U and UNLV studies, more schools are now combining TILT survey data (measuring predictors of student success) with institutional data about retention, grades, and demographics to demonstrate the ways that faculty development programs contribute to institutional goals (chapters 8 and 10). Communications with institutional review boards (IRBs) across the country have helped TILT Higher Ed to revise its protocols to help remove barriers for faculty, faculty developers, and institutional analysis staff to join large SoTL projects (chapters 7, 10, and 11). Insights and input from many IRBs have enabled data analysis of the impact of large-scale implementation of transparent instruction on student learning and student retention through collaborations with state colleges and universities in California, Florida, Indiana, Tennessee, Texas, and Washington, as well as smaller institutions of higher education across the United States.

Some of our authors worked with teams of teachers across multiple institutions who adopted transparent instruction in projects aimed to shrink achievement gaps at their institutions or across their state systems (chapters 9–11). The framework of purpose-task-criteria can even help to unite faculty with leaders at the institutional and national levels around scaling up student success and assessing students' learning. For example, using the same framework to describe the purposes, tasks, and criteria for student learning at the national, institutional, program, departmental, course, and assignment levels provides a direct and tangible link between the everyday work of faculty and the long-term student learning goals that institutions and national organizations promote. Thus the TILT framework can address two great needs in higher education assessment that the National Institute for Learning Outcomes Assessment has identified: more faculty involvement and a sustained culture of assessment (Kuh, Jankowski, Ikenberry, & Kinzie, 2014). As chapter 12 discusses, the framework offers a simple tool for aligning individual assignments and academic work samples with the educational goals of teachers, departments, programs, and institutions and ultimately the desired learning outcomes of national organizations like the Degree Qualifications Profile advocated by the Lumina Foundation or the Essential Learning Outcomes recommended by AAC&U. The Transparency Framework can enrich national conversations about student learning and how to assess it.

The many examples in this book encourage readers to find further applications of the Transparency Framework by making small changes to practice that can offer large benefits in support of increasingly equitable opportunities for success in higher education. Toward that end, all TILT Higher Ed materials and resources are available online at TILTHigherEd.org and are designed to be copied, printed, distributed, adapted, and shared (with citation according to the terms of the Creative Commons Attribution-NonCommercial-ShareAlike 4.0 international license).

References

Aronson, J., Fried, C. B., & Good, C. (2002). Reducing the effects of stereotype threat on African American college students by shaping theories of intelligence. *Journal of Experimental Social Psychology, 38,* 113–125.

Colomb, G., & Williams, J. (1993). Why what you don't know won't help you. *Research in the Teaching of English, 23*(3), 252–264.

Copeland, D. E., Winkelmes, M. A., & Gunawan, K. (2018). Helping students by using transparent writing assignments. In T. L. Kuther (Ed.), *Integrating writing into the psychology course: Strategies for promoting student skills* (pp. 26–37). Society for the Teaching of Psychology. Available from http://teachpsych.org/ebooks/integratingwriting

Gianoutsos, D., & Winkelmes, M. A. (2016, Spring). Navigating with transparency. *Proceedings of the Pennsylvania Association of Developmental Educators,* (pp. 15–19). Available from http://www.pade-pa.org/annual-conference/conference-proceedings

Hart Research Associates. (2013). *It takes more than a major: Employer priorities for college learning and student success.* Washington DC: Association of American Colleges & Universities.

Hart Research Associates. (2015). *Falling short? College learning and career success.* Washington DC: Association of American Colleges & Universities.

Howard, T., Winkelmes, M. A., & Shegog, M. (2019, January). Transparency teaching in the virtual classroom: Assessing the opportunities and challenges of integrating transparency teaching methods with online learning. *Journal of Political Science Education.* doi: 10.1080/15512169.2018.1550420

Ishitani, T. (2006). Studying attrition and degree completion behavior among first-generation college students in the United States. *The Journal of Higher Education, 77*(5), 877.

Kuh, G. D., Jankowski, N., Ikenberry, S. O., & Kinzie, J. (2014). *Knowing what students know and can do: The current state of student learning outcomes assessment in U.S. colleges and universities.* Urbana, IL: University of Illinois and Indiana University, National Institute for Learning Outcomes Assessment.

McNair, T. B. (Ed.). (2016). Transparency and Problem-Centered Learning [Special issue]. *Peer Review, 18,* 1/2. Available from http://www.aacu.org/peerreview/2016/winter-spring

National Research Council. (2000). *How people learn: Brain, mind, experience, and school* (expanded ed.). Washington DC: The National Academies Press.

Paunesku, D., Walton, G. M., Romero, C., Smith, E. N., Yeager, D. S., & Dweck, C. S. (2015). Mind-set interventions are a scalable treatment for academic under-achievement. *Psychological Science, 26*, 784–793.

TILT Survey. (2015–2016). *End-of-term TILT survey responses for UNLV fall 2015 first-time, full-time, first-year students.* Las Vegas, NV: University of Nevada, Las Vegas.

Tough, Paul. (2014). Who gets to graduate? *New York Times Magazine, 18*, 26–30.

University of Nevada, Las Vegas (UNLV) Office of the Vice President and Prov-ost. (2017). *Minimum criteria for syllabi—Academic year 2017–2018.* Las Vegas, NV: University of Nevada, Las Vegas. Available from https://www.unlv.edu/sites/default/files/page_files/27/SyllabiContent-MinimumCriteria-2017-2018.doc

UNLV Data Warehouse/Office of Decision Support. (2018, March 2). *1-year and 2-year retention of fall 2015 full-time, first-time, first-year students.* Las Vegas, NV: University of Nevada, Las Vegas.

U.S. Department of Education. (2014). Graduation rates of first-time, full-time bachelor's degree-seeking students at 4-year postsecondary institutions, by race/ethnicity, time to completion, sex, and control of institution. In *Digest of Education Statistics, Integrated Postsecondary Education Data System (IPEDS).* Washington DC: National Center for Education Statistics and Institute of Edu-cation Sciences. Available from https://nces.ed.gov/programs/digest/d13/tables/dt13_326.10.asp

U.S. News & World Report. (2017, September 12). *Campus ethnic diversity, national universities.* Available from https://www.usnews.com/best-colleges/rankings/national-universities/campus-ethnic-diversity

Walton, G. M., & Cohen, G. L. (2011). A brief social-belonging intervention improves academic and health outcomes among minority students. *Science, 331*, 1447–1451.

Wang, M. C., Haertel, G. D., & Walberg, H. J. (1994). Synthesis of research: What helps students learn? *Educational Leadership, 51*(4), 74–79.

Winkelmes, M. A. (2013). Transparency in teaching: Faculty share data and improve students' learning. *Liberal Education, 99*(2), 48–55.

Winkelmes, M. A., Bernacki, M., Butler, J. V., Zochowski, M., Golanics, J., & Harriss Weavil, K. (2016). A teaching intervention that increases underserved college students' success. *Peer Review, 18*(1/2), 31–36.

Winkelmes, M. A., Calkins, C., & Yu, K. (Forthcoming). Transparent instruction boosts first-year undergraduate students' confidence, belonging and retention. Manuscript in preparation.

Winkelmes, M. A., Christopher, K., Copeland, D., Gravett, E., LaFleur, J., Palmer, M., ... Yong, D. (n.d.). *TILT Higher Ed examples and resources.* Available from TILTHigherEd.org

Winkelmes, M. A., Copeland, D. E., Jorgensen, E., Sloat, A., Smedley, A., Pizor, K.,... Jalene, S. (2015). Benefits (some unexpected) of transparent assignment design. *National Teaching and Learning Forum, 24*(4), 4–6.

PART ONE

THE FUNDAMENTALS OF TRANSPARENT DESIGN FOR FACULTY

WHY IT WORKS

Understanding the Concepts Behind Transparency in Learning and Teaching

Mary-Ann Winkelmes

For thousands of instructors who have participated in transparent assignment design workshops across the United States, a common observation is that the goals of transparent instruction feel both familiar and consistent with their own teaching goals. Indeed, past research on teaching and learning informs the Transparency Framework and can help to explain why it works. The simple purpose-task-criteria framework incorporates the benefits of multiple evidence-based teaching/learning practices. This chapter reviews seven main, foundational ideas about transparent instruction. It also offers examples of what these look like in practice in the context of an academic assignment, as a way of modeling the kind of transparency about concepts in practice that I encourage readers to provide for students.

Explicating the Applicability and Relevance of Academic Work Increases Students' Potential to Succeed and Maximizes Cognitive Bandwidth

A 2016 study demonstrated that students who received transparent instruction that emphasizes the purposes, tasks, real-world applicability (or problem-centeredness) and criteria for academic work experienced elevated confidence, belonging, and metacognitive awareness of skill development (Winkelmes et al., 2016). Confidence and belonging are success predictors that correlate with increased persistence and higher grades (Hausmann, Ye, Schofield, & Woods, 2009; Walton & Cohen, 2011), and scholars have identified metacognition as a key learning skill (National Research Council, 2000; Wang,

Haertel, & Walberg, 1993–1994). Increases in student persistence, as seen in college retention rates for those students who receive transparent instruction compared with those who don't, last at least two years (Winkelmes, Calkins, & Yu, forthcoming). These benefits of transparent instruction are significant, with even larger gains for underserved (first-generation, low-income, underrepresented) students (Winkelmes et al., 2016).

The Transparent Assignment Framework for Students (see Figure I.3) can be used to increase students' understanding of the purposes, tasks, and criteria for their academic work *before* they begin working, while enlightening teachers about where transparency is lacking. Teachers can use the template to frame a class conversation about an upcoming assignment, which has multiple advantages. It puts students in the role of experts about how a teacher can best provide them with transparent instruction—a powerful positive attribution activity that can strengthen success predictors like confidence and belonging. It also gives teachers the information and opportunity they need, at the precise moment they need it, to offer thorough transparency to students about an assignment immediately before students start to work on it. Conversely, a lack of shared understanding can cause cognitive stress; not the kind that is desirably difficult but rather the kind that diminishes equitable opportunity by excluding some students. This not only threatens their confidence and sense of belonging but also reduces their available bandwidth for learning (Verschelden, 2017). The Transparency Framework can help to reduce excess cognitive stress or extraneous cognitive load (Paas, Renk, & Sweller, 2003) by helping students to focus the majority of their time on producing high-quality work rather than on figuring out what that work should look like and how to approach it. "I actually spend a lot more time learning the material rather than devoting a lot of unnecessary time to unscrambling what I'm supposed to be doing," one student at the University of Nevada, Las Vegas, explained (Berrett, 2015, p. A29).

Metacognition Improves Learning

Metacognition, or awareness and understanding of one's thinking processes, enhances learning. Scholars identify metacognition as a key learning skill and an essential, research-based principle for teaching (Ambrose, Bridges, DiPietro, Lovett, & Norman, 2010; McGuire & McGuire, 2015; National Research Council, 2000; Schraw, 1998; Tanner, 2012; Wang, Haertel, & Walberg, 1993–1994). The three main steps of metacognition are planning, implementing/monitoring, and reflecting/revising (Nilson, 2013; Schraw, 1998; Zimmerman, 2002). The three-part Transparency Framework supports metacognition by providing a structured guide for these three metacognitive steps *before* students begin the journey. The first focus area of the framework is the purpose of the assigned academic work. What skills will students practice by doing this work, what knowledge will they gain from doing it, and how do those skills and knowledge offer long-term benefits for the students in real-world contexts beyond the assigned work? When teachers communicate with students about these aspects of an assignment's purpose, they are engaging students in the metacognitive preplanning process and providing a rationale with expected benefits for the assigned work. This coincides with the planning stage of metacognition. The second focus area of the Transparency Framework is the task(s) to be completed. What are students expected to do and how should they do it? This coincides with the implementing/monitoring phase of the metacognitive process. The third and final focus of the Transparency Framework is criteria. What are the expected characteristics of good work, and what do those look like in several real-world examples? When teachers engage students in applying criteria to multiple samples of work in the professional discipline or in the broader community, they are helping students to reflect on quality and to assess the degree to which work meets their established criteria and how it might be improved. This is the reflecting/revising phase of metacognition.

Because the Transparency Framework helps students and their teachers to review all three metacognitive steps *before* the students begin working, it enhances students' awareness of how they might expect to navigate those steps. The framework is a simple, practical guide for metacognition that helps instructors teach students the process of metacognition, while at the same time helping students prepare for a learning experience and then monitor their progress at each step in the process.

Varied, Flexible Assignment Formats and Stakes Appeal to Many Learning Modalities

Instructors seeking to teach with greater transparency may also consider incorporating varied and flexible formats for assignments to maximize inclusion and appeal equitably to students' strengths and learning styles (Burgstahler, 2008; Winkelmes, 2008). Teachers who assign a variety of types of work over the course of an academic term can maximize the chances that every student will experience a moment of working within a learning comfort zone at some moment during the course. It is not necessary to match assignments or teaching strategies to students' learning preferences; in fact, research suggests that students benefit when they experience unfamiliar, challenging, or difficult learning situations (Bjork, 1994; Taylor & Rohrer, 2010; Yan, Clark,

& Bjork, 2016). However, revisiting the same type of assignment multiple times will diminish that equity by privileging one type of learner over others in a course. The reflective process of redesigning an assignment using the Transparency Framework can help instructors recognize a tendency to lean too heavily on a particular type of assignment.

Incorporating lower stakes assignments can also benefit students by encouraging them to take more creative risks when they approach assignments that require them to think in unfamiliar ways or practice developing skills (Elbow, 1997; Jaschik & Davidson, 2010). Students tend to take fewer risks with assignments that count for a large percentage of their course grade. Most teachers do vary the types and weights of assignments, but few share their rationale for doing so with their students; the Transparency Framework promotes the clear articulation of that rationale to students. A quick discussion with students about the purpose of an assignment creates space for sharing this rationale with them, while offering students the opportunity to question and understand, as well as raise their metacognitive awareness through reflection. When students know that assignments in the course will appeal to a variety of learning strengths, their self-awareness about their learning is heightened, and they may feel curious about how much each assignment feels comfortable or challenges them to think differently. Working outside their learning comfort zone may even deepen students' mastery (National Research Council, 2000).

To illustrate how flexible formats can be inclusive for students, consider the case of Miley Nakamura, a Japanese American undergraduate student at Harvard University whose professor required an outline of Nakamura's ideas for her upcoming paper on a production of Andrew Lloyd Webber's *Phantom of the Opera*. The professor reviewed students' outlines and then offered suggestions to help them write their papers. Nakamura's outline took the form of a diagram with overlapping boxes of the sort she learned to use in elementary school in Japan for organizing ideas. But her teacher had expected a more traditional A-B-C, 1-2-3 outline format. To meet her professor's expectations precisely, Nakamura would have needed to diagram her ideas, write the whole paper, and then deduce from that paper an outline that would elicit the teacher's suggestions for how to write the paper she had just completed—a demoralizing and counterproductive process from a student's perspective. Luckily, Nakamura's professor took a more flexible stance and invited a conversation in which Nakamura helped her professor understand the diagram. Then the two discussed ideas for writing the paper. But faculty need not meet every student in person to offer advice about writing a paper. Instead of an outline, a flexible set of questions, such as those listed here, can equally gather the information a professor needs from a student in order to offer advice about a paper:

- What is your topic? What position will you take on that topic?
- What are the major primary and secondary sources essential to this topic? (List full citations.)
- What main pieces of evidence will support your idea(s) about the topic?
- What are possible counterarguments? What evidence might support these?
- What are some possible ways to refute counterarguments? What evidence can be used?
- What problems or questions do you have?

It is not the case that every assignment must consist of low-stakes, open-ended questions. Rather, offering students transparency about the varying types of assignments they will complete and the relative impact these have on the final course grade allows students the opportunity to safely experiment with a variety of learning strategies. Such transparency also maximizes the opportunities that each student will recognize which learning strategies are comfortable, challenging, and most beneficial for them.

Students Benefit From Understanding How We Structure Their Skill Development and Knowledge Acquisition, and How We Offer Feedback

Although many faculty design and arrange their assignments in order to help students develop a set of skills beginning with the simplest ones and building toward the most complex, interdependent skills, they do not always communicate their rationale to students. Research demonstrates that understanding the sequence for their skill development and knowledge acquisition can increase students' self-awareness and even encourage them to monitor their own progress (Ambrose et al., 2010; Colomb & Williams, 1993; Felder & Brent, 2014; Light, 1990; McGuire & McGuire, 2015; Middendorf & Pace, 2004; Perry, 1970). Transparent instruction facilitates the inclusion of clear rationales regarding skill development, not only in assignments but also in other course work and learning materials.

For instance, headings in a syllabus often identify disciplinary content. A more transparent syllabus can also point students to the disciplinary skills they are practicing in any given week of the term (Figure 1.1).

Bloom's taxonomy of educational objectives can offer a basic, cross-disciplinary guide for introducing students to these phases of skill development (Anderson & Krathwohl, 2000). In syllabus headings and assignment instructions, teachers can utilize "question cues" or active verbs related to

Figure 1.1. Syllabus with headings that highlight skills and content.

HIST 251 / ART 495
Tuesday / Thursday 8:30 – 9:45 am

Dr. Mary-Ann Winkelmes
University of Nevada, Las Vegas

INTRODUCTION TO HISTORICAL METHODS / SPECIAL TOPICS IN ART HISTORY:

Art and Politics in Renaissance Italy

This course focuses on strengthening the intellectual skills that are essential to History and Art History, as well as successful professional careers. In the four units of this course, we will consciously practice these skills:

UNIT 1) Understanding the frameworks: contexts, techniques, terms, artifacts as history,
UNIT 2) Analysis and Synthesis: using artifacts, primary and secondary sources to construct the story,
UNIT 3) Evaluating reliability of artifacts and sources, perceptions of value and achievement, evolving contexts,
UNIT 4) Creating new contexts for examining Renaissance artifacts and events.

As we hone these skills, we'll study painting, sculpture, and architecture in the context of various political and social environments in Renaissance Italy: the city-state, the church, the noble court, the neighborhood. We have come to think of Renaissance sculptures, paintings, and decorative objects as artworks. Yet the creators and original users of these works saw them primarily as religious or domestic furnishings, indicators of power or civic pride, gifts or aids to spiritual meditation--many with strong political messages. Artists and patrons we will examine include Michelangelo, Raphael, Leonardo, the Medici, Pope Julius II, Isabella d'Este, and other influential artists and patrons.

...

SCHEDULE OF CLASS MEETINGS AND REQUIRED READINGS

UNIT 1 SKILLS) Understanding the frameworks: contexts, techniques, terms, art as history

Jan 20: Michelangelo's *David* and its meanings over time

Focus questions: Who made it and how? Who commissioned it and why? Who saw it, used it, and how? How does it involve or appeal to viewers? How has its context and meaning changed? What happened to it over time? What does it mean to us now?

Jan 22: Places and purposes of art in daily life in Renaissance Italy

Reading: Paoletti 12-15, 43

Focus questions:

- What are some examples of religious art and architecture in contemporary cultures?
- How might examples of religious art and architecture in Renaissance culture be similar/different?
- How do we define "religious" and "art," and how do our definitions affect the ways we study and understand the history, art, and artifacts of Renaissance Italy?

Jan 27: Materials, Techniques, and Conditions of Artistic Production   …

UNIT 2 SKILLS) Analysis and Synthesis: using artifacts, primary and secondary sources to construct the story

Feb 19: Formal Visual Analysis practice in class   …

Feb 26: Analysis of primary sources: Michelangelo's *Last Judgment*

Reading: primary sources in class

Focus questions:

- Are primary sources more reliable than secondary sources?
- What makes a source reliable?
- When primary sources contradict each other, how to judge?
- When secondary sources contradict each other, how to judge?

Bloom's taxonomy (e.g., *describe*, *interpret*, or *analyze*) to encourage students to pursue specific types of critical thinking.

A single-page assignment sequence chart can also communicate to students about the skills they are developing during a course. Table 1.1 explicates the intention of a team of faculty who collaborated to design an introductory business course at the University of Illinois, Urbana-Champaign. This abbreviated version of the chart lists the team's goals for students' learning on the horizontal axis across the top, borrowed directly from three sources: their accreditors, the Association to Advance Collegiate Schools of Business (Association to Advance Collegiate Schools of Business, 2017), a national survey of employers (Hart Research Associates, 2013), and Bloom's taxonomy of educational objectives (Anderson & Krathwohl, 2000). Due dates for homework assignments appear on the vertical axis at the left. Marked boxes indicate which skills the students are practicing when they work on each homework assignment. At the beginning of the term, homework assignments focus on just one or two relatively simple skills that are critical to students' success in this course. As students master the basic skill sets, they begin using multiple skills simultaneously on assignments in the middle of term. By the end of the term, students are combining multiple, interdependent skill sets in a single assignment. They are prepared to do this because they had opportunities to practice each skill independently earlier in the term.

Just as assignments can guide students' skill development in an incremental sequence, so can faculty feedback guide that development at each phase toward the next developmental step. Conscientious teachers often feel it is their duty to offer a student everything they know about how the students' work could be improved. But too much feedback during a student's development of basic disciplinary skills can be overwhelming and counterproductive (Svinicki, 2008). At more advanced levels of development, students can benefit from more detailed feedback about how to improve their work. The Transparency Framework promotes a specific, delimited focus for instructor feedback through the inclusion of criteria for effective completion of assignments, as well as through the articulation of discrete tasks. Instructors should focus their feedback on students' development of skills with respect to the criteria provided.

Accessible Criteria Can Encourage Students' Self-Monitoring

Once students are aware of the path for skill development that their professor intends, instructors can encourage them to monitor their own learning progress. The Transparency Framework encourages instructors to include clear

TABLE 1.1

Assignments Sequence Chart for an Introductory Business Course

Due Dates for Assignments	Use of Information Technology[ac]	Communication: Oral, Written[ac]	Teamwork: Understanding Group and Individual Dynamics in Organizations[bc]	Understanding Domestic and Global Economic Environments[a]	Multicultural and Diversity Understanding[a]	Analytic Skills[ab]	Applying Learned Concepts to Practical Situations[b]	Understanding Professional Responsibility, Including Ethical Reasoning Regarding Self, Organizations, Society[ab]	Research: Locating, Evaluating, and Selecting Useful Information and Resources[b]	Reflective, Self-Evaluative Thinking Skills[ab]
8/31		x								
9/1		x								
9/7	x	x	x							
9/11	x			x						
9/26				x				x		
10/9						x		x		
10/23						x		x		
11/6					x			x		x
11/13							x	x	x	
12/4							x	x	x	x
12/10							x	x	x	x

[a]Association to Advance Collegiate Schools of Business (2017).
[b]Anderson & Krathwohl (2000).
[c]Hart Research Associates (2013).

Note. Reproduced with permission of Mary-Ann Winkelmes.

assessment criteria that can help students engage in such self-monitoring. A simple checklist for introductory-level students, or a detailed rubric for students working at a more advanced level, can help students track their success while they are working on a project or assignment. North Carolina State University's guidelines for students writing a lab report (Carter, 2004) (Figure 1.2) and the Higher Education Funding Council for England's Core Assessment Criteria for Essays (Harrington et al., 2006) (Figure 1.3) both fall between these two poles, providing more detail than a simple checklist but less than a full rubric. Faculty often find that they spend less time grading and responding to students' work when students are aware of the established criteria while working on a project.

Considering Multiple Examples of Criteria in Practice, Before Students Begin Working, Helps Students to Begin Their Work at the Same Starting Line

The Transparency Framework suggests that instructors provide students with multiple examples (for discussion) of real-world work that meets or approaches the criteria for their own assignments *before* they begin working. This component is critical to providing all students with an equitable opportunity to succeed with an assignment, because checklists and rubrics, no matter how detailed they are, can't illustrate what the finished work would look like in practice and because any single example limits students' understanding of multiple ways to succeed.

Annotated examples like Carol Augspurger's (Figure 1.4) illustrate what it looks like when specific criteria from a checklist or rubric are met in practice. Her example demonstrates in detail what it looks like to do some of the things that a checklist might include: "use inverted triangle to organize," "first give big picture/context" to see the "importance of study highlighted," and review "prior studies relevant" to this one. However, a single example to illustrate how criteria can be met in practice is inadequate. Students with only one example may follow it too closely. Furthermore, most of the teachers in our Association of American Colleges & Universities (AAC&U) study and subsequent cohorts did not have annotated examples of work available for sharing.

Fortunately, an efficient alternative to preparing annotated examples offers even greater advantages for students. When teachers bring annotated examples to share, they usually put themselves in the role of explaining how a particular sample of work is good. But when teachers bring samples of work that they did not annotate (photographs of a construction project for an architecture course or a paragraph from a journal in the academic discipline), students can take responsibility for evaluating the work by applying a

Figure 1.2. LabChecklist: SelfGuide.

The Introduction in my Lab Report . . .
- starts out by stating (in a sentence or two) the scientific concept the lab is about and then describes what I know about that scientific concept that is relevant to the lab (typically one or two paragraphs).
- sets down in sentence form the main lab objective(s) and then describes what these objectives will help me learn about the scientific concept of the lab (typically one paragraph).
- states the hypothesis and then explains how I arrived at the hypothesis, using what I know about the scientific concept of the lab as the basis for my reasoning (typically one or two paragraphs).

The Methods in my Lab Report . . .
- provides a concise, easy-to-follow description of the specific procedures I followed in the lab.
- gives enough detail of both the materials and the procedure used so that the experiment could be repeated just as I did it.

The Results in my Lab Report . . .
- begins with a sentence or two describing the overall findings of the lab.
- visuals (tables or graphs or other figures) that are appropriate to the data and are arranged in an order that best tells the "story" of the data.
- consists of a paragraph for each visual and structures each paragraph by (1) summarizing in a sentence or two the overall trend shown in that visual and then (2) supporting the summary by including any specific details from the visual that are important for understanding the results.
- clearly refers to the appropriate visuals in the paragraphs (Table 1, Figure 2, etc.).
- reports the data from the experiment only, successfully avoiding any explanations or conclusions about the data.

The Discussion in my Lab Report . . .
- begins with a statement of whether or not the overall results support, do not support, or support to some extent my original hypothesis (in the Introduction).
- points to specific data from the findings as evidence for deciding whether or not the hypothesis is supported.
- uses what I have learned about the scientific concept of the lab to explain in a convincing way why or why not the data support my hypothesis.
- addresses other issues that may be appropriate, such as (1) any problems that occurred or sources of uncertainty in the lab procedure; (2) how the findings compare to the findings of other students in the lab and an explanation for any differences; (3) suggestions for improving the lab.

The Conclusion of my Lab Report . . .
- directly states what I have learned about the scientific concept of the lab from doing the experimental procedure.
- gives enough details of what I have learned to be convincing.
- describes anything else I may have learned from doing the lab and writing the report (something about the lab procedure, methods of analyzing data, etc.).

© Copyright NC State University, 2004. Sponsored and funded by National Science Foundation (DUE-9950405 and DUE-0231086). Rev. MF 5/26/05; https://labwrite.ncsu.edu/lc/lc-selfguide.htm
Note. Reproduced with permission of Michael Carter, North Carolina State University.

Figure 1.3. Higher Education Funding Council for England core assessment criteria for essays.

Assessment Plus: Using Core Criteria to Guide Judgements about the Quality of Students' Work

Core Criteria Descriptions and Guidance Notes

1. Addressing the question	The relevance of the content of the essay to the question or title set. • Good essays select relevant material (knowledge, concepts, interpretation, theoretical models, others' perspectives). • Better ones make it clear throughout how the material is relevant to the question.
2. Using evidence	The use of externally sourced material, such as research findings, facts, quotations, or other forms of information. • Good essays include information from outside sources that backs up the points made in the essay. • Better ones explicitly highlight or interpret the evidence to support a more general claim or idea or point being made in the essay.
3. Developing argument	The construction of a coherent and convincing set of reasons for holding a particular point of view; the following of an analytical path leading from a starting point to a concluding point. • Good essays contain expressions of positions on the issues raised by the essay. • Better ones develop arguments throughout the essay, with each element building on the last.
4. Critical evaluation	Determining the value, significance, strengths and/or weaknesses of something (e.g., research findings, theory, methodological approach, policy, another's argument or interpretation).

	• Good essays contain evaluative assertions or descriptive points about the strengths and weaknesses of elements referred to in the essay.
	• Better ones contain systematic, reasoned explanations for the evaluative points being made.
5. Structuring	The formal arrangement of the essay content into paragraphs.
	• Good essays have clearly recognisable introductory and concluding paragraphs, and paragraphs in the main body of the essay each have a clear, single concept or point as their main focus.
	• Better essays have a paragraph structure that supports the development of ideas within the essay, so that the structure of the essay is linked to the developing argument.
6. Use of language	The use of words, grammar, and punctuation to formulate an utterance appropriate to the purpose and context.
	• Good essays are free from errors in spelling, punctuation and grammar, and would be acceptable pieces of writing in the wider world.
	• Better essays adopt academic styles and conventions, and approximate to the appropriate academic 'register'.

Assessment Plus

Assessment Plus: Using assessment criteria to support student learning
HEFCE funded consortium project

www.writenow.ac.uk/assessmentplus

Source. Higher Education Funding Council for England (n.d.).
Note. Reproduced with permission of Katherine Harrington, London Metropolitan University.

Figure 1.4. Annotated introduction of Plant Biology paper.

Plant Biology Paper, Example

Carol Augspurger, School of Integrative Biology, University of Illinois at Urbana-Champaign

Use "inverted triangle" to organize introduction. *First, give big picture/context.*	INTRODUCTION (4–5 paragraphs)
Topic sentence of paragraph; all sentences in paragraph relate to this topic.	Both extrinsic and intrinsic factors affect the relative population size of species of small mammals in local habitats. Extrinsic factors may include the amount of food availability (Bell 1989), presence of competing species (Holt et al. 1995), and the presence
Background information.	of predators (Batzli and Lin 2001). Intrinsic factors may relate to their diet and food preferences (Heskie 2004), competitive ability (Holt et al. 1995), and body shape (Hoffmeister 1989)
Key references included.	that affects their speed and agility in escaping predators. Differences in
No direct quotations—only paraphrases with sources. *Proper literature format used.*	these factors are expected to result in varying population sizes of species of small mammals among local habitats. Understanding the factors that affect a species population size is important because it allows us to predict how changes in the environment will affect its population dynamics and the community structure.
Importance of study highlighted. (Why should reader care?)	Augspurger et al. (2008) found that the relative population sizes of small mammals differed in successional old fields of contrasting age. Specifically, their five years of live trapping showed that voles have a large population in a field abandoned one year ago, while
Prior studies/observations (data) relevant to specific study.	shrews have a larger population size in a field abandoned five years ago. Mice have a slighter greater population in a 1-year field.

Note. Reproduced by permission of Carol Augspurger.

checklist of criteria to the real-world work examples and debating the degree to which the work fulfills each criterion. With the teacher's guidance, such conversations lead to a shared understanding of what it looks like when work samples meet or exceed or fall short of an established set of criteria. In our Transparency in Learning and Teaching (TILT) studies, the result was that students collaboratively evaluated examples of work in the discipline in real-world forms that teachers suggested, like construction projects, theatrical performances, art installations, and newspaper and journal articles in a variety of disciplines. *Before* students began working on their own projects, they all shared the same information about what good (and not so good) work from the discipline looks like in practice. Thus, students began their projects equitably at the same starting point, with the same shared information and expectations for their work. Putting students in the role of collaborative evaluators may also contribute to success predictors like increased confidence and sense of belonging in college.

To ensure that students begin their work at the same starting line, with equitable access to information about what good work looks like, it is necessary for teachers to offer multiple examples of work that students can evaluate. Multiple examples can help students to understand a variety of ways to meet the criteria for their work. Teachers can engage students in analyzing the varying degrees of success in multiple examples to ensure that students begin their own work with a fuller understanding of how criteria can be approached and met in practice.

Peer Instruction Increases Understanding Efficiently and Encourages Positive Attribution Activities, and Knowing This Will Enhance Students' Peer Learning Experiences

Just as the Transparency Framework encourages the inclusion and evaluation of multiple "real-world" examples, it can also facilitate the incorporation of peer instruction, such as peer evaluation of work in progress. Evaluating someone else's work objectively is often easier than evaluating one's own. Peer instruction, in the context of a take-home assignment or in-class activity, offers students an understanding of someone else's way of thinking about problems or topics in the discipline, as well as an opportunity to evaluate someone else's work. Research supports peer instruction as a way to help students master course content more quickly, increase the accuracy of their understanding, and increase their confidence in their understanding (Crouch & Mazur, 2001; Mazur, 1996). Likewise, testing one's understanding through activities like peer instruction, as opposed to simply reviewing content, can enhance mastery, increase metacognition, and deepen learning (Roediger, Putnam, & Smith, 2011).

Although many faculty structure peer learning opportunities, they do not always tell students their rationale for it. Offering students additional transparency about the rationale for a peer learning exercise, by using the purpose-task-criteria framework to introduce the exercise, can increase students' motivation because they understand the benefits to them in advance of their participation. Furthermore, when students understand the teacher's purpose is to increase their confidence, accuracy, or ability to understand course content from another perspective, their metacognitive capacity to monitor their progress toward that goal will increase. Equally important, increasing students' confidence and sense of belonging through peer learning activities can help to diminish factors like stereotype threat or microaggressions that compromise students' capacity to learn (Aronson, Fried, & Good, 2002; Dweck, 2006; Spitzer & Aronson, 2015; Verschelden, 2017; Walton & Cohen, 2011).

Conclusion

The Transparency Framework (see Figures I.2 and I.3) is a simple tool that incorporates the benefits of these seven foundational principles and helps faculty and students to frame conversations about academic work. The vocabulary of purpose (including skills to be practiced and knowledge to be gained), tasks to complete, and criteria (for evaluating multiple real-world examples and for students' self-monitoring the success of their own work underway) is accessible to students and faculty across disciplines. The framework is a tool that incorporates multiple educational strategies and encourages conscious reflection on them both before and during the assigned work, by predicting and then following the three-part metacognitive process of preplanning, implementing, and reflecting/revising. The complexity of these teaching/learning strategies and the foundational, research-based principles in which they are grounded become readily accessible to faculty and students across disciplines at all levels of expertise through the deceptively simple Transparency Framework that guides communication around the purposes, tasks, and criteria for academic work.

EDITORS' HIGHLIGHTS

For instructors considering incorporating transparent instruction, consider the following points from this contributor:

- Transparent instruction is grounded in research on evidence-based practices for improving students' learning experiences.
- The Transparency Framework is a helpful, accessible tool for incorporating the benefits of multiple, evidence-based teaching/learning practices in a simple three-part framework of purpose, tasks, and criteria.

References

Ambrose, S., Bridges, M. W., DiPietro, M., Lovett, M. C., & Norman, M. K. (2010). *How learning works: 7 research-based principles for smart teaching* (pp. 126–127). San Francisco, CA: Jossey-Bass.

Anderson, L., & Krathwohl, D. (Eds.). (2000). *A taxonomy for learning, teaching and assessment: A revision of Bloom's taxonomy of educational objectives.* New York, NY: Pearson.

Aronson, J., Fried, C. B., & Good, C. (2002). Reducing the effects of stereotype threat on African American college students by shaping theories of intelligence. *Journal of Experimental Social Psychology, 38*(2), 113–125.

Association to Advance Collegiate Schools of Business (AACSB). (2017). Curriculum content. In *Eligibility Procedures and Accreditation Standards for Business Accreditation* (pp. 34–36). Tampa, FL: AACSB World Headquarters. Available from http://www.aacsb.edu/-/media/aacsb/docs/accreditation/standards/business-accreditation-2017-update.ashx?la=en

Association to Advance Collegiate Schools of Business (AACSB). (2018). *Eligibility procedures and accreditation standards for business accreditation.* Available from https://www.aacsb.edu/-/media/aacsb/docs/accreditation/business/standards-and-tables/2018-business-standards.ashx?la=en

Berrett, D. (2015, September 25). The unwritten rules of college. *Chronicle of Higher Education.* Available from https://www.chronicle.com/article/The-Unwritten-Rules-of/233245

Bjork, R. (1994). Memory and metamemory considerations in the training of human beings. In J. Metcalfe & A. Shimamura (Eds.), *Metacognition: Knowing about knowing* (pp. 185–205). Cambridge, MA: MIT Press.

Burgstahler, S. (Ed.). (2008). *Universal design in higher education: From principles to practice.* Cambridge, MA: Harvard Education Press.

Carter, M. (2004). *LabChecklist: SelfGuide.* Raleigh, NC: North Carolina State University.

Colomb, G., & Williams, J. (1993). Why what you don't know won't help you. *Research in the Teaching of English, 23*(3), 252–264.

Crouch, C. H., & Mazur, E. (2001). Peer instruction: Ten years of experience and results. *American Journal of Physics, 69*(9), 970–977.

Dweck, C. (2006). *Mindset: The new psychology of success.* New York, NY: Random House.

Elbow, P. (1997). High stakes and low stakes in assigning and responding to writing. *New Directions for Teaching and Learning, 69,* 5–13.

Felder, R., & Brent, R. (2014). Want your students to think creatively and critically? How about teaching them? *Chemical Engineering Education, 48*(2), 113–114.

Harrington, K., Elander, J., Lusher, J., Norton, L., Aiyegbayo, O., Pitt, E., . . . Reddy, P. (2006). Using core assessment criteria to improve essay writing. In C. Bryan. & K. Clegg (Eds.), *Innovative assessment in higher education* (pp. 110–119). New York, NY: Routledge.

Hart Research Associates. (2013). *It takes more than a major: Employer priorities for college learning and student success.* Washington DC: Association of American Colleges & Universities.

Hausmann, L. R., Ye, F., Schofield, J. W., & Woods, R. L. (2009). Sense of belonging and persistence in white and African American first-year students. *Research in Higher Education, 50*(7), 649–669.

Higher Education Funding Council for England. (n.d.). *Essay feedback form using core criteria.* Available from https://www.reading.ac.uk/web/files/EngageinFeedback/Blank_essay_feedback_sheet.pdf

Jaschik, S., & Davidson, C. (2010, May 3). No grading, more learning. *Inside Higher Ed.* Available from http://www.insidehighered.com/news/2010/05/03/grading

Light, R. (1990). *The Harvard assessment seminars: First report.* Cambridge, MA: Harvard University Graduate School of Education.

Mazur, E. (1996). *Peer instruction: A user's manual.* New York, NY: Pearson.

McGuire, S. R., & McGuire, S. (2015). *Teach students how to learn: Strategies you can incorporate into any course to improve student metacognition, study skills, and motivation.* Sterling, VA: Stylus.

Middendorf, J., & Pace, D. (2004). Decoding the disciplines: A model for helping students learn disciplinary ways of thinking. *New Directions in Teaching and Learning, 98,* 1–12.

National Research Council. (2000). *How people learn: Brain, mind, experience and school.* Washington DC: National Academy Press.

Nilson, L. B. (2013). *Creating self-regulated learners: Strategies to strengthen students' self-awareness and learning skills.* Sterling, VA: Stylus.

Paas, F., Renkl, A., & Sweller, J. (2003). Cognitive load theory and instructional design: Recent developments. *Educational Psychologist, 38*(1), 1–4.

Perry, W. G. (1970). *Forms of intellectual and ethical development in the college years: A scheme.* New York, NY: Holt, Rinehart, and Winston.

Roediger, H. L., Putman, A. L., & Smith, M. A. (2011). Ten benefits of testing and their application to educational practice. In J. P. Mestre & B. H. Ross (Eds.), *The psychology of learning and motivation: Cognition in education* (pp. 1–36). Oxford, UK: Elsevier.

Schraw, G. (1998). Promoting general metacognition awareness. *Instructional Science, 26*, 113–125.

Spitzer, B., & Aronson, J. (2015). Minding and mending the gap: Social psychological interventions to reduce educational disparities. *British Journal of Educational Psychology, 85*(1), 1–18.

Svinicki, M. (2008). When does enough feedback become too much? *National Teaching & Learning Forum, 17*(3), 12.

Tanner, K. B. (2012). Promoting student metacognition. *CBE Life Sciences Education, 11*(2), 113–120.

Taylor, K., & Rohrer, D. (2010). The effect of interleaving practice. *Applied Cognitive Psychology, 24*, 837–848.

Verschelden, C. (2017). *Bandwidth recovery: Helping students reclaim cognitive resources lost to poverty, racism, and social marginalization.* Sterling, VA: Stylus.

Walton, G. M., & Cohen, G. L. (2011). A brief social-belonging intervention improves academic and health outcomes among minority students. *Science, 331*, 1447–1451.

Wang, M. C., Haertel, G. D., & Walberg, H. J. (1993–1994). Synthesis of research: What helps students learn? *Educational Leadership, 51*(4), 74–79.

Winkelmes, M. A. (2008). Building assignments that teach. *Essays on Teaching Excellence: Toward the Best in the Academy, 19*(8). Available from https://podnetwork.org/content/uploads/V19-N8-Winkelmes.pdf

Winkelmes, M. A., Bernacki, M., Butler, J. V., Zochowski, M., Golanics, J., & Harriss Weavil, K. (2016). A teaching intervention that increases underserved college students' success. *Peer Review, 18*(1/2), 31–36.

Winkelmes, M. A., Calkins, C., & Yu, K. (Forthcoming). Transparent instruction boosts first-year undergraduate students' confidence, belonging and retention.

Yan, V. X., Clark, C. M., & Bjork, R. A. (2016). Memory and metamemory considerations in the instruction of human beings revisited: Implications for optimizing online learning. In J. C Horvath & J. Hattie (Eds.), *From the laboratory to the classroom: Translating science of learning for teachers* (pp. 61–78). New York, NY: Routledge.

Zimmerman, B. J. (2002). Becoming a self-regulated learner: An overview. *Theory Into Practice, 41*(2), 64–70.

2

HOW TO USE THE
TRANSPARENCY
FRAMEWORK

Mary-Ann Winkelmes

T his chapter guides readers through the process of making assignments transparent for students. It offers advice for instructors revising or starting from scratch and thinking about implementing the Transparency Framework (see Figure I.2 and Figure I.3) in their own classrooms. It focuses on clarifying the purposes, tasks, and criteria for an assigned piece of academic work, and how to make it transparent, relevant, and equitably accessible for students.

Purpose

The first step to making an assignment, exercise, or any piece of academic work transparent for students is to define its purpose explicitly, in language that is accessible to disciplinary novices as well as experts. Most faculty design assignments and class activities thoughtfully, with a rationale and a specific learning goal for every required piece. These purposes may include practicing disciplinary methods, applying discipline-specific tools, or learning essential disciplinary knowledge. But many faculty do not explicitly share these rationales with their students. Students' metacognition and learning can increase when they know what skills they will practice and what knowledge they can expect to gain before beginning the assigned work. Without an understanding of the learning gains they will experience, students may view an assignment as merely an arbitrary list of required tasks with no rationale apart from providing material upon which to base their grade. To help you identify the most critical skills and knowledge that provide the foundation for an assignment, consider what might happen if you described your assignment to a disciplinary stranger. How would this person answer the following questions about your assignment?

Five years after completing the assignment:

- What knowledge should students retain from doing this assignment?
- What skills should students be able to perform because they practiced them while doing this assignment?
- How will the skills and knowledge still be essential in students' lives five years later?

Posing these questions from the perspective of someone outside of the discipline or thinking ahead with a five-year time frame may help you define how the learning gained from a particular assignment will benefit students in your course and beyond. When you listen to a colleague from another discipline identify the targeted skills and knowledge for an assignment in this way, several realizations can occur. First, the knowledge and skills that seemed obvious to you as a disciplinary expert are more difficult to discern for the disciplinary stranger—even a stranger who holds a doctorate in another discipline. Second, the knowledge to be gained is sometimes short-term knowledge that will have evolved or transformed after five years. Third, there might be too many skills for the student to practice simultaneously in a way that will lead to high proficiency. Research suggests that young adults can hold no more than four or five ideas in short-term working memory (Cowan, 2010), and most teachers and coaches would choose to have their students focus simultaneously on just one or two that the student is aiming to master. When teachers work to create transparent purpose statements, their first drafts might contain an overwhelming amount of detail about skills to be practiced and knowledge to be gained. They often remedy this problem in a second draft that breaks a large assignment into two or three smaller ones that connect or accumulate together. This scaffolding allows students to consciously focus on acquiring some preliminary knowledge and skills, receive some feedback from peers or the teacher, and then apply that feedback to the next step of the assignment where they focus on a different skill and additional knowledge.

Additional considerations you can review when crafting the purpose statement for an assignment prompt include the knowledge and skills you are seeking to enhance. Consider the following:

- Does your purpose statement specify content knowledge or skills that students will gain from doing this assignment?

- Does your purpose statement link those skills and knowledge to the larger context of
    - recent topics of class sessions?
    - this part of the course?
    - the whole course?
    - the major?
    - the discipline?
    - your institution's main learning outcomes?
- Does your purpose statement indicate the relevance and/or usefulness of this knowledge to the students' lives beyond the course, beyond the major, or beyond college?
- Would this assignment benefit from segmentation into several assignments, each one focused on a discrete set of skills that should be mastered to ensure students' successful completion of the next assignment in the sequence?

Task

The second step in offering transparency to students about academic work is to clarify the task in terms of productive steps for students to follow and counterproductive steps they should avoid. Some teachers fear this might make the work too mechanical for students or stifle their creativity. What if you want to provide students with absolutely no instruction about the task? Engineering and performing arts or studio art faculty in our studies have sometimes worried that providing a defined task would limit students' creativity and stifle their achievement. Indeed, students sometimes benefit from challenging learning conditions, as research on desirable difficulty suggests (Bjork, 1994; Diemand-Yauman, Oppenheimer, & Vaughan, 2011). When teachers in our studies held such views about the justifiable rationale for withholding guidance about the task from their students, we asked them to incorporate language like the following in their purpose statement: "The purpose of this assignment is for you to struggle and feel confused while you invent your own process to address the problem." This information may preserve students' academic confidence and sense of belonging, encouraging their persistence even in moments when they are unsure if they are working effectively or successfully.

Another common concern for some instructors is whether transparency about the task might be *too* helpful to students, making it too easy for them to complete their assignments. Does it coddle students and reduce their motivation to excel? Published reflections from faculty in our studies who shared such concerns indicate that the quality of students' work was higher than they anticipated or that students met the teachers' goals quickly, leaving time for more challenging work and greater achievement by the end of term (Kang, Kelly, Murray, & Visbal, 2016; Whitehead, 2016; Winkelmes et al., 2015). To help you think through the many steps involved in completing the task for your selected assignment, consider asking a colleague from another discipline to describe every step that would be taken from the very beginning of work on the assignment to the moment of submitting it. Colleagues from outside of the discipline will often list steps you didn't anticipate and may want to include in the task portion of your assignment prompt. Conversely, colleagues may list unproductive steps you will counsel your students to avoid. When crafting the task portion of an assignment prompt, consider the following cues:

- Does your description of the task
  - identify the very first thing students should do when they begin working on the assignment?
  - the very next thing they should do?
  - the next, and so on, until they submit their finished work?
  - help students to avoid wasting their time on unnecessary steps or unproductive time expenditure?
  - help students to focus their time efficiently on producing the highest quality work possible in the time given?
- Would students benefit from some practice exercises in class to prepare them to perform the task outside of class on the graded assignment?

Criteria

The third step for designing a transparent assignment is to offer students a set of criteria for success, along with multiple examples from real-world work in the discipline. The design of our initial (2014–2015) Association of American Colleges & Universities (AAC&U) study presumed that teachers would have existing samples of past students' work, annotated like Carol Augspurger's biology paper in chapter 1 (see Figure 1.4), along with permission to share them. When we realized that many teachers did not have such examples readily available, we encouraged them to find several examples of work in their discipline to bring to a class discussion with their students. The result was better than we anticipated. Instead of telling students what was good about past students' work, teachers asked students to apply their assignment's criteria to the real-world examples. Students then worked to understand what it looks like in practice when real-world work from their disciplinary communities either approached or met the criteria for their own assignment. Teachers guided the discussions and helped students to evaluate multiple examples of work, preparing them to evaluate their own progress when they would soon be working on their own assignments. Some faculty reported that this resulted in higher quality student work, less procrastination by students, fewer last-minute requests for guidance, and fewer questions or disputes about grades (Copeland, Winkelmes, & Gunawan, 2018; Howard, Winkelmes, & Shegog, 2019; Kang et al., 2016; Whitehead, 2016; Winkelmes et al., 2015).

To help you draft criteria statements for your assignment prompts, keep in mind that students should be able to answer the following questions affirmatively:

- Are you confident you are doing the task effectively?
- Are you confident you are doing excellent work?
- Do you have multiple successful, real-world work examples from this discipline or examples of concrete strategies you could use for improvement?
- In order to answer yes to the previous questions, what further examples and information would you need?

The most important question is the last one, and although your colleagues inside or outside of the discipline can try to answer on behalf of students, students themselves will provide the most accurate responses. Students can offer insights about what types of examples from which real-world contexts are helpful, whether some examples should illustrate moderate success or a lack of success, and how many examples they need to discuss with you before they are ready to begin working independently. This communication will inform how you can transparently provide what students need to begin their work from the same starting point as they think about how to approach the assignment.

Additional considerations when drafting the criteria statement for an assignment prompt may include the following:

- Can students use the criteria while they are working on the assignment to determine whether they are completing the assignment efficiently and effectively?
- Do the criteria take the form of a checklist students can use to evaluate their efforts while they are working on the assignment?
- Can you help students apply the checklist by evaluating and annotating some samples of real-world work in class, so they understand how

each criterion would look in practice? (These annotated examples may then be shared as a reference for students to use while they work on their own assignments.)

- Can you provide a set of concrete strategies that students could apply to improve their work while it is underway? Would a rubric (e.g., Valid Assessment of Learning in Undergraduate Education [VALUE] Rubric) be helpful to students while they work on this assignment? (AAC&U, 2017)

- Does the rubric provide a helpful amount of information (not overwhelming or counterproductive) for students at this phase in their learning?

The final step in offering transparency around academic assignments to students requires faculty to offer their students transparency about transparency and to seek out the expertise of the students themselves. Sharing the rationale behind any evidence-based teaching strategy can enhance students' metacognitive awareness while increasing their attention to monitoring their own learning process (as discussed in chapter 1). You can further enhance students' metacognitive preparation by engaging them in parsing the assignment. Try giving students the Transparency Framework for Students (see Figure I.3) and using it to frame a conversation in which students answer questions about the purposes, tasks, and criteria for an upcoming assignment. This helps students learn to analyze assignment prompts and ask for greater transparency, while simultaneously preparing them to think metacognitively about their learning gains as they work on a specific assignment. Further, it improves the instructor's success in offering transparency by providing one last opportunity to offer additional clarity for the whole group of students in response to some students' questions or misunderstandings about the intended purposes, tasks, and criteria before they begin working on the assignment. No matter how well the teachers in our studies prepared their assignments, followed Transparency in Leadership and Teaching (TILT) guidelines for assignment design (see Figure I.2), or gathered feedback from colleagues, they discovered that students are the best experts on how to make an assignment transparent to them.

You can be confident that you have offered a transparently designed assignment only after such a discussion ensures that all students begin working on the assignment with the same starting-line information about how to accomplish the work. Teachers from our initial TILT studies report they continue to revise their already transparent assignments as they work with new groups of students who offer different questions and insights.

Examples of Transparent Assignments: Before and After

An example of one of the assignments from the University of Nevada, Las Vegas (UNLV) study before and after it was revised to offer greater transparency can shed light on the work you will do when you decide to make an assignment more transparent to students. The unrevised, less transparent version of an interview assignment from a communications course appears in Figure 2.1.

The purpose of this original, unrevised assignment is difficult to locate. The knowledge and skills that students will gain by doing this assignment as well as their value and relevance are not readily accessible. Buried and implied in part 4 of the assignment instructions, and declared in part 6, section 3, the purpose of this work is one that can motivate students: "learn about your

Figure 2.1. Less transparent interview assignment from a communications course.

Intro Communications Course
Interview Assignment

1. Select a professional in your prospective academic discipline and/or career field that is considered an expert in an area in which you are interested.

2. Secure an interview with the professional for a date and time that is convenient for both for you.

3. Prepare 8 to 10 questions to ask the professional about their knowledge of a particular academic discipline/career field.

4. Conduct a 20 to 30 minute, face-to-face interview to gather knowledge that will help you make an informed decision about the major/career you are considering. You will want to audio/video record the interview with the interviewee's permission.

5. Prepare a typed transcript of the questions and answers using the audio/video recording

6. Write a 400 to 500 word reflection paper in which you address the following items:

   a. Who you selected and why?

   b. What you learned from them that is most interesting?

   c. What this assignment helped you learn about your major/career decision?

   d. What questions you still have?

7. Submit the typed transcript and reflection paper to your instructor.

Note. Reproduced by permission of Katherine Johnson.

major/career decision." Even the most experienced college professors struggle initially to find this purpose in the text of the assignment. Finding the assignment's purpose would be far more challenging for an incoming new-majority college student.

This assignment's purpose is equally obscure in regard to the skills the student will practice, not because they are difficult to locate but because there are so many of them. In fact, students who complete this assignment will need to use the following skills: audio-recording, transcribing, identifying a professional in a field that interests them, spoken and written communication skills appropriate to a professional setting, arranging an appointment, devising interview questions, listening, responding with follow-up questions, analyzing responses, synthesizing ideas, organizing thoughts, evaluating and selecting ideas for further analysis, extracting lessons learned, and writing. How many of those skills did the authors of this assignment want the students to practice simultaneously? It is unlikely the teachers intended for students to focus equally on 15 or more skills simultaneously. Were some of those skills more important learning goals than others? The way this assignment is written makes it impossible to identify with certainty the skills that the teaching team most wanted their students to practice consciously. This version of the assignment privileges those students who know how to parse an assignment, those who have access to people who know what college papers look like in a communications course, and those with the means to seek out the help of such people.

By contrast, the revised version of the assignment (Figure 2.2) offers students greater transparency about the purposes for their work. Those purposes are explicated at the beginning of the assignment under the heading "Purpose," with subheadings "Skills" and "Knowledge." The motivating benefits of doing this work are clear and accessible to students: "The purpose of this assignment is to help you make an informed decision about the major/career you are considering." Students will gain knowledge about "issues facing professionals in a field." The assignment directs students to focus on a small number of skills they can consciously practice while they are working on the assignment: "accessing and collecting information from appropriate primary and secondary sources . . . synthesizing information to develop informed views . . . composing a well-organized, clear, concise report."

The tasks in the revised assignment are listed in sequential order and remain mostly unchanged from the original draft. The revised assignment offers several due dates that break these tasks into smaller sequential pieces so students can consciously focus on developing two or three skills/ideas at a time, and receive and act upon feedback at several stages during their work on the project.

Following the tasks, criteria appear in the form of a rubric that students can use to monitor their success while they are working on the assignment.

Figure 2.2. More transparent interview assignment from a communications course.

University of Nevada, Las Vegas
COLA100E, Interview Assignment
Due dates:
- Sept 30—Draft interview questions
- October 15—Transcript of interviews
- November 17—Report

Purpose: The purpose of this assignment is to help you make an informed decision about the major/career you are considering.

Skills: This assignment will help you practice the following skills that are essential to your success in school and your professional life:
- Accessing and collecting information from appropriate primary and secondary sources
- Synthesizing information to develop informed views
- Composing a well-organized, clear, concise report to expand your knowledge on a subject in your major.

Knowledge: This assignment will also help you to become familiar with the following important content knowledge in this discipline:
- Issues facing professionals in a field
- Scholarly research formats for documenting sources and creating reference pages (i.e., bibliographies).

Task: To complete this assignment you should:
1. Select two professionals in your prospective academic discipline and/or career field who are considered experts in an area in which you are interested.
2. Secure an interview with the professionals for a date and time that is convenient for both of you.
3. Prepare 8–10 questions to ask the professionals about their expertise in a particular academic discipline/career field. The questions must be based on a review of the field using 5 credible sources as defined by the librarian in our research module. Sources should be cited using APA formatting.
4. Conduct a 20–30-minute, face-to-face interview with each professional to gather knowledge that will help you make an informed decision about the major/career you are considering. You will want to audio/video record the interview with the interviewee's permission.
5. Prepare a typed transcript of the interviews.
6. Compare and contrast the information provided by both professionals in an **8-page (1.5 spaced, 12 point Times New Roman font, 1 inch margins) report** that documents the advantages and disadvantages of a career in the selected field.

Criteria for success: Please see the attached rubric.

Note. Reproduced by permission of Katherine Johnson.

Faculty can engage students in applying criteria from a rubric or simple checklist to examples of similar real-world work, like excerpts the teacher selects from published interviews, for example. A brief discussion in class allows students to consider how the criteria for their own assignment can apply to such real-world examples. Such an exercise also helps students to see how real-world examples can fall short of the expectations for their own assigned work. The criteria statement in the assignment has been improved in subsequent years:

> You will have succeeded on this assignment if you conduct written and spoken communications with an experienced professional in your desired field, if you learn from any mistakes you made and effective strategies you used during those communications, and if you learn something you find useful about pursuing a career in that field.

The more transparent version of this assignment was one of many in the UNLV study that contributed to students' increased confidence, belonging, metacognitive awareness, and higher retention rates up to two years later (as discussed in the introduction). Although the assignment, like many in our study, still gets revised to make it more transparent for new groups of students, the more transparent version of it offered here was transparent enough for students to experience significant benefits in our study.

The big differences between the draft and the revised version demonstrate the changes that faculty often make when they revise an assignment to make it more transparent for students. First, the learning goals and the purposes of the work are explicitly defined, including disciplinary knowledge to be gained and skills to be practiced. Second, a checklist, rubric, or other criteria are provided before students begin working, and teachers and students discuss how well several samples of real-world work manage to meet those criteria. And third, multiple due dates divide the assignment into smaller parts, with specific learning purposes for each part. The list of tasks that constituted the entire text of the original assignment remains mostly the same. These changes help students to maintain a metacognitive focus on how they are internalizing knowledge specific to the discipline and on practicing discrete skills that are useful for their lives during and after college. Faculty may offer feedback themselves or structure peer feedback opportunities at checkpoints during the project. Students can correct course and improve their work as needed while the project is underway, enabling higher quality work and greater achievement in the completed projects.

Faculty can often accomplish these kinds of changes in less than half an hour, as in the workshops for the faculty in our study. Although the before-and-after examples offered in this chapter come from a communications course, these changes apply across all disciplines. A calculus problem set assignment, for example, might include a revised purpose statement explaining that all the problems on the assignment will help students practice calculating and depicting the rate at which change happens—skills that students might later use when considering things like their own earnings or the cost of living in a city where they might want to settle. A science research poster assignment in a mandatory introductory science course might include a revised purpose statement that explains the benefits of the assignment for those who don't plan to become scientists: "This assignment will help you practice how to judge the reliability of scientific information about health or diet that you encounter in popular media." Examples of many assignments across the disciplines before and after they were revised to make them somewhat more transparent are available online (TILT Higher Ed, 2014), where the collection of first and second revisions demonstrates that teachers continue to find ways to include more transparency for new groups of students over time.

Because most assignments already include some description of tasks, the bulk of the effort to make an assignment more transparent focuses on communicating the knowledge to be gained, the skills to be practiced, and what the criteria look like in practice when they are achieved. Sharing these in a way that makes them equitably accessible to students is not unreasonably difficult or time-consuming. A checklist for designing transparent assignments (Figure 2.3) may be helpful as you embark upon the design or revision process.

Challenges and Variations

The sample assignments offered in this chapter are visual artifacts from a fuller communication among teachers and students about the purpose-task-criteria framework for academic work. They illustrate only a part of the conversation. Not all of the teachers in the AAC&U study, the UNLV study, or subsequent cohorts chose to write out their assignments in this specific order. Sometimes there are only spoken instructions. Often, teachers provide both written instructions and a discussion in an effort to provide greater access to students who might have missed that one class discussion about the assignment, or who would benefit from seeing the purpose-task-criteria framework for their work in written form. When the assignment is a short, in-class peer exercise that takes place during a class meeting, teachers sometimes discuss the purpose, tasks, and criteria with students while jotting down ideas on a PowerPoint slide or whiteboard or shared document where students can view

Figure 2.3. Checklist for designing a transparent assignment.

Self-Guided Checklist for Designing a Transparent Assignment

PURPOSE:

Knowledge:

○ Does your purpose statement specify content knowledge that students will gain from doing this assignment?

○ Does your purpose statement link that particular knowledge to the larger context of
  - recent topics of class sessions?
  - this part of the course?
  - the whole course?
  - the major?
  - the discipline?
  - your institution's main learning outcomes?

○ Does your purpose statement indicate the relevance and/or usefulness of this knowledge to the students' lives
  - beyond the course? beyond the major? beyond college?

Skills:

○ Does your purpose statement specify a skill or skill set that students will practice while doing the assignment?

○ Does your purpose statement link that particular skill/skill set to examples/contexts where this skill is important in the context of
  - recent class sessions?
  - this part of the course?
  - the whole course?
  - the major? the discipline? your institution's main learning outcomes?

○ Does your statement indicate the relevance and/or usefulness of this knowledge to the students' lives
  - beyond the course? beyond the major? beyond college
  - Would this assignment benefit from segmenting it into several assignments, each one focused on a discrete set of skills that should be mastered to insure students' successful completion of the next assignment in the sequence?

(Continues)

Figure 2.3. (*Continued*)

TASK

o Does your description of the task:
  - identify the very first thing students should do when they begin working on the assignment?
  - the very next thing they should do?
  - the next, etc.

o Does your description of the task help students to avoid wasting their time on unnecessary steps, unproductive time expenditure?

o Does your description help students to focus their time efficiently on producing the highest quality work possible in the time given?

o Would students benefit from some practice exercises (in the form of a pre-task) in class to prepare them to perform the task outside of class on the graded assignment?

CRITERIA:

o Can students use the criteria while they are working on the assignment to determine whether they are completing the assignment efficiently and effectively?

o Do the criteria take the form of a checklist students can use to evaluate the quality of their efforts while they are working on the assignment?

o Does the checklist specify characteristics of high-quality work for this assignment?

o Can you help students apply the checklist to evaluating some sample work in class, so they understand how each criterion would look in practice?

o With your guidance, can the students collaboratively annotate several examples of work to indicate where/how the work satisfies the criteria? (These annotated examples may then be shared as a reference for students to use while they work on their own assignments.)

o Would a rubric (AAC&U VALUE examples) be helpful to students for this assignment?

o Does the rubric provide an amount of information that helps students at this phase in their learning?

o Does the rubric provide an overwhelming or counterproductive amount of information for students at this phase in their learning?

o Did you provide examples of good work, annotated to identify exactly where and how this work satisfies your criteria?

o Can you provide students with examples in class so they and you can test out your criteria checklist or rubric to be sure students know how to apply the criteria to multiple examples of work, and eventually their own work?

the emerging key points before they get to work, and check them again while their work is underway.

Our studies have demonstrated that when teachers communicate with students about purposes, tasks, and criteria for academic work in their own way and at their own discretion, students benefit significantly and equitably. We intentionally offered a Transparency Framework to guide teachers' implementation of transparency rather than a strict protocol, because we wanted our research to demonstrate what happens when teachers apply transparency with different groups of students in ways that felt consistent with the teachers' judgment and their own teaching practices. In other words, we wanted to test and document what happens in reality when teachers apply transparency at their own discretion.

Although transparency can help students, too much transparency may be unnecessary or overwhelming. You can adjust the amount of detail, providing less information about purposes and criteria for introductory students and more for advanced students. For introductory students, a full rubric with multiple columns and rows may offer more detail about criteria than students need or understand. A simple checklist and an opportunity to discuss and apply the criteria to multiple real-world examples *before* beginning their own work may provide enough help. Introductory students may benefit from a more detailed description of tasks, whereas upper-level or graduate students need less detailed guidance on each step to be taken and more information about criteria. Teachers tend to offer less detail about purposes, tasks, and criteria for low-stakes assignments and in-class exercises, whereas they offer more purpose-task-criteria information about final projects and other high-stakes work that can substantially affect a student's course grade.

Ultimately, as teachers across the country have discovered, students are the best judges of how transparent an academic assignment is to them. Teachers who use the Transparency Framework for Students (see Figure I.3) to frame in-class conversations about the work to be undertaken report that students will find ways to clarify the purposes, tasks, and criteria for the work that the teachers never predicted. Subgroups or sections of students in the same large course will find different ways to help their instructor make the work more transparent to them. Even teachers who meticulously follow the guidelines find that their students can offer insights about how to make the work more transparent at the moment the work is assigned and discussed with the class group. Students are the ultimate experts on how teachers can make an assignment transparent to them, and discussing assignments with students before they begin working can ensure that the students spend the bulk of their time working efficiently and meeting the criteria for their work, and teachers will subsequently spend less time correcting, coaching, guiding revisions, or defending grades.

Many of the teachers in our studies went on to revise and improve the transparent assignments in subsequent terms, and they gradually incorporated transparency into more assignments and class exercises, and even into their syllabi. They perceive that more instances of transparent instruction encourage even higher student achievement. A simple way to build additional instances of transparent instruction is to offer one preparatory in-class activity before each assignment, where students can practice the skills and grapple with some of the knowledge they need for the assignment and gather peer feedback as well as coaching from their teacher. The sequencing worksheet (Table 2.1) offers an example of how you might sketch out a plan for building a sequence of transparent assignments and in-class exercises through a whole term that focuses on building students' mastery of increasing complex skills and knowledge in a course. In the table, I completed the worksheet for the assignments in my Art and Politics in Renaissance Italy course.

Each graded assignment focuses on a specific skill set, beginning with simpler skills at the beginning of term and working toward more complex, compound skills as the term progresses. The content focus for each assignment develops chronologically in this example across the fifteenth and sixteenth centuries. Low-stakes activities in class offer students a chance to try out the work they will do in higher stakes, graded assignments out of class. This provides teachers with an opportunity to guide and correct students before they begin working independently outside the class setting.

The main skill sets that students will develop over a term (identified in the far left column on the sequencing worksheet) can be reinforced via headlines in the syllabus that correspond to the skills and knowledge identified on the sequencing worksheet and in the purpose statement for each assignment or class activity. For example, in my Art and Politics course, the main skill sets that students practice are highlighted in the first paragraph of the syllabus, and again throughout the calendar of class meetings. Each of the main skill sets is the focus of one of the course's four units. The sequence of skill development listed in the syllabus (see Figure 1.1) mirrors the sequence illustrated in the sequencing worksheet for course activities and assignments in Table 2.1.

Conclusion

Although this chapter offers multiple examples and guidelines, it is important to recognize that a relatively small amount of transparent instruction can offer significant benefits for students. You do not need to revise every syllabus, in-class activity, or assignment to reap those gains. In our AAC&U and UNLV studies, we asked teachers to revise only two assignments in a term to make them more transparent, relevant, and accessible for students. That was enough to provide students with significant increases to their confidence, sense of belonging, metacognitive awareness, and retention up to two years later, with even larger gains for underserved students. Two discussions in a term about the purposes, tasks, and criteria for their academic work can prepare students to seek out transparency in other assignments and in other courses.

For assistance in designing assignments, learning exercises, and course materials that offer transparency equitably to students, consult the guidelines in this chapter, this book, and the multiple examples available on the TILT website (TILT Higher Ed, 2014), and also consider engaging your peers. Ultimately, keep in mind that students are the best source of information about how to offer them transparency around the purposes, tasks, and criteria for their academic work.

EDITORS' HIGHLIGHTS

For faculty members thinking about redesigning an assignment using the Transparency Framework, consider the following points from this contributor:

- Small changes lead to big improvements. Start by revising just two assignments in a course so that all students begin with an equitable understanding of the purposes, tasks, and criteria for their work before they begin doing it. Consult examples in this book, TILT Higher Ed online resources, your peers, and most importantly your students, as you aim to offer students transparency about their academic work.
- Ask your peers (both from your discipline and outside of your field) for their feedback about your revised assignments. The input gained from a colleague might reveal a new way of thinking about your assignment; moreover, conversations about teaching and learning, although often rare, are almost always welcome.
- Engage students in seeking the purposes, tasks, and criteria for their academic work. This increases their metacognitive ability to monitor their own learning and helps teachers to provide transparent instruction effectively. Students are the best experts on how to make academic work transparent to them.

TABLE 2.1

Sequencing Worksheet for Course Activities and Assignments

GOAL: SKILLS 5 years out Bloom; DQP; GenEd	GOAL: CONTENT KNOWLEDGE 5 years out	ACTIVITY OR ASSIGNMENT	CUES Bloom, Felder (page 2)	ASSESSMENT FROM	STAKES %	TIME-SAVERS
Understanding the frameworks: contexts, techniques, terms, artifacts as history	Michelangelo's *David*, Ancient models for Renaissance Legitimacy, Daily Life in Renaissance Italy	In-class formal analysis of art exercise	Identify, describe	Peers and teacher	Low	Review of skills/knowledge goals, explicate their relevance; Guidelines/checklist provided
Understand Renaissance art-making techniques and tools, terms, social history of art		Take-home paper: formal analysis of artwork	Identify, locate, describe	Teacher	Medium	Annotated examples provided; In-class annotation of examples, using the checklist
Analysis and Synthesis: using artifacts, primary and secondary sources to construct the story	Art and politics in Renaissance republics, religious orders, dynasties	In-class analysis of primary, secondary sources	Separate, compare, summarize	Peers and teacher	Low	Review of skills/knowledge goals, explicate their relevance; Build skills in a sequence; In-class narration of skills in use
		Take-home assignment: annotated bibliography explaining how each source helps you	Choose, cite, decide, describe	Peers	Low	Peer feedback on drafts, using checklist feedback targeted to phase
				Teacher	Medium	

Learning outcome	Topic	Activity	Cognitive skills	Assessor	Stakes	Feedback
Evaluating reliability of artifacts and sources, perceptions of value and achievement, evolving contexts	Politics of preserving, pricing, and selling Renaissance art	In-class activity: reconstruct the painting of Michelangelo's *Last Judgment* from conflicting primary sources and contemporary conservation analysis	Compare, make a judgment, interpret, debate, choose	Peers and teacher	Low	Review of skills/knowledge goals, explicate their relevance Build skills in a sequence in-class narration of skills in use Peer feedback on drafts, using checklist Feedback targeted to phase
		Take-home paper; likely original context/use for your selected artwork	Compare, make a judgment, interpret	Teacher	High	
Creating new contexts for examining Renaissance artifacts and events	Student-designed art exhibitions	Presentations and feedback	Identify, describe, compare, judge, interpret, design create	Peers and teacher	Medium	Review of skills/knowledge goals, explicate their relevance
		Final paper		Teacher	High	In-class narration of skills in use peer feedback suggests revisions

References

Association of American Colleges & Universities (AAC&U). (2017). *VALUE: Valid assessment of learning in undergraduate education*. Washington DC: Association of American Colleges & Universities. Available from https://www.aacu.org/value-rubrics

Bjork, R. A. (1994). Memory and metamemory considerations in the training of human beings. In J. Metcalfe & A. Shimamura (Eds.), *Metacognition: Knowing about knowing* (pp. 185–205). Cambridge, MA: MIT Press.

Copeland, D. E., Winkelmes, M. A., & Gunawan, K. (2018). Helping students by using transparent writing assignments. In T. L. Kuther (Ed.), *Integrating writing into the psychology course: Strategies for promoting student skills* (pp. 26–37). Washington DC: Society for the Teaching of Psychology. Available from http://teachpsych.org/ebooks/integratingwriting

Cowan, N. (2010). The magical mystery four: How is working memory capacity limited, and why? *Current Directions in Psychological Science, 19,* 51–57.

Diemand-Yauman, C., Oppenheimer, D., & Vaughan, E. (2011). Fortune favors the bold (and the italicized): Effects of disfluency on educational outcomes. *Cognition, 118*(1), 111–115.

Howard, T., Winkelmes, M. A., & Shegog, M. (in press). Transparent teaching in the virtual classroom: Assessing the opportunities and challenges of integrating transparent teaching methods with online learning. *Journal of Political Science Education.*

Kang, Y., Kelly, J., Murray, C., & Visbal, A. (2016). Transparency and problem solving: The UHD experience. *Peer Review, 18*(1/2), 24–27.

TILT Higher Ed. (2014). *Transparency in Learning and Teaching.* Available from www.tilthighered.org

Whitehead, D. M. (2016). Faculty evidence. *Peer Review, 18*(1/2), 37–38.

Winkelmes, M. A., Copeland, D. E., Jorgensen, E., Sloat, A., Smedley, A., Pizor, P.,... Jalene, S. (2015). Benefits (some unexpected) of transparent assignment design. *National Teaching and Learning Forum, 24*(4), 4–6.

3

FACULTY VOICES
AND PERSPECTIVES
ON TRANSPARENT
ASSIGNMENT DESIGN

FAQs for Implementation and Beyond

Allison Boye, Suzanne Tapp, Julie Nelson Couch,
Robert D. Cox, and Lisa Garner Santa

A s the first chapters of this book establish, the Transparency in Learning and Teaching in Higher Education (TILT Higher Ed) project appeals to faculty, educational developers, and administrators alike for its accessible and easily implemented model as well as its wide-reaching benefits for students. Like other educational developers, including those featured in this collection, we also saw the project as a gateway for engaging with faculty. Through the creation of small faculty learning communities (FLCs), we were able to delve more deeply into the faculty perspective. In this chapter, we share the reflections of faculty on our campus who put the Transparency Framework into practice in their own classrooms and answer some common questions that other interested faculty might have as they consider the model for their own use. Although the faculty highlighted here are from a single institution, they reflect diverse disciplines, experiences, and class types and sizes, and their perspectives are representative of the varied experiences of instructors writ large.

Context

Texas Tech University is a large emerging research institution with a population of approximately of 37,000 undergraduate students, 12 colleges and schools, more than 150 undergraduate degrees, 100 graduate degrees, 50 doctoral degrees, and approximately 1,500 full-time faculty. The Teaching, Learning, and Professional Development Center (TLPDC) at Texas Tech University was begun in 1998. The mission of the TLPDC is to support Texas Tech's commitment to teaching and learning excellence by providing professional development workshops; guidance on service-learning courses; graduate student development fellowships and programming; faculty development focused on science, technology, math, and engineering (STEM) disciplines; and teaching consultations for any member of the Texas Tech University teaching community.

In the summer of 2016, the TLPDC invited a select group of Texas Tech faculty members to join us in a brief FLC to think about how to apply principles from the TILT initiative to an assignment in one of their fall classes. We promoted the project with a simple e-mail:

> The Transparency in Learning and Teaching Project is led by Mary-Ann Winkelmes from University of Nevada, Las Vegas and is a partner with the Association of American Colleges & Universities; the project has also been highlighted in *The Chronicle of Higher Education* and many other publications. The goal of this project is to implement a transparent teaching framework that helps to promote your students' understanding of how they learn. It's a simple concept to reframe an assignment in a way that focuses on the how and why of the assignment. Winkelmes' research has shown that for students, there are statistically significant gains in short-term and long-term learning benefits, and of particular interest to us, students show greater awareness of critical thinking skills after participating in transparent teaching environments. (S. Tapp, personal communication, May 25, 2016).

This initial FLC offering was so successfully received and easily implemented that our center for teaching and learning (CTL) colleagues created four more FLCs, including groups with a focus on graduate student instructors, STEM faculty, faculty teaching online, and a group representing multiple disciplines.

We know that faculty who might be interested in implementing transparent assignment design in their own classes often have similar concerns before embarking on the revision process. Our work with faculty on the Texas Tech campus shows that many of those concerns are quickly allayed by the value of the project. We surveyed members of the five FLC groups to identify their perceptions about the TILT project ($N = 15$, response rate 45.45%) and interviewed three faculty members further. The three faculty members featured in this chapter include Robert Cox, a STEM professor from Natural Resource Management who teaches undergraduate lectures and labs; Lisa Garner Santa, a flute professor from the School of Music who primarily teaches applied music through private lessons and uses a foundational flute technique assignment with all students; and Julie Nelson Couch, a literature professor from the Department of English. What follows are comments gleaned from responses to an anonymous survey and further interviews with these three faculty partners.

What Are Faculty Members' Initial Impressions of Transparent Assignment Design?

We found that faculty had a range of reactions to the project in the beginning, from "I think I'm already doing this" to "Wow, I really need this!" On one end of the spectrum, some faculty might feel that their assignments are already sufficiently effective and clear to students. For instance, Garner Santa, the flute professor, noted that her first thought was "My syllabus is already transparent." However, upon further inspection of the transparent assignment components, she soon realized that, indeed, her assignments could be improved. She noted:

> I realized how confusing my syllabus must seem for a new student who didn't already understand my expectations. I teach applied music, basically private lessons, to a wide level of skill, from freshmen to graduate. Typically, each student is assigned repertoire, études, and exercises based on individual strengths and deficiencies; however, a foundational flute technique assignment is presented each semester for all to master. I decided to apply the transparent design to the common assignment, and even more specifically, to only the semester technique assignment for the incoming freshman class. I thought they would gain the greatest benefit from the clarity of expectations regarding preparation and assessment supported by the new syllabus design.

Other faculty perceived that the design seemed like plain old good teaching rather than some sort of gimmick and were excited to see how it could benefit their students. Cox, from Natural Resources Management, remarked that

> it simply seemed to be good teaching practice. There wasn't any "trick" or new technique to master, just an emphasis on sound instructional design. I thought it seemed pretty intuitive: carefully explain what you expect, and why you expect it, and then provide examples of how to complete the assignment.

Similarly, Nelson Couch, the English professor, revealed that she was "excited to implement the pragmatic suggestions" in hopes that they might help her students better comprehend the analytical writing process. She detailed:

> In the past, I had been frustrated by students' lack of understanding of my expectations for writing essays. I was particularly frustrated at the gap between what I had expected of these assignments and what the students actually did. I would receive essays that summarized rather than analyzed the text for example, or essays that did not offer a strong thesis statement. These flawed approaches to analytical essays are typical and the bane of English professorial grading. I saw this Transparency Project as a potentially effective way to close the comprehension gap, to make explicit to students what I was asking for and give them the steps to achieve it.

Other faculty we surveyed anonymously offered similar insights, such as "I felt like adding transparency would help students buy into what can easily be a very dry topic" and "I saw a great opportunity to be more clear in my expectations." Clearly, it did not take long for our faculty to recognize the simplicity of the transparent assignment design concept and buy into the potential it held for their students' success.

What Assignment Changes Do Faculty Make, and What Realizations Do They Have?

Some faculty might be reticent to take on a substantial redesign of assignments they feel they have perfected. However, our faculty revealed that upon reflection and thoughtful revision as facilitated by the Transparent Assignment Framework (see Figures I.2 and I.3), they found meaningful and valuable changes to make that they had not previously considered, and came to some powerful realizations about how they had been and *could be* communicating with students.

Clarifying Guidelines and Adding Scaffolding

Many changes our faculty made were simple, taking the form of clarified grading criteria or refined guidelines for completion. Nelson Couch added more methodical instructions for her essay assignment, including a "step-by-step process for planning, outlining, and writing the essay" (Figures 3.1 and 3.2); she also chose to eliminate the single final deadline and instead implement sequenced deadlines for individual tasks, delineated on a clear timetable (Table 3.1).

Figure 3.1. Original English 4311 assignment, fall 2016.

Julie Nelson Couch
English 4311, Studies in Poetry

(LESS TRANSPARENT)

CRITICAL ESSAY ON A SELECTED COTTON NERO POEM, 4-6 PAGES (18 PTS): For this assignment, you will choose one of the four poems in the manuscript and offer a close reading and interpretation of it in a well-written essay. On one of the days we are reading the poem you choose, you will offer a preliminary argument (thesis) as your forum response for that day. The forum response should also include a brief summary of one secondary article on the poem. The essay should incorporate the student's interpretation and at least the one secondary source. The **final draft** of the essay will be due the last day scheduled for that poem. **NOTES**: Students should plan ahead and also begin scheduling these due dates the first full week of school. Students must choose different poems for the Presentation assignment and this Critical Essay.
Date Range For Essays: Sept 3--Nov 7

Note. Reproduced by permission of Julie Nelson Couch, Texas Tech University.

This scaffolding of an assignment into smaller sequential pieces is a common outcome for faculty who apply the transparent framework for the first time (see chapter 2).

Through the revision process, Garner Santa also realized that she had not been providing concrete details about the grading process for her students' flute technique assignment, so in her revision, she added "basic instructions on preparation, as well as a very clear rubric on assessment." Clarifying grading criteria might seem like a relatively insignificant addition, but the literature on rubrics confirms that they are useful for teaching as well as evaluating, helping students to focus, feel less anxious, and earn better grades (Andrade, 2005; Andrade & Du, 2005). Rubrics and clear grading criteria can likewise facilitate student self-assessment alongside the feedback process for instructors (Andrade & Du, 2005; Jonsson & Svingby, 2007). In her experiences with transparent assignment design, Garner Santa likewise saw all of these benefits come to fruition for her own students.

For others, the changes were even more fundamental. Cox had not previously distributed a physical assignment handout to his students, so the revision process encouraged him to articulate and describe the entire assignment for students more systematically. He noted:

Figure 3.2. Task description from revised English 4311 assignment, fall 2016.

I. **TASK: To complete this assignment, you will:**
    A. Prepare a Close Reading of the Poem:
    1. Read and reread the entire poem, taking notes and making connections. Much of this preparation will be completed through class preparation and class meetings.
    2. Select **one** of the 20 sections of the poem to analyze.
    3. Consider the following questions as you begin to analyze the poem:
        a. What are the contexts (including genre, manuscript, the poem as a whole) of the section?
        b. Who is speaking?
        c. Going line-by-line, what features of syntax, juxtaposition, imagery, allusion, patterns, repetition, language, and/or tone contribute to the meaning of the passage?
        d. NOTE: You may choose to analyze one of the translations or the Middle English version.
    4. Read back through the section and your notes to draw an interpretative conclusion. Articulate your conclusion as a **thesis statement**. While your essay focuses on one section of the poem, your thesis should offer a meaning that applies to the poem as a whole. For example, the thesis could propose the function of the chosen section within the larger poem.
    5. Write out a **preliminary outline** of your close reading.

    B. Prepare a Secondary Source:
    1. Use the MLA database to find a **relevant critical article** on *Pearl*.
    2. Determine and then write out, in your own words, the **main argument** of the article; this summary should be written as a three-sentence **annotation**.
    3. Work out how to incorporate the article into your interpretative essay. Insert the article—its argument and/or your response to the article—into your **essay outline**.

    C. Write Your Essay:
    1. Compose a **four- to six-page**, well-organized, well-written, clear, specific, interpretative essay on your chosen section of *Pearl*. Your essay should be typed, double-spaced, and in Times New Roman font with one-inch margins.
    2. Doublecheck quotes for accuracy. Incorporate proper MLA citations and include a Works Cited page for all sources used in the essay.
    3. Upload your essay to Blackboard. All uploaded files should be named appropriately as follows: **YourLastName_Assignment Name** (e.g. Jones_PearlEssay1stdraft).
    4. After Peer Review, revise your essay according to the feedback you received.
    5. Upload your final essay draft to Blackboard.

Note. Reproduced with permission of Julie Nelson Couch, Texas Tech University.

TABLE 3.1

Sequence of Due Dates From Revised English 4311 Assignment, Fall 2016

Date	Task Description
September 6	1. **Introduction to Assignment In-Class**: Go over assignment and grading rubric. Discuss close reading. Analyze and annotate sample essays. Compile a checklist of the features of a successful essay.
September 13, 11:00 AM	2. Submit **chosen section.** (NOTE: one student per section)
September 15, 11:00AM	3. Submit **annotated MLA citation of chosen critical article**.
September 20, 10:00 AM	4. Write and submit a **preliminary thesis statement** and **outline**. The outline should include the article's relation to your analysis.
September 22, 11:00 AM	5. Write the **first draft** of your essay and upload to Blackboard for Peer Review.
September 22	6. **In-Class Peer Review**
September 27, 11:59 PM	7. Revise Draft. Submit **final draft** of your essay via Blackboard.
October 6	8. After receiving your graded draft, complete a short reflection handout on the learning experience afforded by this assignment, including personal goals for improvement.

Note. Reproduced with permission of Julie Nelson Couch, Texas Tech University.

I didn't really change the purpose or the work of the assignment, but I significantly changed *how* I assigned it, and how I explained it to the students. Before participating in the TILT program, I simply explained the assignment during lecture, took questions about it, and allowed the students to proceed with their work. After participating in the TILT program, I created an assignment handout following the TILT Framework to explain the Purpose, Task, and Criteria for Success. I reviewed the handout in class, and we discussed it in class.

Rethinking Goals

Other participating faculty found themselves adding information about the goals and rationale for their assignments, which many had never actually articulated for students before. Additionally, some discovered that the revision process prompted them to reconsider their own goals for their assignments at a foundational level and, as a result, facilitated some essential realizations about their teaching in general. One faculty member surveyed wrote,

Thinking of the lesson in these three components (purpose, task, criteria) raised the bar for the lesson itself. Adding [those components] in demands more of the teaching and application portions of the lesson. My prepared explanations and examples became more thorough and better sequenced. I began thinking more about sequencing and clarity as a result.

Nelson Couch likewise found clarity for her own purposes as an instructor through the revision process, commenting that "the step-by-step process was extremely helpful . . . helping me to articulate what I was really looking for in the assignment." She added, "When I had to spell out what it takes to analyze a text, it gave me the words to teach the skills not only on the written assignment but also orally in class."

Adopting the Students' Perspective

The transparent assignment design process also helped our faculty to see their assignments from the students' perspective and make discoveries about their own faulty assumptions and miscommunications. Cox in particular highlighted the way the framework helped fill in the wide gaps he had been leaving for his students to fill in on their own—often in error. He observed:

I realized how poorly presented and poorly executed the assignment had been. The fact that I orally explained the assignment to the students in the classroom setting but provided no handouts or examples left a lot of room for them to misinterpret and misunderstand what the purpose of the assignment really was.

Through the revision process, our faculty also discovered that the Transparency Framework helped them bridge the preparation gap for their students—a gap that continues to widen in higher education (Petrilli & Finn, 2015). Indeed, one study of over 900 two- and four-year colleges from 44 states revealed that 96% of schools enrolled students who required remediation (Butrymowicz, 2017); further, the National Assessment of Educational Progress found that although preparedness rates of high school graduates has floated between 35% and 40% since the 1990s, the proportion of high school graduates *attending* college is now significantly higher than the proportion of those *prepared* for college (Petrilli & Finn, 2015). As such, it follows that transparent assignment design can and does play a role in helping clarify expectations for any less prepared students. The benefits for underserved students are even greater than the statistically significant benefits for all students in a national study (Winkelmes et al., 2016). One of our survey respondents voiced this, commenting that transparent instruction "seems like a reasonable response to a perceived or real decrease in student readiness." Nelson

Couch, for instance, gained a new appreciation for the leaps her own upper level students were having to make in completing her assignments, acknowledging that she had faultily assumed that students already knew how to analyze a literary text. She commented, "I realized I was being too obscure and assuming student knowledge that was not necessarily present." She added:

> In an unrevised assignment . . . I had just stated: include a secondary article. What I really wanted, I realized, is to teach students how to navigate the relevant database, how to choose an appropriate article, and how to determine the thesis of the article. I now spell all of that out and demonstrate those steps in class.

Garner Santa too became aware of "how overwhelming it must be for a new student" to sort through and make sense of the material she had previously only included on the course syllabus.

How Much Time and Effort Did It Take to Rework Your Assignments?

A major concern that many instructors might have about implementing the Transparency Framework is the time and effort involved in the development process. It is true that developing and articulating the purpose, task, and criteria components of an assignment does take some time. The faculty highlighted here indicated that the time they spent on their assignment revisions ranged from a few hours to a full day of work. Garner Santa indicated that she spent two hours creating the assessment rubric, and Nelson Couch surmised that she spent three to four hours redesigning the assignment. Cox estimated that he spent a full day creating his assignment handout, which is perhaps not surprising given that he had not previously utilized a detailed assignment handout. The good news is that although our faculty admit that some extra time was involved, they all felt the payoff was much greater, as their comments discussed later show, resulting in reduced confusion and improved performance from their students, and ultimately saving time in the end for both students and instructors.

How Did Students Respond to and Perform on the Newly Transparent Assignments?

The primary goal of transparent assignment design is, of course, to help students find more success in the classroom, so perhaps one of the most important questions interested faculty might ask involves student performance. Although the research from a national study indicates that this process supports student gains (Winkelmes et al., 2016), we were interested in what our faculty "on the ground" would have to say about their own students' results. And in fact, many of our participating faculty reported that they saw marked improvement in their students' responses to the newly revised assignments; 63% of survey comments regarding student response to the revised assignment indicated that students appeared to learn more, showed improved understanding, and/or performed more successfully. Just as research shows that transparency fosters significant success for all students, but especially for more at-risk student populations (Winkelmes et al., 2016), our faculty likewise found their students not only performed better but faculty also had fewer—if any—students who simply misinterpreted the task altogether. Cox, for example, observed:

> Overall students performed much better on the revised assignment. The quality of the finished work was higher, and there were fewer groups that missed the mark completely. In a class of 10–15 groups, I've found that 3–4 groups usually completely misunderstand the assignment and turn in something that doesn't meet the intent. The redesigned assignment had only one group in this category.

Nelson Couch echoed this result, remarking that "it seems that students who would have given up in the past worked hard and submitted essays that earned passing grades. It seemed that all the students, not just the strong writers, 'got' the assignment."

Garner Santa experienced some of the most notable successes with her flute studio students. Although it was routine for many students to fail their midterm technique assignment, she found that with application of the transparent assignment design, more students than ever were not just passing, but doing so at very high levels. She noted:

> Unquestionably, this freshman class was the most prepared and successful in the completion of the assigned technique. Typically in October . . . several students would fail the midterm technique exam, primarily because they did not understand the expected level of mastery. They were definitely familiar with the exercises but would make many mistakes. This resulted in students feeling frustrated and overwhelmed. Tears routinely would follow. After the implementation of the transparent design, the success rate of the students skyrocketed, many scoring 100%. Not a single student failed, nor [was] a single tear shed.

Garner Santa also noticed that her students had formed study groups in which to practice their technique together—another unprecedented behavior that was facilitated by the addition of more explicit criteria that students used to evaluate each other's work and undoubtedly contributed to their overall success with the assignment.

What Difficulties Did You Encounter With the Revision Process and New Assignment?

As with any project, the transparent assignment design process might not be a perfect "fit" for all instructors in a single format, and many faculty might be interested in any roadblocks or impediments that others encountered in their own implementation. Remarkably, our participating faculty had very few suggestions to make, if any, with 54.5% of respondents remarking that they found nothing difficult at all about the endeavor.

Staying Concise and Adjusting to Suit Individual Teaching Styles

Several instructors noted a desire to achieve greater concision using the framework without diminishing the clarity or transparency of the assignment. One faculty member acknowledged that the redesign doubled the size of the lesson, which necessitated cutting some other material, but that "students learned that topic more deeply."

Like other faculty in the national study, Nelson Couch found ways to fine-tune the Transparency Framework to fit her own teaching practices:

> In later versions of transparent assignments, I have made the instructions more concise while remaining true to the transparency model. Specifically, I made the list of items under *Purpose* shorter. I also switched the order: putting *Tasks* first and then *Purpose*. I found that starting with the practical sequence of tasks held the students' attention. Once I had introduced the students to their role in fulfilling the assignment, I then transitioned logically to the purpose of the assignment.

Time

Several faculty also remarked on the increased time and effort involved in the revision and presentation of the assignment. Garner Santa found that, although the transparent design process took more time than previous assignment descriptions, the process remained reasonable and the results outweighed any cost of additional time. She commented: "The redesign was a simple process. Perhaps most time consuming was the creation of the grading rubric, but the results were so substantial, it was worth every minute spent." Another participating faculty member who responded to our anonymous survey offered a similar comment: "Transparency redesign takes time and effort, but to me it was time and effort well spent." Cox had only one suggestion regarding the usage of the framework—that the process "be more widely considered by instructors," asserting that "it's a simple change that can make a big difference for students!"

What Did You Find Most Useful About the Transparent Assignment Design Process and Implementation?

Our participating faculty clearly responded very positively to the implementation of transparent assignments and found that the exercise offered numerous benefits to both teacher and student. In fact, all of the faculty respondents to our anonymous survey indicated that they found transparent assignment design to be either somewhat (27%) or significantly helpful (72%), and that they would probably (18%) or definitely (82%) revise future assignments using the Transparency Framework.

Reflection

Perhaps not surprisingly, our faculty welcomed how the Transparency Framework fostered reflection, assessment, and improved communication with students. Garner Santa shared, "I had been utilizing the same format for my masterclass syllabus for many years, so participating in the Transparency Project provided an impetus to evaluate the syllabus' effectiveness." Cox echoed this sentiment, remarking that even though "it can sometimes be painful to evaluate yourself . . . . the TILT process makes it as painless as possible" and "the most useful part of the process was the opportunity to critically evaluate my own teaching and look for ways to improve." Other participating faculty surveyed likewise valued the reflection and clarification facilitated by the process, offering comments such as "I have found myself rethinking all of my lessons, making sure that I am always clear about my goals in a given class" and "I found it useful for forcing me to be more explicit about the steps required of a learning activity and to be more mindful of the learning assumptions I bring to the activity that makes the learning more frustrating and potentially unsuccessful for students."

Time Management

Transparent assignment design appears to have potential for not only improving student understanding but also fostering more measured and responsible approaches to time management and completion. Nelson Couch—as well as her students—communicated a newfound appreciation specifically for multiple deadlines and scaffolding of assignments. She wrote:

> I found the greatest strength of the assignment redesign to be the incorporation of mini-deadlines before the final draft is due; a sequence of tasks with real deadlines empowers students to avoid procrastination in writing an essay. Many of my students have told me that having a deadline for a preliminary draft successfully kept them from procrastinating, making writing the final draft go much more smoothly. One student praised the sequence because it allowed more time for his idea to grow and develop before he was writing the final draft.

Similarly, another responding faculty member offered that their students, like others, appeared to demonstrate better understanding of the assignment, but they also worked on the assignment more diligently throughout the semester "rather than only trying to complete it right at the end of the semester, as in previous years."

How Has This Process Changed Faculty Approaches to Assignments and Teaching in General?

A remarkable if perhaps unintended result of the transparent assignment redesign process is the ripple effect it seems to have for faculty beyond just a single chosen assignment. Most obviously, the revision process inspired many of our participating faculty to redesign *all* of their assignments. One survey respondent, for instance, wrote, "I have already redesigned using the transparency design for my spring course—all assignments therein." The transparent assignment design process also seemed to encourage faculty to monitor their own assumptions and be more generally cognizant of the student perspective. One faculty member observed, "I learned to watch for assumptions about learning that my previous learning activity assignments may have included. I realized how important it is to articulate the process, the stages of work involved in assignments that are abstract and synthesizing." Another wrote, "I realized that I tend to make connections in my head that I do not articulate (or at least do not articulate well) to my students," and noted the realization that framing influences student perception of assignments and course material.

The transparent design process also highlights the fundamental value of clarity and time in cultivating deeper student learning, as several of our faculty found themselves expanding their lessons. Nelson Couch in particular shared that this process has encouraged the use of more class time to discuss expectations with students, and she works harder at modeling those expectations. She offered:

> I now take much more time in class to go over detailed assignment instructions and give students a chance to ask questions. I am also always on the lookout for examples. . . . For instance, in a reading I always assign in my graduate Research Methods class, I point out how the author maps out her review of the criticism as an exemplary model of how they can present their critical review in their own research projects. The article itself is assigned for its content, but now I also point out its effective formal features.

And although clarity and time may seem like simple concepts, as our faculty's experiences demonstrate, they can yield meaningful results for their students. Another faculty respondent insightfully summarized: "I do think that students perceive clarity as caring."

Conclusion

In general, implementing transparency appears to foster more purposeful and reflective teaching. Cox, for instance, reflected that being involved with the TILT project has made him "more thoughtful and conscious" about his teaching. Other faculty likewise noted improved intentionality in their teaching. This very act of reflection, which plays a crucial role in increased and continued teaching effectiveness (Bell, 2001; Brookfield, 1995; Bullough & Gitlin, 1991; Hammersley-Fletcher & Orsmond, 2005; Loughran, 2002), has much bigger consequences for instructors beyond simply offering clearer assignments; indeed, it can lead to better teaching.

As our faculty partners' experiences demonstrate, transparent assignment design and the reflective processes that accompany it offer the potential for immense rewards for both students and instructors. For faculty who may be considering implementing the practice in their classrooms, or for faculty developers interested in promoting the practice on their own campuses, we hope that the questions answered here might offer some guidance, encouragement, and even excitement for an easy change that can make a big impact.

EDITORS' HIGHLIGHTS

For faculty members considering implementing transparent assignment design, consider the following points from these contributors:

- You will spend extra time to redesign your assignments, but the payoff is worth it and ultimately saves you time when your students submit work that more closely meets your expectations.
- This process will help you rethink your assignments from a student perspective and will help you recognize assumptions you may be making about your students.

References

Andrade, H. G. (2005). Teaching with rubrics: The good, the bad, and the ugly. *College Teaching, 53*(1), 27–31.

Andrade, H. L., & Du, Y. (2005). Student perspectives on rubric-referenced assessment. *Practical Assessment, Research, and Evaluation, 10*(3), 1–10.

Bell, M. (2001). Supported reflective practice: A programme of peer observation and feedback for academic teaching development. *The International Journal for Academic Development, 6*(1), 29–39.

Brookfield, S. D. (1995). *Becoming a critically reflective teacher.* San Francisco, CA: Jossey-Bass.

Bullough, R. V., & Gitlin, A. D. (1991). Educative communities and the development of the reflective practitioner. In B. R. Tabachnick & K. M. Zeichner (Eds.), *Issues and practices in inquiry-oriented teacher education* (pp. 35–55). London, UK: Falmer Press.

Butrymowicz, S. (2017, January 30). Most colleges enroll many students who aren't prepared for higher education. *The Hechinger Report.* Available from http://hechingerreport.org/colleges-enroll-students-arent-prepared-higher-education/

Hammersley-Fletcher, L., & Orsmond, P. (2005). Reflecting on reflective practices within peer observation. *Studies in Higher Education, 30*(2), 213–224.

Jonsson, A., & Svingby, G. (2007). The use of scoring rubrics: Reliability, validity, and educational consequences. *Educational Research Review, 2*(2), 130–144.

Loughran, J. J. (2002). Effective reflective practice: In search of meaning in learning about teaching. *Journal of Teacher Education, 53*(1), 33–43.

Petrilli, M. J., & Finn, C. E. (2015, April 8). College preparedness over the years, according to NAEP. *Flypaper* (Thomas B. Fordham Institute). Available from https://edexcellence.net/articles/college-preparedness-over-the-years-according-to-naep

Winkelmes, M. A., Bernacki, M., Butler, J. V., Zochowski, M., Golanics, J., & Harriss Weavil, K. (2016). A teaching intervention that increases underserved college students' success. *Peer Review, 18*(1/2), 31–36.

PART TWO

TRANSPARENT DESIGN FOR FACULTY DEVELOPERS

4

TRANSPARENCY AND FACULTY DEVELOPMENT

Getting Started and Going Further

Allison Boye and Suzanne Tapp

In October 2017 at the annual Professional and Organizational Development Network (POD) in Higher Education meeting in Montreal, Canada, a group of educational developers representing approximately 25 institutions gathered to talk about their work with the Transparency in Learning and Teaching in Higher Education (TILT Higher Ed) project. As the conversation progressed and participants listened to each other's successes and challenges with TILT, it was apparent to all that participation in this project, whether through smaller, low-stakes implementation or as part of larger, institution-wide directives or multi-institution collaborations, was a positive, game-changing experience for faculty, students, and faculty developers. This purpose of this chapter is to provide an overview of the scope of work carried out by centers of teaching and learning (CTLs) involved to varying degrees in TILT and to provide a range of experiences and possibilities for those interested in getting involved with TILT at their institutions.

Low-Stakes Implementation

For educational developers who are interesting in dipping their toes into the TILT waters, there are several readily accessible low-stakes options.

Webinars and Online Videos

As educational developers shared their entry into and current status with the TILT project at the meeting in Montreal, many noted that they began their participation in TILT by viewing a short video about TILT or watching or even cohosting a webinar with Mary-Ann Winkelmes. The TILT Higher Ed website provides a variety of videos under the heading "TILT Higher Ed Examples and Resources" (TILT Higher Ed, 2014) for such purposes, including short summaries of TILT's impact and data, short descriptions of the purpose-task-criteria framework, a train-the-trainers conversation, a webinar for institutional leaders, and webinars for faculty who are working to design or revise transparent assignments. Similarly, resources including workshop slides, handouts, checklists, and assignments are also available for use, duplication, and customization to institutions. Publications, blogs and news media, and adaptations from across the United States are also available for reference. These online resources provide an incredibly easy entry into the TILT project for interested CTLs, requiring little effort and no additional cost to introduce faculty to the Transparency Framework.

Individual Consultations

Many CTLs count one-on-one consultations as a primary focus of their work with faculty colleagues (Brinko, 2012). Whether these conversations center around classroom observations and discussions about teaching, syllabus creation, and strategies for overcoming challenges or broader issues of departmental curriculum reform or college-level assessment projects, the work of an educational developer is often built around relationships and asking thoughtful questions to identify goals and challenges to teaching effectiveness (Little & Palmer, 2011). Faculty developers at institutions such as the Community Colleges of Spokane in Washington noted that the TILT framework has proven to be a helpful tool in consultations with both new and experienced faculty members. Xavier University representatives described attending a workshop at the 2016 annual POD conference that explained the principles of TILT seen through various case studies at institutions (Boye, Tapp, & Winkelmes, 2017). This catalyzed their use of the TILT framework with new faculty and in consultations. At our home institution, Texas Tech University, the practical application of assignment transformation and the promise of improved student success have been very appealing to faculty and instructors. This theme seemed to be shared by many others, as seen throughout this book, who were able to use TILT as a starting point to bigger opportunities.

Stand-Alone Workshops or Series

The TILT framework has been incorporated into many CTLs' programming as individual workshops or as part of a larger series. The Center for Teaching

Excellence at Duquesne University, for example, incorporated TILT into orientation sessions, short workshops, and flipped workshops. In our experience, these workshops fall into the low-stakes category because they require relatively little preparation on behalf of the facilitator. Reading this book provides an excellent foundation, and the materials previously referenced (the webinar and handouts) as well as materials created by Duquesne (found in chapter 6), are easily adaptable. At Texas Tech, we organize our TILT workshops with selected portions of a video featuring Mary-Ann Winkelmes to offer an overview of the foundational concepts supporting TILT as well as the research emerging from the project. We then walk through the purpose-task-criteria framework and, most importantly, look at sample "before and after" assignments provided at the TILT Higher Ed website under "Examples and Resources" (TILT Higher Ed, 2014). We have found it to be particularly helpful to ask participants to work together to analyze the less transparent "before" assignments and identify problematic components, and then repeat the process by identifying changes made in the more transparent version of the assignment. As a follow-up to this workshop, we also offer an optional hands-on version, in which participants are invited to bring their own assignments and engage in a peer workshop process to review the revisions with a partner or in small groups. Often, an interdisciplinary pairing proves to be the key to clarifying directions and recognizing underlying assumptions within the assignment that might not be accessible to students. This workshop opportunity is open to our teaching community and the condensed process differs from our smaller and more intensive faculty learning community approach explained in a following section.

Medium-Stakes Implementation

For educational developers who are interested in or more comfortable with implementing the TILT project at slightly higher levels than webinars or individual consultations, there are many relatable examples available. Several institutions and CTLs have found ways to weave TILT components into existing programming, build learning communities, or create larger programs around them.

Faculty Learning Communities

One simple yet far-reaching strategy for bringing the TILT project into your CTL is through the creation of faculty learning communities (FLCs) focusing on transparency. Cox (2004) defines an *FLC* as a small group of cross-disciplinary faculty or staff who engage in an active and collaborative program with a focus on teaching and learning. Faculty developers at Elon University in North Carolina had great success with interdisciplinary assignment design groups as well as informal FLCs and working groups (see chapter 5). CTL directors in Indiana also implemented FLCs centered on TILT with modest funding (see chapter 11). At Texas Tech University, we likewise found the formation of FLCs to have immense impact for our participating instructors as well as our center. (See chapter 2 for more details on faculty response and impact.) We used our first foray into the TILT project as an opportunity to reconnect with faculty who had once been highly involved with our center or to connect with other faculty with whom we had been eager to work further. Our model was simple: we met with our FLC 3 times—once prior to the start of the semester to introduce the TILT framework and research, a second time to allow them to "workshop" their revised assignments in process with one another, and a third time at the end of the semester to discuss the implementation of their revised assignments and their reflections on the experience. We were also able to secure small stipends ($300) for each of our 10 participating faculty as an incentive for helping us try out the new model.

This model was easily implemented and so successful in generating broader interest that four new learning communities comprising volunteers from our own campus and other regional campuses gathered the following year to work together without stipends. One group consisted of full-time faculty members from various disciplines; another solely of graduate student instructors; a third group of science, technology, engineering, and math faculty; and the fourth was facilitated online with regional off-campus instructors. FLCs such as these offer faculty an opportunity to connect more deeply with others across disciplines and to engage with the Transparency Framework with more focus and reflection than a stand-alone workshop, but without the need for a great deal more time and resources from CTLs, offering meaningful impact with comparatively little effort.

Conferences or External Guest Speakers

Hosting conferences or bringing in guest speakers to present to faculty can be an alternative way to introduce the TILT project and framework to larger groups on campus. At Texas Tech, Mary-Ann Winkelmes engaged our faculty in an interactive keynote session as part of a conference, which concluded with a panel discussion of faculty members who shared their experiences with TILT. The credibility of an external speaker often appeals to faculty and to CTL staff alike by bringing a variety of expertise and perspectives to an institution. Such visits carry the risk that new ideas may not take hold after their primary representative visits and then departs. Bringing in guest speakers also carries added costs, including speakers' honorariums; travel and hotel fees; and, for some, the costs and logistical complications associated with reserving larger/off-campus venues or hosting a major event. As such, this approach has slightly higher stakes than utilizing a webinar, though the face-to-face, personal interaction brings much added value.

Institutes or Other Programming Initiatives

Another popular approach utilized by CTLs is to integrate the Transparency Framework into some of their existing programming initiatives. Georgia Southern University, Brown University, and George Washington University, for instance, incorporated the framework into their course design/redesign institutes for faculty. Stetson University in Florida likewise integrated it into their certificate in teaching and course design, and the University of St. Thomas in Minnesota is utilizing the framework in their Inclusive Classroom Institute. Albion College in Michigan similarly wove it into programming for new faculty, and Keene State College in New Hampshire is adopting it in their first-year writing initiative. Some participants included stipends (as we did at Texas Tech with our pilot FLC) or mini-grants to faculty to incentivize participation, though that may not be fiscally feasible for all interested CTLs or institutions. Such examples, along with others in this book, indicate the Transparency Framework complements a variety of teaching and learning initiatives or other forms of campus programming, and the convenience of incorporating it into existing infrastructure is very appealing for many. Further, the use of such extended programming likely also widens the impact of the project beyond a one-off workshop or even a conference, and can involve the collection of data that includes large and meaningful sample sizes, as described in the next section.

Higher Stakes Implementation

A few institutions are engaging with the TILT project on an even larger scale, through gathering student and faculty data for scholarship of teaching and learning (SoTL) projects, impact studies, and assessment of institution-level programming or multi-institution partnerships. Measuring the impact of faculty development work on student success is historically very difficult because so many variables affect students' learning experiences. TILT's online student surveys and protocols have evolved to accommodate institutions' and CTLs' efforts to measure the impact of faculty development programs on student success. New protocols, as approved by UNLV's institutional review board (IRB) and those at additional schools, facilitate collaborations with institutional analysis staff or registrar staff to link objective measures of student success (e.g., student retention data and grades) with student predictors of success from TILT survey data. These higher stakes approaches demonstrate the excitement and enthusiasm that the project can inspire but also the requirement of more commitment by CTLs or other stakeholders in terms of both time and resources.

Data-Collecting Initiatives

The TILT project obviously offers an enticing opportunity for participants to gain insight into how their students learn, as well as the impact of their engagement with transparent assignment design. For individual faculty or faculty teams like FLCs, TILT offers free access to online surveys that can be shared with students at the beginning and end of term to gather students' views about their learning experiences. After an instructor requests access to use a TILT survey, TILT communicates directly with the institution's IRB chair to share past approvals and arrange any new ones that might be needed. After approvals are secured, TILT provides the instructor with a survey link to share with students, and after grades are submitted, TILT sends a confidential, individual instructor report.

On a larger scale, educational developers are collaborating with faculty members and staff to connect empirical data about student performance and retention. One early project of this sort is detailed in chapter 7 by participants from the University of Tennessee, Knoxville. Missouri Western University and Reed College are also involved in data-collection projects related to TILT, whereas at Texas Tech (chapter 3) and some California state institutions (chapter 10), faculty surveys were created to gather data about the impact of TILT on faculty practice and satisfaction.

A major consideration for those who might be interested in collecting student data is the need for approval from their IRB. If one seeks information on student grades or retention data, the IRB approval process could be rigorous in order to protect student privacy, as it was for researchers at the University of Tennessee, Knoxville. A hallmark of the TILT project is a philosophy of sharing materials. TILT shares all its IRB-approved documentation, including all modifications and reciprocal agreements over a period of 10 years, to offer interested researchers and IRB members a range of examples already approved by multiple institutions. The potential knowledge to be gained from such scholarly endeavors within and across institutions is vast and thus very appealing to many participants. We encourage scholars interested in pursuing IRB approval to contact the editors of this book for further discussion of communications with IRB staff at a variety of institutions.

Large Institutional Initiatives

A few institutions have decided to incorporate the TILT project into larger campus initiatives for even wider impact. Albion College in Michigan and Xavier University in Ohio, for instance, have included the Transparency Framework in targeted sessions for new faculty members. Tennessee Tech has taken it one step further and integrated the Transparency Framework into a course redesign initiative as part of their quality enhancement plan (QEP). Chapter 8 likewise offers a detailed look at the work done at UNLV incorporating transparent assignment design in courses, advising, and faculty development programs, and measuring the impact of that work on important student success goals that are part of the institution's strategic plan.

Clearly, the Transparency Framework inspires and excites many faculty developers and administrators with its accessible plan and promise of improved student success, and it easily dovetails into larger initiatives. For those hoping to implement the framework on a larger scale, buy-in from university administration is imperative, as is the ability to collaborate and partner with other units on campus.

Multi-Institutional Initiatives

Perhaps the highest stakes form of implementation comes in the form of multi-institutional collaborations and consortia. For example, the University of North Florida is part of a multi-institution consortium that is collaborating with the TILT project, including a qualitative analysis of student writing samples; Stetson University is likewise considering joining that consortium as they include the Transparency Framework as part of their certificate in teaching and course design. The California State University System has also included the Transparency Framework as a component in their graduation initiative, and institutions in the state of Indiana's Liberal Education and America's Promise (LEAP) network focus their inclusive excellence initiative on the TILT project (see chapters 10 and 11).

Conclusion

As evidenced by the many examples listed in this chapter and highlighted in the book, the TILT project can be adapted to fit an institution's campus culture and context. Its scalability in terms of involvement and cost as well as the proven outcomes seen in the research from TILT researchers around the United States offer CTLs a tangible way in which they might customize TILT to influence teaching and learning on their own campuses.

EDITORS' HIGHLIGHTS

For faculty developers interested in how TILT might influence their programming or interactions with faculty, consider the following points from these contributors:

- Many of the TILT projects initiated at CTLs and highlighted in this chapter began with conversations at the POD Network conference about the TILT project and are a good reminder of the power of sharing ideas and networking.
- For those who are new to the Transparency Project, there are generous online resources available from TILT Higher Ed to jumpstart workshops and CTL implementation.

References

Boye, A., Tapp, S. & Winklemes, M. A. (2017, November). *Transparency in teaching and learning project meeting.* Session presented at Professional and Organizational Development Network in Higher Education Conference, Montreal, Canada.

Brinko, K. (Ed.). (2012). *Practically speaking: A sourcebook for instructional consultants in higher education* (2nd ed.). Stillwater, OK: New Forums Press.

Cox, M. (2004). Introduction to faculty learning communities. *New Directions for Teaching and Learning, 97,* 5–23.

Little, D., & Palmer, M. S. (2011). A coaching-based framework for individual consultations. *To Improve the Academy, 29,* 102–115.

TILT Higher Ed. (2014). Transparency in Learning and Teaching. Available from www.tilthighered.org

5

DESIGNING TRANSPARENT ASSIGNMENTS IN INTERDISCIPLINARY CONTEXTS

Deandra Little and Amy Overman

A s educational developers, we often design new programming for faculty colleagues in order to share effective teaching methods and strategies that have been demonstrated to improve student learning and performance, and to promote intentional reflection on one's own teaching practices and beliefs. We have found the Transparency in Learning and Teaching in Higher Education (TILT Higher Ed) project offers an excellent opportunity to model effective, evidence-based design principles and formats (e.g., Fink, 2013) while demonstrating transparent teaching, or an "explicit conversation . . . about the processes of learning and the rationale for required learning activities" (Winkelmes, 2013, para. 4; see also Winkelmes, 2015; Winkelmes et al., 2016). When we encountered the Transparency Framework in 2015, we found it and the research findings persuasive. Moreover, we found the overarching metaphor of "TILTing"— as opposed to dismantling, overhauling, or rebuilding—aligned well with one of our center's primary objectives to "foster innovative, evidence-based teaching and learning practices and critical reflection through programs & services designed for faculty working in a range of teaching and learning contexts" (Elon University Center for the Advancement of Teaching & Learning, 2017). This focus on making intentional "minor adjustments" (Winkelmes, 2013, para. 4) resonated with our frequent recommendations that colleagues considering course or assignment improvements should focus on small, targeted changes that build over time—or "strategic tweaks"—to better determine which variables most help improve student learning within a course.

At our Center for Teaching and Learning (CTL), we adapted the TILT Higher Ed framework to our faculty needs and institutional culture and created a series of workshops and interdisciplinary assignment design groups. We discovered that the framework also began to inform our individual consultations and eventually developed into scholarship of teaching and learning (SoTL) projects. In this chapter, we introduce our local context, describe the series of offerings we developed based on the TILT framework, and explain what we learned about adapting the framework to our institutional and CTL context and what impact we have noticed on our CTL as a result.

Who We Are: TILT and Our Disciplinary Backgrounds

The TILT framework seemed like a promising tool to introduce to our faculty colleagues at Elon. In particular, the focus on transparent assignments appealed to us for three reasons: because it synthesizes a deep base of research (from various areas) on effective assignments; because it offers an accessible, straightforward, and easy-to-remember formula to be applied to assignments; and because it offered a hook for each of us disciplinarily in addition to our roles as educational developers.

As a literature professor, Deandra Little has an interest in research on writing assignments and on students and faculty as writers, and as a developer, she has been interested in compelling ways to talk about meaningful course design and assessment for a long time. The Transparency Framework for assignment design concisely distills some of the research on effective writing instruction (summarized in Bean, 2011), writing or multimedia assignments and cognitive load (e.g., Brünken, Plass, & Leutner, 2004), and learning to write distinct disciplinary genres (Carter, 2007) into key principles that are readily adaptable for faculty across disciplines. Research on writing, for example, demonstrates that teaching student writers to "think rhetorically" (Bean, 2011, p. 40)—or to understand audience, purpose, and genre—helps them transfer knowledge from one context to another. Clearly explaining purpose, task, and criteria helps students target their attention on the most important and complex aspects of the assignment, while reducing the extraneous cognitive load caused by a confusing format or unclear description (Brünken et al., 2004). The focus on clarifying the purpose, task, and criteria also builds on what we know about productive course design, which starts by articulating the goal—or why, which might also be understood as the larger course purpose—before specifying which assignments and activities—or tasks—best align with the goal or outcome (Biggs, 1996; Fink, 2013; Wiggins & McTighe, 2005). Finally, the reminder to include the criteria for evaluation is a nice prompt to enact findings from research on assessment and effective feedback practices (e.g., Walvoord & Anderson, 2011).

As a cognitive neuroscientist and developer, Amy Overman is particularly interested in how the Transparency Framework aligns with science of learning research and offers an easy entry point for faculty to align teaching practices with what we know about how learning works. For example, scientific research has shown that experts perceive information to which novices are blind, such as organizing principles (Chi, Glaser, & Rees, 1982). As faculty, we are experts and can see the purpose, task, and criteria of our assignments and courses clearly. However, our students are often unaware of these until we explicitly point them out. Additionally, scientific research has shown that working memory capacity is limited (see Cowan, 2005, for an extensive consideration of working memory capacity limits). When we give students transparent assignments we reduce the demand on working memory so students can focus on thinking deeply about the assignment, rather than devoting precious resources to interpreting our intent as teachers or wondering why they have been asked to do the work and how it relates to the class content.

Where We Work: TILT and Our Institutional Context

The first and most central part of our mission as a CTL is to "promote intentional, evidence-based, and inclusive teaching and learning practices" (Elon University Center for the Advancement of Teaching & Learning, 2017), and the Transparency Framework connects to all three aspects: transparent assignment design requires critical reflection on purpose and task, and the research findings suggest that transparent teaching increases predictors of success for all students (e.g., academic confidence, sense of belonging) and particularly does so for underrepresented, first-generation, and low socioeconomic status students (Winkelmes et al., 2016). Many other teaching centers share some or all of these values and so the TILT Higher Ed framework has a high potential for alignment with other centers' missions as well as to the core values of the educational developers themselves and the institutions where they work.

That the framework is "consistent with research-based best practices in higher education" (Winkelmes, 2013, para. 4) was an important consideration for us as we developed programming for our faculty colleagues. It will not be surprising that our center, like others, prioritizes sharing strategies and methods drawn from research on teaching and learning. We try to make evidence-informed decisions (Felten, Little, Ortquist-Ahrens, & Reder, 2013) about what workshops or programs to offer, considering evidence that draws on higher education scholarship, learning science, and educational development as well as evidence from the program assessment data we collect. When planning a program, we start with the following questions:

- What literature or models are we drawing on to design or deliver this program?
- What studies or theories about teaching and learning inform the content?
- What evidence from the literature on educational development does the program format or structure rely on?

After evaluating the research base, we consider local, contextual evidence, specifically whether the new topic speaks to existing needs or interests and what evidence we have that it connects to a campus concern or initiative or a departmental- or field-based one. The TILT framework aligns with our university's strategic plan in which we make an "unprecedented commitment" to focus on diversity and inclusion (Elon University, 2018). Part of that commitment means bringing in more students who may be underrepresented, first generation, or of low socioeconomic status, and therefore ensuring access and success continue to be concerns for faculty and administrators. TILT provides a way to address some of those concerns at the ground level of teaching and learning. Each class in which a faculty member incorporates transparency is a class in which access, success, and retention are supported, and the framework overlays other promising strategies (described further in the chapter) for enhancing the learning environment for all students which have been well received at our campus. For readers considering how to adopt the TILT framework at your institution, we encourage you to examine commonalities between your university's strategic plan and the TILT framework, both as a way to articulate the value of transparent teaching and learning to administrators (and possibly secure further financial support for programming) and as a way to articulate value to faculty members and create investment in adopting the approach.

Significantly, TILT Higher Ed also aligns with the evaluation system of our university. Teaching is given "top priority" as a criterion for evaluation of faculty (Elon University, 2017). The faculty handbook includes the following in the list of indicators of effective teaching: "demonstrating a commitment to improvement of teaching," "demonstrating an ability to communicate effectively with students," "challenging students to be engaged learners," and "facilitating intellectual opportunities for students" (Elon University, 2017) all of which dovetail with the TILT approach to teaching. Furthermore, our liberal arts emphasis encourages interdisciplinary and cross-departmental collaborations, which is one of the reasons we emphasized cross-disciplinary groups when implementing workshops, learning communities, and assignment alignment working groups.

In sum, the TILT Framework met our criteria for evidence arising from the literature and also from our institutional context. We encourage readers to use a similar evidence-based decision-making process as you decide how to bring conversations about transparent teaching to campus. You might consider incentivizing adoption of TILT by framing it in terms of your particular institution's evaluation system and/or curricular and student needs, as well as to consider whether discipline-based or cross-disciplinary programming will best fit with your institutional size, culture, and faculty norms for engaging with colleagues.

Workshops

We first introduced the TILT framework on our campus in spring 2015 with a workshop called "Creating Transparent Assignments to Enhance Student Learning." The workshop allowed us to test the framework for "proof of concept" on our campus to see how our colleagues responded to it and what they learned from applying it to their assignments. The workshop began with a brief description of the TILT Higher Ed project and findings on the benefits to students and unexpected benefits to instructors who used it, including that the main research goal of the project was "to study how faculty transparency about the design and problem-centered nature of student assignments would affect students' learning experiences and the quality of students' work" (Winkelmes, 2015, p. 1). In response to requests from our CTL and others, the TILT website now shares short videos as well as PowerPoint slides and handouts that developers can use to describe the project's research findings as well as its assignment design activities.

Workshop participants found the benefits to students and faculty that we shared (as reported by Winkelmes et al., 2016) to be persuasive, including that students experienced increased motivation, decreased resistance to assignments, and fewer questions about the work; moreover, the quality of student work improved. They seemed particularly interested in the unexpected benefits to faculty, namely that the resulting transparent assignments were easier to explain and to grade, because the purpose and expectations were clear, and that the clarity had the potential to increase student buy-in and reduce grade disputes. They were also interested to learn that faculty in the study began using the framework to introduce and conclude class meetings and to structure whole course syllabi, not just assignments within courses.

After an overview of the project, we focused on the transparent assignment intervention, explaining that a group of faculty in the TILT project had focused their efforts on redesigning two assignments to ensure they were clarifying the following key features:

- The purpose of the assignment, specifically the knowledge students would gain and the skills they would practice

- The task, or the steps they would follow
- The criteria by which student work would be judged

After sharing the research and framework, we invited triads of participants to use the framework to analyze and provide feedback on assignments or assignment ideas their colleagues brought to the session. Convinced of the power of the decoding the disciplines model (Middendorf & Pace, 2004) for helping bring to the surface the tacit knowledge we apply to our fields as experts, we deliberately instructed participants to form triads with colleagues from disciplines different than their own. Our interactive workshops frequently include moments for peer review, where we invite colleagues to play the role of *critical friend* (loosely based on the Critical Friend protocol from K–12 teaching; see Costa & Kallick, 1993; Mitchell & Sackney, 2000). In this case, reviewers were prompted to take a student's perspective while reviewing a colleague's assignment, using the following questions as a guide:

- *Purpose:* What seems to be the purpose of this assignment? What content knowledge or skills does it require or reinforce?
- *Task:* What do students need to do to successfully complete the assignment?
- *Criteria for Evaluation:* What is expected of students in order to succeed on this assignment? What will distinguish an excellent from a poor performance?

The peer feedback was an important part of the session. We had originally included it as a way for participants to practice using the framework to analyze assignments, because transparency can seem straightforward conceptually, but more challenging to "see" in one's own assignments or syllabus. We found, however, that the peer review had additional benefits, as respected colleagues from other departments voiced their confusion over how to interpret an assignment, or their concerns that "as a student" they would not know what aspects of it should be judged more or less important. For example, colleagues from statistics and English helped each other understand how clear their assignments were and where they might be using discipline-specific jargon or expecting, as experts, a demonstration of knowledge, problem-solving, or skills that was not explicitly articulated. This helped make clear the tacit assumptions instructors were making about students' prior learning or experience. Further, it encouraged instructors to highlight those moments in the class where the required knowledge or skills were introduced or practiced before students would use them in a take-home assignment. In addition to some things we had anticipated (e.g., that colleagues would find the research and framework compelling and find the discussion about their assignments helpful), we also found that the assignment's purpose was frequently more challenging for some participants to explain than other aspects of the assignment. After the peer review, we were able to discuss why that might be so and the importance of explaining purpose in order to help increase a sense of relevance necessary for student motivation and to help demystify assignments for students new to college or new to our disciplines.

After one of the coauthors presented on the workshop at the 2016 Professional Organization and Development (POD) Network Conference, we were invited to give the workshop to faculty at another college in our region, which has a similar liberal arts, teaching-focused mission; there, faculty participants had a similar positive reaction to the framework and its application to assignments. At the end of the 2017 workshop, some participants expressed interest in attempting this alignment in their own classes, similar to the informal faculty learning communities we developed as a result (described in the next section).

In both experiences, peer review using the TILT framework sparked thoughtful conversations about long-term learning goals and intentional teaching choices, while simultaneously making visible the differences between student and faculty (or expert and novice) perspectives. As we describe further, we also found that focusing on transparent assignments quickly led to discussions about transparent courses more broadly. We recommend that in presenting TILT, developers emphasize the alignment of course goals and objectives with assignments and emphasize the expert/novice divide.

Informal Faculty Learning Communities

Recognizing what the evidence tells us about the lower level of impact that one-time workshops provide (Chism, Holley, & Harris, 2012), we attempted to deepen the impact of the workshop by considering other ways to introduce transparent assignments with targeted groups of faculty and in longer term programming, including short- and long-term informal faculty learning communities and working groups.

New Faculty

Although a workshop was effective in reaching a core group of faculty and sharing the framework with colleagues at another college, we realized that in our university context we could potentially affect even more students by sharing the TILT framework with new faculty. Each year approximately

35 to 40 new faculty participate in our new faculty orientation, which consists of presemester programming and a monthly new faculty meeting. Many of our new faculty arrive excited about teaching but with limited teaching experience and/or teaching experience that took place in a large-class setting at a research-intensive university, which differs significantly from our teaching-focused university with class sizes of 33 or smaller. Additionally, incoming faculty are from various disciplines, which allowed us to continue to incorporate interdisciplinary perspectives.

We began weaving the TILT framework into new faculty programming to frame discussions of assignment design during a summer, 2-day Course Design Institute. We have also incorporated it into a 90-minute session on balancing academic challenge with appropriate support when teaching, grading, and giving feedback. Both of these have been excellent fits for the TILT framework. In 2016, when we introduced TILT in the monthly session, we also invited new faculty to participate in informal interdisciplinary learning communities. Three groups of a total of 10 new faculty participants met to share assignments and give and receive transparency-focused feedback. One unexpected benefit we observed was that when groups applied the framework, it opened up a robust discussion of a range of topics important to effective assignment design and grading.

For example, focusing on the purpose of the assignment helped participants clarify what skills or knowledge their assignments were prioritizing and figure out how to talk about that with students. Many of the faculty were surprised to realize how much of their knowledge and the language they used was specific to their disciplinary training and was opaque to their colleagues from other disciplines (including the facilitator). Again, this led to "ahas" about how their knowledge and language are perceived by students, who are novices to the discipline and novices to college-level learning.

Additionally, during discussion of the task and criteria aspects of the assignments, new faculty had realizations about how the differences between their prior experiences and their new institutional context and local student demographics would necessitate adjustments in the transparency of their assignments. They took time to consider what a novice learner in their new institutional context might find difficult; how this compared to students in their prior context; and, therefore, what aspects of the assignment were most important to clarify; and what grading and feedback was appropriate. For example, one participant had experience with larger classes as a teaching assistant at a research-intensive state university where students did not expect the level of feedback that our students expect. The TILT framework helped him to communicate more clearly to his students about assignment expectations. As a result, students avoided common pitfalls, and he was able to use his time to give more detailed, tailored feedback to each individual.

Furthermore, the focus on tasks and criteria allowed the facilitator to prompt a discussion about what prior opportunities faculty provided for students to practice using the skills and knowledge they would need to apply in order to meet the instructors' criteria for success in the assignments. This led to realizations and strategy sharing about the structure of the entire course, such as where scaffolding could be better built into the course, how assignment sequencing could be improved, and what types of feedback are most effective and how to balance that with faculty time demands.

Faculty reported that they felt comfortable because the group was composed of other new faculty who faced some of the same challenges in transitioning to our university. In addition to creating clearer, more transparent assignments, a helpful side effect was that faculty in their first year at Elon learned more about our students and university in the process. Thus, we met both the need for new faculty orientation and the need for increased assignment transparency with the same programming. For readers considering how to apply the TILT framework for your institution, we encourage you to consider using this "multiplier" approach (Stanford University, 2013) to meet overlapping needs with a single programming opportunity.

Assignment Alignment Working Groups

As noted previously, an unexpected outcome of the informal new faculty learning communities was that our discussion of assignment design often broadened to encompass aspects of the entire course. Based on this observed desire of faculty to discuss course design, not just assignment design, we created assignment alignment working groups (AAWGs), in which we blend backward design (Fink, 2013) with the TILT framework (Winkelmes et al., 2016). After inviting faculty to sign up on a campus-wide electronic mailing list, a CTL facilitator creates small, cross-disciplinary groups of two to four faculty who meet three times over the course of a semester. A CTL faculty member facilitates each group meeting, during which members create or revise a major assignment or several smaller assignments to make them more transparent. Before each meeting, participants receive reflection questions to prepare for the meeting. In these groups, faculty consider (a) the transparency of their assignments, (b) the transparency of their semester-long learning goals, and (c) how to revise or develop assignments so that they align with their semester-long learning goals. AAWG group facilitators also prompt group discussions on ways to help students understand the relationship of each assignment to the broader aims of the class and on how to translate the implicit goals of the class into explicit information for students.

In the final meeting(s) of an AAWG, faculty share their original and revised assignments and syllabi with other participants (see Figures 5.1 and 5.2).

Figure 5.1. Original Economics 310 assignment, first page, spring 2017.

Assignment #7 ECO 310 (10 points)	NAME: _____

1. (*2 points*) Find and collect data for your home state (if your home state is North Carolina, then pick any other state). Fill in the amounts in the table and then perform the calculations (round to one decimal place). Data on population can be found at census.gov and data on the labor market can be found at bis.gov

Working-Age Population	
Labor Force	
Employed	
Unemployed	
STATE:	

  a. **The employment-population ratio**
   Answers vary. Employment/working-age population = emp-pop. ratio
  b. **The labor force participation rate**
   Answers vary. LP/working-age population = LPPR
  c. **The unemployment rate**
   Answers vary. Unemployed/LP= u-rate

2. (*1 point*) According to the article I posted to Moodie, discuss two potential reasons men could be "leaving" the workforce? Do you see this as a potential problem? Why or why not?

   Answers vary. Generally, the article mentions incarceration, technology displacing traditionally male occupations, and (in a very minor way) staying at home to take care of their family.

Note. Reproduced by permission of Brandon Sheridan, Elon University.

Figure 5.2. Revised Economics 310 assignment, first page, fall 2017.

Problem Set #5: Labor Market   ANSWER KEY_____
ECO 310

Purpose: The primary purpose of this assignment is to help you gain a deeper understanding of the labor market. You will (1) use data to calculate labor market statistics, (2) diagram and explain labor market policy, and (3) apply some of this theory to your own life.

Task: Complete the following problems, as outlined. Be sure to show your work and provide written explanations for all problems. Writing out each step you take in your calculations is a useful tool to help you learn formulas and explaining your steps can help identify gaps in your understanding.

Criteria for Success: Exemplary work will provide a complete description of steps taken, including showing all work for any calculations performed. Adequate work will provide only answers, with no explanation or written steps outlining how you arrived at that answer.

---

1. Find and collect data for your home state (if your home state is North Carolina, then pick any other state). Fill in the amounts in the space provided and then perform the calculations (round to one decimal place). Data on population can be found at census.gov and data on the labor market can be found at bis.gov. Copy and paste the exact links where you obtained your data here:

Working-Age Population	
Labor Force	
Employed	
Unemployed	
STATE:	

   a. **The employment-population ratio**
       Answers vary. Employment/working-age population = emp-pop. ratio

---

Note. Reproduced by permission of Brandon Sheridan, Elon University.

During each meeting, we divide the time equally across participants, so each can use that time to meet teaching needs. Often this takes the form of feedback on assignments and syllabi given by the other participants, but each group also typically spends time considering verbal messaging around transparency, such as discussing how to set the tone for the class on the first day by having a conversation with students about transparency.

Many of the same realizations noted in our description of the new faculty learning communities were also present in the AAWGs. One major difference was the depth of the comments and reflection in the working groups. Having only three people meeting multiple times for the AAWGs allowed for deeper discussions of the course and assignments than the slightly larger groups of new faculty who met only once. Additionally, the multiple working group sessions meant that working groups were able to actually revise and share assignments and courses rather than just talking about what they might do. In contrast to the new faculty groups, in the AAWG there was more time and commitment to really grapple with how to change the language and articulate expectations. Groups suggested specific language changes to each other and demonstrated collaboration, even helping each other wordsmith or plan out assignment sequencing. In short, there was more of a collaborative vibe to completing the actual work than among the new faculty groups, which were collaborative in spirit but not in action.

Important to us was that faculty who participated in these working groups reported that they received positive responses from students based on their course revisions. Participating in the AAWG also helped them clarify what the objectives of their courses were and what explicit and implicit messaging they were sending students about those objectives through their assignments. For readers considering how to frame the TILT framework to increase faculty interest and investment, it may be helpful to share the potential benefits to faculty in parallel with sharing the benefits for students.

Unanticipated Outcomes of Our Work With the TILT Framework

Working with the TILT framework offered our CTL significant benefits, including some positive outcomes that we had not anticipated, such as involvement with SoTL projects and an opportunity to reframe our approach to programming.

SoTL Consultations Resulted From the TILT Faculty Learning Communities

As an outgrowth of the new faculty learning community and AAWGs, two faculty from mathematics and economics expressed an interest in conducting

SoTL projects related to transparency. We consulted with them to help them begin a project comparing two sections of the same course within each of their departments—one that incorporated transparent assignments and one that did not. This is currently in progress. Gathering data via the TILT survey about students' perceptions of their learning experiences and aligning that with evidence of their learning mastery (through course grades or retention in the major) can help us to measure the impact of this SoTL study.

Impact on Other Individual Consultations

One unplanned effect of working with the TILT framework is that thinking about purpose-task-criteria became a lens through which we started to view other aspects of our work, such as the development of programming that we offer through our center. Thus, we began to infuse the TILT framework into our existing approaches to developing programming. We went on to codify this process and presented a session on it—"Practicing What We Preach: A Process for Planning Evidence-Based Programming"—at the POD Network conference (Overman & Little, 2017), which blended the TILT framework, a heuristic for program planning (based on Felten et al., 2013), and backward design (Fink, 2013). Chapter 8 in this book describes how the TILT framework serves as a strategic plan for the University of Nevada, Las Vegas's faculty development services.

The TILT framework has also impacted our everyday interactions with faculty. It has become a standard "go-to" sharing piece for consultations about many aspects of teaching because of the accessibility of the framework, its generalizability to any discipline, and perception by faculty that they could use it to make small, strategic tweaks that would lead to better outcomes for students.

Other Lessons Learned and Suggestions for the Future

We conclude with a few overarching lessons learned from our reflections on adopting the TILT framework into our CTL programming and from our analysis of faculty feedback from those sessions, from their revised assignments, and from their reports of other measures of satisfaction or change in student learning, performance, or perceptions of the learning environment. We have been systematically collecting feedback on the AAWG; the number of faculty who have participated is still small, but preliminary analysis parallels the larger TILT study: some faculty report improved student end-of-term evaluations on items related to clarity of assignments, and others report improved class climate around assignments.

Other specific takeaways from our implementation experiences with TILT Higher Ed at our institution include the following:

- *The importance, and challenge, of defining purpose:* Faculty who were already familiar with the idea of transparency in task and criteria often had not considered adding the purpose to their assignments. They were eager to discuss the purpose and sometimes they were challenged when trying to identify it. One AAWG participant, for example, described the benefit of being more transparent about purpose in terms of "honesty," sharing that

  one aspect that helped a lot was being honest with the students why they were doing all the assignments. The course . . . is data-intensive, and earlier, students were having difficulty in seeing what use they had learning all those data-analysis techniques. By wording questions in a way that showed their relevance, students understood and appreciated why they were doing all those assignments.

  We learned to lead with talking about purpose, rather than lingering on the idea of transparency, which many faculty often initially reported that they were already doing.
- *The importance of actually analyzing teaching artifacts rather than just discussing transparency as a concept:* On a related note, across all the spaces where we introduced TILT Higher Ed, we learned how important it is to analyze and discuss specific teaching and learning products or practices. Through discussing and examining assignments, faculty learned they were often not being as transparent as they initially thought, once they heard the perspectives of their peers from other disciplines.
- *The value of cross-disciplinary peer feedback for uncovering the novice/expert divide:* Instructors' ability to assess the relative degree of transparency in their assignments was greatly enhanced by the cross-disciplinary groups. One AAWG participant described the largest benefit as having "fresh eyes of readers outside of my academic discipline" because

  it is enlightening to hear people with different specialties communicate possible confusion in my assignment description about terms and phrases I might take for granted that everyone should know. . . . These colleagues are probably more akin to students who are learning the discipline and don't "speak the language" every day.

- *The importance of connecting to faculty self-interest:* In addition to considering student motivation, we were reminded how important it can be to emphasize the benefit of new teaching strategies like TILT for our faculty colleagues (e.g., more joy in teaching because more students understand the expectations and fewer students dispute grades or feedback) as well as how this strategy might relate to the evaluation system at the university.
- *The value of working with sustained groups over time:* The faculty learning communities that worked together for longer periods reported stronger benefits. In contrast, the one member of the only group that did not sustain members throughout the semester reported, "The one thing I hope could be improved is the participation of all the participants. By the end, only I was there." Determining meeting times at the first session and building in reminders and accountability e-mails from the facilitators helped most groups reap the benefit of developing teaching ideas with colleagues over the course of the semester.

Conclusion

Overall, we found that our adoption of the TILT framework for workshops and cross-disciplinary faculty working groups not only positively affected individual faculty members and our assignment design programming but also benefited our CTL more broadly, including in unexpected (but welcome) ways. We now find ourselves infusing the language of transparent teaching into other consultations and programming. We also use it to inform our programming, as we try to practice and model transparent educational development to facilitate learning and growth for our students and our faculty and staff colleagues. Overall, we found that TILT Higher Ed offered a range of generalizability of application that we had not previously expected and that has enhanced our educational development work.

EDITORS' HIGHLIGHTS

For educational developers considering implementing transparency-based programming, consider the following points from these contributors:

- Lead with a focus on the "purpose" component of the Transparency Framework.
- Employ a "multiplier approach" to programming to serve several purposes with a single program.

References

Bean, J. C. (2011). *Engaging ideas: The professor's guide to integrating writing, critical thinking, and active learning in the classroom.* San Francisco, CA: Wiley.

Biggs, J. (1996). Enhancing teaching through constructive alignment. *Higher Education, 32*(3), 347–364.

Brünken, R., Plass, J. L., & Leutner, D. (2004). Assessment of cognitive load in multimedia learning with dual-task methodology: Auditory load and modality effects. *Instructional Science, 32*(1), 115–132.

Carter, M. (2007). Ways of knowing, doing, and writing in the disciplines. *College Composition and Communication, 58*(3), 385–418.

Chi, M. T. H., Glaser, R., & Rees, E. (1982). Expertise in problem solving. In R. S. Sternberg (Ed.), *Advances in the psychology of human intelligence* (pp. 1–75). Hillsdale, NJ: Erlbaum.

Chism, N. V. N., Holley, M., & Harris, C. J. (2012). Researching the impact of educational development. *To Improve the Academy, 31*(1), 129–145.

Costa, A., & Kallick, B. (1993). Through the lens of a critical friend. *Educational Leadership, 51*(2), 49–51.

Cowan, N. (2005). *Working memory capacity.* Hove, UK: Psychology Press.

Elon University. (2017, November 4). First level criterion–teaching. *Faculty handbook.* Retrieved from http://elon.smartcatalogiq.com/2017-2018/faculty-handbook//evaluation-system/criteria-for-evaluation/first-level-criterion-teaching

Elon University. (2018). *Strategic plan.* Available from https://www.elon.edu/e/administration/president/strategic-plan-2020/diversity.html

Elon University Center for the Advancement of Teaching & Learning. (2017, November 4). *Advancing effective teaching & engaged learning.* Available from https://www.elon.edu/u/academics/catl/

Felten, P., Little, D., Ortquist-Ahrens, L., & Reder, M. (2013). Program planning, prioritizing, and improvement: A simple heuristic. *To Improve the Academy, 32,* 183–198.

Fink, D. L. (2013). *Creating significant learning experiences: An integrated approach to designing college courses.* New York, NY: Wiley.

Middendorf, J., & Pace, D. (2004). Decoding the disciplines: A model for helping students learn disciplinary ways of thinking. *New Directions for Teaching and Learning, 98,* 1–12.

Mitchell, C., & Sackney, L. (2000). *Profound improvement: Building capacity for a learning community.* Lisse, Netherlands: Swets & Zeitlinger.

Overman, A. A., & Little, D. L. (2017, October). *Practicing what we preach: A process for planning evidence-based programming.* Session presented at the 42nd Annual POD Network Conference, Montreal, Canada.

Stanford University (Producer). (2013). *Rethinking time: The power of multipliers with Jennifer Aaker* [Video file]. Available from https://womensleadership.stanford.edu/time

Walvoord, B. E., & Anderson, V. J. (2011). *Effective grading: A tool for learning and assessment in college*. New York, NY: Wiley.

Wiggins, G., & McTighe, J. (2005). *Understanding by design* (2nd ed.). Alexandria, VA: Association for Supervision and Curriculum Development.

Winkelmes, M. A. (2013). Transparency in teaching: Faculty share data and improve students' learning. *Liberal Education*, *99*(2), 48–55. Available from https://www.aacu.org/publications-research/periodicals/transparency-teaching-faculty-share-data-and-improve-students

Winkelmes, M. A. (2015). Recent findings: Transparency and problem-centered learning. In *New York Centennial Forum Resources*. Washington DC: Association of American Colleges & Universities. Available from https://www.aacu.org/sites/default/files/files/LEAP/CentForumWInkelmesHandout.pdf

Winkelmes, M. A., Bernacki, M., Butler, J. V., Zochowski, M., Golanics, J., & Harriss Weavil, K. (2016). A teaching intervention that increases underserved college students' success. *Peer Review*, *18*(1/2), 31.

6

INTEGRATING TILT INITIATIVES THROUGHOUT A CENTER FOR TEACHING AND LEARNING

Educational Developer and Instructor Insights

Steven Hansen, Erin Rentschler, and Laurel Willingham-McLain

In this chapter, we will describe how the Center for Teaching Excellence (CTE) at Duquesne University implemented Transparency in Learning and Teaching (TILT) across a variety of center programs as part of our Small Changes Advancing LEarning (SCALE) initiative. We also share insights about the impact of this work on both participating instructors and our center staff. Founded in 1989 as a faculty initiative, the CTE "helps Duquesne faculty and graduate student teaching assistants excel as teacher-scholars deeply invested in student learning" (Duquesne University, n.d.) We serve Duquesne's teaching staff of about 500 full-time and nearly that many part-time faculty, as well as graduate student teaching assistants (Institutional Research and Planning, 2017). Classified by the Carnegie Institute as a higher research activity doctoral granting institution, Duquesne has 9 schools, including liberal arts, sciences, education, health sciences, and other professional programs. Duquesne University is a private, urban, midsized Catholic university serving about 9,400 students and located in downtown Pittsburgh, Pennsylvania. The university, founded to serve the working poor in the late 1800s, still identifies walking alongside marginalized populations as central to its mission. Duquesne University's broad vision of global citizenship begins at home in our classes. Indeed, our faculty discuss and write about what it means for them to "walk with learners" (Hansen, Quiñones, & Margolis, 2015, p. 99).

The TILT initiative relates directly to all of our center's goals for faculty and graduate students, which are seen in the following statements:

1. Implement sound instructional strategies focused on student learning by embracing evidence-based pedagogical ideas and a spirit of innovation.
2. Create well-designed courses and curriculum that incorporate strong learning-assessment strategies resulting in deep learning.
3. Succeed as teacher-scholars engaged in pedagogical development and academic research in whatever stage they are in (tenure-track, tenured, nontenure-track, adjunct, teaching assistants).
4. Approach personhood holistically with a view to understanding their students and themselves as people balancing personal and academic demands.
5. Feel like they belong and contribute to a community that values teaching excellence, collaboration, and diversity (Duquesne University, n.d.).

TILT promotes sound instructional and learning-assessment strategies. It is accessible and useful to instructors at any stage, it can deepen student learning while also lightening work of providing rich feedback to students, and it helps all students and particularly those from underserved populations. In addition, participants in Duquesne's TILT programming are providing peer leadership to one another. The Transparency Framework offers a clarity of purpose and simplicity of structure and at the same time invites instructor creativity and contextualization of course assignments. This combination serves our center well, because it is feasible and energizing for the CTE's staff of three full-time educational developers and two graduate assistants. Likewise, providing the tools and terminology to help instructors see their assignments in a new light increases faculty confidence in their ability to effect change—something that is particularly helpful for new faculty, graduate students, and adjunct faculty who may have less flexibility in designing courses and curricula.

TILT tied a number of threads together for us at the center, including core curriculum, student retention, evidence-based pedagogical practices, and a broadening of CTE impact while recognizing faculty time constraints. At the same time that we began collaborating with Mary-Ann Winkelmes around TILT, we were approached by enrollment management to explore ways we might help foster student retention efforts at the university. Concomitantly, we were reading James Lang's (2016) essays on small teaching, collected as a special report in the *Chronicle of Higher Education*, and *Nudge* by Thaler and Sunstein (2009). We decided that implementing small changes could have big impacts. TILT offers a small way for faculty to make evidence-based improvements requiring only the redesign of a couple of assignments that can both save grading time and potentially contribute to retention.

In 2016 we launched the SCALE initiative to explore teaching methods that are achievable by instructors in varied contexts, based on principles of learning, open to instructor creativity, and known to benefit students equitably. Any CTE offering that aligns with these criteria is advertised as a SCALE initiative. To date, we have featured outside speakers, various types of workshops, book studies, and blog posts as part of our SCALE emphasis. Our goal is that instructors will implement research-based small changes into their teaching, reflect on the impact the changes make on student learning, and experience small successes by using SCALE ideas. Transparency fits perfectly under the broader umbrella of small changes. In fact we used it in launching the multiyear SCALE program.

CTE TILT Programming

In 2016, Mary-Ann Winkelmes presented a synchronous Web conference on transparent assignment design to a group of Duquesne University faculty. This initial event provided us with three important resources: an online video and documents introducing transparency, a group of Duquesne faculty peer leaders, and their examples of assignments to use in future programming. We have followed up in numerous ways, including brief orientation topics, micro workshops, flipped workshops with hands-on assignment revision, and assignment *wrappers* during which instructors engage in guided reflection. The transparency approach has also influenced CTE consulting. Furthermore, participants have had the opportunity to make their work public through the CTE blog *The Flourishing Academic* and through the national TILT website and workshops.

Each of our TILT offerings has its roots in educational strategies known to promote student learning in higher education. We have repurposed these educational strategies for a faculty audience (Table 6.1). Our rationale is threefold: (a) the variety of programming creates awareness among a broad group of faculty and graduate student teaching assistants regarding the importance of transparency and its potential impact on student learning and faculty performance; (b) the varied session types and goals model for faculty how the same knowledge and skills can be taught using multiple educational strategies, each with positive learning outcomes and relevance to learners with diverse levels of experience; and (c) the repurposing of educational strategies for TILT is a highly beneficial and efficient approach to leverage

TABLE 6.1
Overview of TILT Offerings and Educational Strategies,
Center for Teaching Excellence, Duquesne University

CTL Offering	Educational Strategy	Rationale
Web Conference	Synchronous Videoconferencing	Promotes faculty awareness of TILT by having a nationally recognized scholar via a cost-effective video conference with interactivity and application
Orientation Segment	Microlearning	Introduces incoming faculty to the framework and benefits of TILT in a brief orientation segment to create awareness and stimulate participation in other offerings
Micro Workshop	Microlearning	Permits time-constrained faculty to discover TILT in a 35-minute interactive workshop with a 1-page handout that introduces them to the benefits, framework, and resources
Flipped Workshop	Flipped Instruction: Asynchronous + face-to-face	Repurposes the recording of the synchronous online workshop to allow faculty to learn asynchronously and then attend a face-to-face hands-on session to workshop an assignment
Wrapper Session	Metacognitive Wrapper	Encourages faculty to self-assess an assignment in their course through a guided reflection worksheet and small group discussion using the TILT framework

impactful faculty development for a CTL working in a resource-constrained campus climate (Truong, Juillerat, & Gin, 2016). As we explore each TILT programming type in the following sections, we will briefly highlight the educational strategy, rationale, and our recent experience.

Web Conference

Wang and Hsu (2008) outline five advantages to synchronous webinars—affordability, immediate feedback, incorporation of real-time multimedia, multilevel interaction (i.e., presentation, interaction of participants with presenter, and collaborative group work among participants), and the ability to archive the session for later use. As an educational strategy, synchronous online formats offer "a high degree of interactivity and instructor immediacy" (Marquart, Fleming, Rosenthal, & Hibbert, 2016, p. 188) and allow "instantaneous feedback" (Watts, 2016, p. 27) to participants from the instructor.

In consultation with our colleagues in the Office of Retention and Advisement, we sent a special invitation to faculty teaching core curriculum courses. By focusing on general education requirements, we targeted faculty teaching predominantly first- and second-year undergraduates who could benefit from transparent expectations in early college-level assignments. We seek to help students better understand the purpose of the core curriculum, which they often see as extraneous to their major areas of study or as redundant to work they did in high school.

During the session, participants heard an introduction to the TILT framework and the research that undergirds it. They then worked through a sequence of tasks alone and in pairs in order to rethink one of their assignments. They tested their communication of the assignment purpose with "disciplinary strangers" to check for clarity with someone outside their field. After the web conference, participants who submitted a revised or new assignment following TILT principles received a $150 stipend from CTE. We obtained permission to use many of these assignments in our center's work—for example, in workshops, orientations, blog posts, and consultations (see sample in Appendix 6A).

Micro Workshop and Orientation Segment

Micro workshops, in contrast to traditional educational development workshops, focus on a single concept in an abbreviated period of time. Microlearning and microcontent originate from online learning and the accumulation of digital information, but the concepts and rationale for microlearning and microcontent are applicable to educational development programming. Buchem and Hamelmann (2010) define *microlearning* as "short, fine-grained, interconnected and loosely-coupled learning activities with microcontent" (p. 2). Similarly, they define *microcontent* as information dealing with "a single main topic" or "concept" (p. 2). The need for microlearning and microcontent arises from the necessity to support lifelong learning "that can be easily integrated into everyday activities" (Buchem & Hamelmann, 2010, p. 1).

Our single-topic, 30-minute workshops gave faculty an opportunity to engage in educational development activities over lunch. In the Just a TAD—Transparent Assignment Design—micro workshop, participants heard a brief overview of TILT research and its three components. They then considered an assignment with which their own students struggle, explained its purpose to a faculty member outside their field, and asked each other questions for clarification. A brief primary handout, aligning with the format of a micro session, provided an overview of TILT, listed the participant tasks, recommended resources, and announced a related upcoming "wrapper" session (discussed further in a separate section later in the chapter). Other handouts included the TILT checklist and two examples of assignments Duquesne University faculty had revised (see micro workshop handout and evaluation in Appendix 6B). At the end, participants completed a combined evaluation about the workshop type and topic. To describe the session they selected the words *helpful* (9 respondents), *manageable* (7), *clarifying* (5), *effective* (3), and *energizing* (1). Participants also added the words *affirming, enlightening,* and *very practical*. In sum, they emphasized how practical TILT is and indicated their confidence in using it. All 14 respondents reported that it was "very likely" they would implement strategies from the workshop that semester.

Similarly, we introduced transparent assignment design through microlearning in a 15-minute orientation segment for new part-time faculty. We focused on articulating the purpose of assignments. When asked what aspect of the orientation they found most helpful, a quarter of the respondents indicated transparent assignment design. Transparent design also lends itself to the "Be the Spark" segments of full-time faculty orientation. In 5 to 10 minutes, CTE staff offered practical tips intended to whet new faculty appetites for engaging in practices that align with teaching and learning research. During each "spark" segment, we drew 2 names and gave out books related to the topic.

Flipped Workshop

The concept of flipped instruction combines a set of pedagogical strategies that "move most information-transmission teaching out of class" and "use class time for learning activities that are active and social" (Abeysekera & Dawson, 2015, p. 3). The benefits of flipped instruction are "profoundly human" because the instructor has more time to engage students during class (Tucker, 2012, p. 1). "Increased student-teacher interactions give teachers more opportunities to provide feedback to students," and, ultimately, flipped instruction allows the instructor to "carefully observe students, identify their learning needs, and guide them to higher levels of learning" (Goodwin & Miller, 2013, p. 79).

The original Web conference video and materials featuring Mary-Ann Winkelmes are available through Duquesne's intranet. The first 50 minutes of the video serve as prework for a flipped workshop. Faculty can be introduced to the framework and research basis at their own pace prior to a face-to-face session, during which CTE staff and faculty peer leaders with TILT experience guide participants in revising or designing assignments.

Wrapper Sessions

In Duquesne's wrapper sessions, faculty participate in individual and small group reflective practice. The concept is based on the metacognitive value of exam wrappers, or "short activities that direct students to review their performance (and the instructor's feedback) on an exam with an eye toward adapting their future learning" (Lovett, 2013, p. 22). Analogously, assignment wrappers ask faculty members to review the purpose, task, and criteria of a course assignment, with an eye to keeping what worked well, revising as needed, and creating more transparent future assignments for their students. CTE staff introduce participants to the wrapper concept and then explain the session guide (see Appendix 6C). After participants have time alone to reflect on the assignment, we facilitate small group discussion to highlight successes and provide an opportunity for peer colleagues to offer feedback and support. To date, we have conducted wrapper sessions on three topics: assignments, courses, and student evaluations of teaching. In keeping with CTE's focus on community and peer leadership, wrapper sessions feature seasonal refreshments as well as mutual encouragement and learning by participants.

Flourishing Academic *Blog Posts*

Faculty have authored blog posts for CTE's *Flourishing Academic* (via WordPress), sharing examples of transparent assignment redesign and making their work public for colleagues at Duquesne and beyond. These posts serve as early steps in the scholarship of teaching and learning. Some participants have also shared sample assignments on the national TILT website.

Consultations

The TILT framework is an immensely useful tool in consultations with faculty seeking to improve student performance on assignments or consulting on course design and learning assessment. We have used it to preview upcoming workshops as well as to follow up on them. The following summary points to faculty insights coming from sessions and consultations.

Instructor Insights

CTE regularly collects feedback from faculty and staff who use our services. Our Impact Survey looks at three years of programming and targets *frequent users,* generally defined as having attended three or more workshops, been a member of a faculty learning group, participated in a retreat, or accumulated two hours of consulting with CTE. Additionally, we collect feedback after every session to (a) capture what participants have learned and (b) determine their immediate plans/hopes for implementing their new ideas. Finally, to collect faculty insights about transparent assignment design specifically, we gathered insights from participants in related programming.

In the 2017 Impact Survey, 14 of 64 respondents referenced transparent assignment design in the open-ended item "Name one or two changes you made based on something learned from CTE programming." With ever-growing responsibilities, faculty do not have time to make change for the sake of change. Many Duquesne faculty have embraced transparency because we have framed it as small changes to what they are already doing. As one instructor indicated in postsession feedback, "Smaller changes seem far better! They don't lead to destroying things that are here, but build upon them. It's not the 'throw out' culture and making change just for change['s] sake." Implied in this instructor's comment is the notion that sometimes changes can be seen as attempts to follow a new trend without taking into consideration what is already in place. Likewise, another faculty member indicated on the 2017 Impact Survey, "I can utilize the ideas I have and combine them with things others have already tried and validated. [This] gives me the language to discuss and understand the techniques I try in class." These sentiments also reflect our SCALE initiative in which we encourage faculty to make small impactful changes to benefit students in their academic work.

Smaller changes prove beneficial to not only students but also faculty. They lead to more and other types of alterations in designing the learning experience. For example, one faculty member explained,

> Transparent Assignment Design has helped me to understand the importance of sample assignments. Not only can students use them to see exactly what a good version of the assignment at hand looks like, I can also use them in classes for a variety of activities (i.e., learning introduction and conclusion strategies, proofreading activities, etc.).

The TILT framework promotes pedagogical changes beyond particular assignments by giving faculty a flexible structure that encourages their creativity and confidence. For instance, faculty no longer feel the need to replicate others' assignments but rather express confidence that they can create their own assignments, clearly connecting student learning to their lives and careers.

CTE Staff Reflections

Promoting student learning through evidence-based educational development is a primary goal of CTE, and the TILT framework certainly meets this goal (see chapter 1). But it also offers much more. We have witnessed impacts of TILT beyond its benefit to students. The Transparency Project has been energizing for CTE staff, because it has contributed to community building, campus climate, and a recognition of something profoundly human in its enactment. In terms of community building, TILT programming from the first video conference to the most recent wrapper session has fostered a sense of community among our faculty participants. It has become an accessible point of entry into peer leadership for faculty, regardless of status. Graduate student instructors, part-time faculty, and tenure-track faculty alike have become peer leaders by sharing their experience with colleagues at workshops or by writing blog posts about transparent assignment design. We are amazed by the way TILT gives faculty members in differing stages of their academic careers a voice to speak a common educational language using the Transparency Framework.

The Transparency Project strikes at an even more fundamental level than the instructional community. People are looking for transparency in all aspects of life, including the university and the contemporary political climate. Whether TILT creates a sensitivity to the language of transparency or it actually empowers people to advocate for transparency, we have witnessed the language of transparency being used more frequently by faculty in relation to university decision-making to promote a more democratic, less hierarchical climate. Ultimately, transparency addresses equity, and it contributes to our intensely human capacity to walk alongside another person. One faculty participant noted that

> when students complain about something I ask them to do, it isn't necessarily because they don't want to be challenged to learn new material; rather, it's more likely they don't understand either how to do the assignment or how the assignment contributes to their learning.

The TILT framework helped humanize this faculty member's perspective on students facing difficulty in learning.

Conclusion

It is in the process of writing this chapter that we have noticed how the TILT framework relates to such a wide variety of issues and opportunities we face. So simple on the face of it, we are surprised at how it addresses the needs of various groups: students, graduate student instructors, faculty, and

CTE staff. As we look at the way our program has emerged over the past 18 months, we anticipate being able to plan more intentionally for faculty entry points and pathways, from an introduction to TILT, to revising 1 or 2 transparent assignments, to seeing an impact on many aspects of teaching, to reflecting on practice in community, indeed, to faculty making their work public beyond the classroom.

EDITORS' HIGHLIGHTS

For CTLs considering implementing transparency-based programming, consider the following points from these contributors:

- Emphasize to faculty that a transparent approach is a small but significant change to assignment design.
- Utilize a variety of workshop formats and follow up with faculty who successfully incorporate transparency by asking them to write about their experiences in CTL newsletters and blog posts.

References

Abeysekera, L., & Dawson, P. (2015). Motivation and cognitive load in the flipped classroom: Definition, rationale and a call for research. *Higher Education Research & Development, 34*(1), 1–14.

Duquesne University. (n.d.) *About CTE.* Available from https://www.duq.edu/about/centers-and-institutes/center-for-teaching-excellence/about-cte

Buchem, I., & Hamelmann, H. (2010). Microlearning: A strategy for ongoing professional development. *eLearning Papers, 21*(7). Available from https://www.openeducationeuropa.eu/sites/default/files/old/media23707.pdf

Doyle, T. (2011). *Learner-centered teaching: Putting the research on learning into practice.* Sterling, VA: Stylus.

Goodwin, B., & Miller, K. (2013). Research says: Evidence on flipped classrooms is still coming in. *Educational Leadership, 70*, 79.

Hansen, S., Quiñones, S., & Margolis, J. (2015). Spiritan pedagogies in practice: Possibilities, tensions and characteristics of walking with learners. *Spiritan Horizons, 10*, 99–113. Available from http://www.duq.edu/Documents/catholic-social-thought/CSS/Horizons/Horizons%202015-%20final-%20cover%20and%20pages.pdf

Institutional Research and Planning. (2017, August). *2016–2017 fact book.* Available from http://www.duq.edu/about/departments-and-offices/finance-and-business/planning-budgeting-and-institutional-research/fact-books/2016---2017-fact-book

Lang, J. (2016). *Small teaching: Everyday lessons from the science of learning.* San Francisco, CA: Jossey-Bass.

Lovett, M. C. (2013). Make exams worth more than the grade: Using exam wrappers to promote metacognition. In M. Kaplan, N. Silver, D. LaVague-Manty, & D. Meizlish (Eds.), *Using reflection and metacognition to improve student learning: Across the disciplines, across the academy* (pp. 18–52). Sterling, VA: Stylus.

Marquart, M., Fleming, M., Rosenthal, S. A., & Hibbert, M. (2016). Instructional strategies for synchronous components of online courses. In S. D'Agustino (Ed.), *Creating teacher immediacy in online learning environments* (pp. 188–211). Hershey, PA: Information Science Reference.

Thaler, R. H., & Sunstein, C. R. (2009). *Nudge: Improving decisions about health, wealth, and happiness.* New York, NY: Penguin.

Truong, M. H., Juillerat, S., & Gin, D. H. C. (2016). Good, fast, cheap: How centers of teaching and learning can capitalize in today's resource-constrained context. *To Improve the Academy, 35,* 180–195.

Tucker, B. (2012). The flipped classroom. *Education Next, 12*(1). Available from https://search.proquest.com/docview/1237826701?accountid=7098

Wang, S. K., & Hsu, H. Y. (2008). Use of the webinar tool (Elluminate) to support training: The effects of webinar-learning implementation from student-trainers' perspective. *Journal of Interactive Online Learning, 7*(3), 175–194.

Watts, L. (2016). Synchronous and asynchronous communication in distance learning: A review of the literature. *Quarterly Review of Distance Education, 17*(1), 27.

ORIGINAL AND REVISED MUTANT PHENOTYPES ASSIGNMENTS

Original Assignment

BIOL 111L
C. elegans Mutant Phenotypes Assignment
Name_____

For each mutant, complete the following:

1. How does this mutant differ from the wild type worms you've been observing?
2. Hypothesize: what developmental defect (molecular, structural, physiological) could underlie the phenotype? (It does not matter if you're correct as long as it's a plausible explanation!)
3. Find (& cite) a peer-reviewed study that explains the root cause of the phenotype.

[Students were also provided with images of worms for this assignment.]

Note. Used with permission of Kasey Christopher, Biological Sciences, Duquesne University

Redesigned Mutant Phenotypes Assignment

Purpose: The purpose of the exercise is twofold: first, to simulate the process developmental biologists go through in the laboratory when observing a novel mutant, and second, to help you think about downstream physiological effects of loss of function of various genes.

This assignment will help you practice the following **skills**:

✓ Observing and describing a mutant phenotype as compared to wild-type organisms
✓ Formulating a hypothesis to explain a biological phenomenon
✓ Critical thinking and experimental interpretation
✓ Finding, citing, and summarizing research from a peer-reviewed scientific journal

This assignment will help you gain the following **knowledge**:

✓ Familiarity with the appearance and physiology of the *C. elegans* nematode
✓ Understanding of the functional roles of a variety of organs and tissues of the *C. elegans* nematode
✓ Understanding of the links between embryonic development and adult phenotypes

Task: This exercise asks you to think about a series of *C. elegans* mutants. All of these mutants survive to adulthood, but display phenotypes that are based on underlying developmental defects. For each mutant, examine the images and watch the associated video (linked on Blackboard). Then, answer the following questions for each mutant:

1. Describe the phenotype of the mutant. How does it differ from wild-type worms?
2. Hypothesize: How do you think this phenotype arises? (What process or structure might be defective in the mutant? What type of gene/protein function might be missing?) It does not matter if you're correct as long as it's a plausible explanation.
3. Find a peer-reviewed primary journal article that explains the true cause of the phenotype (see resources under Criteria for further information). Cite the paper, and describe what the root cause of this phenotype is. Some questions to consider: what is the normal function of the mutated gene? What happens when that gene is mutated? Why does the loss of function create the observed phenotype?

[Students were also provided with images of worms for this assignment.]

Criteria for Success: As scientists, we should strive for specificity and accuracy. As such, I encourage you to avoid vague descriptions or unclear hypotheses. Note that in the example given below, the student clearly describes the appearance of the worm's movements and how they contrast with wild type, rather than simply stating that it moves aberrantly. Furthermore, her hypothesis (though ultimately incorrect) provides a direct physiological mechanism by which the phenotype could arise. Finally, she identifies the actual underlying cause and cites the related peer-reviewed primary journal article. Note also the citation style used; this is the example you should follow in your own assignment.

Example answer for *unc-22* mutant (www.youtube.com/watch?v=o6g2ZA mCrlo):

1. Instead of normal sinusoidal movement, the *twitcher* mutant worm shows uncoordinated movements in which it constantly twitches its head back and forth.
2. I hypothesize that there is a defect in the nervous system of the *twitcher* worm, which doesn't allow it to properly control its muscle movements.
3. *unc-22* encodes a protein called twitchin, which is required for the normal function of muscle tissue in *C. elegans*. Twitchin interacts directly with the myosin motor protein and therefore is critical for contractile motions of the muscle. In the absence of twitchin (when the *unc-22* gene is mutated), muscle contraction is uncoordinated and therefore the animal twitches.
4. Source: Moerman, D. G., Benian, G. M., Barstead, R. J., Schriefer, L., Waterston, R. H. 1998. Identification and intracellular localization of the *unc-22* gene product of *Caenorhabditis elegans*. Genes Dev. 2:93–105.

Reminders regarding peer-reviewed sources: www.wormbook.org is a peer-reviewed online encyclopedia of *C. elegans* development that you may find helpful in beginning your search for information, but note that this is *not* a source of **primary** journal articles. As such, it would not be appropriate to cite as your source, but it is a reputable repository of information and could certainly help you find the right paper to cite! More generally, an excellent way to identify appropriate sources is to use the Gumberg Library website to search the ScienceDirect or Google Scholar databases, as we discussed in class last month. Wikipedia, blogs, and other websites (even if hosted by a university) are <u>not</u> peer-reviewed primary sources. Please stop by office hours if you'd like a quick refresher on how to identify appropriate papers.

Note. Used with permission of Kasey Christopher, Biological Sciences, Duquesne University

JUST A TAD—TRANSPARENT ASSIGNMENT DESIGN

Microworkshop Handout

Imagine

A simple practice you can do that strongly promotes student performance on assignments.

In several national studies of courses using the transparent assignment design,

- Students report in pre/post surveys significantly increased *academic confidence* and *sense of belonging* (compared to students in courses not using the transparent assignment design)
- This finding is statistically more significant for students from underserved populations.
- Prior research connects academic confidence and sense of belonging with student persistence and grades.

What is it?

A systematic way to be transparent about the **purpose, task, and criteria** of assignments to promote students' learning. It can apply to all kinds of assignments, small and big.

Checklist for transparent assignment design

Two examples from Duquesne faculty

Application

- Think of an assignment your students have struggled with.
- Turn to a partner and describe the **purpose** of the assignment: outline the *content, skills, real-life relevance*.
- Ask one another questions for clarifying the assignment's purpose.

Micro-workshop evaluation

Learn more

- Transparency in Learning and Teaching Project (TILTHigherEd.org)
- View a video of Mary-Ann Winkelmes presenting the Transparent Assignment Design to Duquesne faculty (DORI CTE site, multi-pass required). The first 51 minutes and handout present the model.
- Berrett, Dan. "The Unwritten Rules of College." *Chronicle of Higher Education*, September 21, 2015.
- Winkelmes, Mary-Ann, Matthew Bernacki, Jeffrey Butler, Michelle Zochowski, Jennifer Golanics, and Kathryn Harriss Weavil. "A Teaching Intervention That Increases Underserved College Students' Success." *Peer Review* (Winter/Spring 2016).

Assignment wrapper: Announcement for upcoming session

You are in the midst of grading a lot of student work. How about taking a minute to step away and reflect on a student assignment you gave recently? What worked well? What disappointed or frustrated you? How much time did it take to grade? What do you want to keep the same next time? Change up a bit? CTE colleagues will help you reflect on the assignment. You'll have time to think quietly as well as talk with colleagues.

Center for Teaching Excellence
SCALE UP Micro-Workshop Session Evaluation
Just a TAD—Transparent Assignment Design

1. Please circle the word(s) that best describe(s) your experience of the workshop.
   Energizing   Manageable   Effective   Helpful   Clarifying
   Add your own word, if you'd like:

2. How likely is it that you'll incorporate one of the strategies discussed today into your course this semester?
   Very likely   Somewhat likely   Not likely

3. Is there anything else you'd like us to know about your experience of this session?

CTE ASSIGNMENT WRAPPER FALL 2017

A. Circle <u>all</u> the phrases that correspond with your **overall impression** of how the assignment went.

    Student performance was: outstanding   strong   mediocre   weak or _____

    Students seemed to feel: eager   confident   complacent   confused angry or _____

    The assignment I gave was: very clear   confusing in places   unclear or _____

    Overall:

    I knew what I was expecting and it worked out well.

    I'm really happy about this assignment.

    It worked for most of the students.

    I'd give this assignment again with a few changes.

    I feel like completely reworking the assignment.

    It felt like a waste of time.

    I felt unsure about the way I was grading the assignment.

    Or _____

B. Think back to the assignment. What was your **purpose? What knowledge and skills** did you want the students to show?

C. **List the tasks** you imagined the students doing in order to perform well on the assignment. What timeline and ordering of the tasks did you expect? Compare your expectations to the tasks students actually seemed to do. Was there a good match?

D. In what ways did you **communicate the quality of work** you expected from students?

E. Take a closer look at **student performance:**
   1. To what extent did students generally demonstrate the knowledge and skills you were hoping for?
   2. What strengths and gaps in learning did you notice?
   3. Look across the students' performance. Did it vary widely? If so, who excelled? Who didn't perform very well? What patterns do you see?

F. What worked well about this assignment so that you want to **keep** it and even **apply** it to other assignments?

G. What parts might you **revise**?

Remember!
"Those who do the work, do the learning" (Doyle, 2011)
By crafting careful assignments and reflecting on them,
you are taking student learning seriously.

Adapted from Transparent Assignment Design, Transparency in Learning and Teaching in Higher Education, TILTHigherEd.org

By the Center for Teaching Excellence, Duquesne University, November 2017, www.duq.edu/cte

7

USING PRINCIPLES FROM TILT FOR WORKSHOP DESIGN AND MEASURING THE IMPACT OF INSTRUCTIONAL DEVELOPMENT

Taimi Olsen, Ellen Haight, and Sara Nasrollahian Mojarad

There is a growing national call to more clearly evaluate and link the relationships among educational development, instructional practices, curriculum improvements, and student learning (Beach, Sorcinelli, Austin, & Rivard, 2016; Brown & Kurzweil, 2017). To help connect these components and demonstrate the impact of instructional development on teaching practice and student learning, the Teaching and Learning Center (TLC) at the University of Tennessee, Knoxville (UT), adopted surveys from the Transparency in Learning and Teaching (TILT) initiative and gathered complementary, campus-specific data. The purpose of this chapter is to describe how the contributors used the TILT framework of purpose-task-criteria to design a program focused on incorporating evidence-based teaching strategies (EBTS). In addition, the chapter focuses on assessing the effectiveness of instructional development and documenting the work of a teaching and learning center through data collection evaluating the program's impact. Finally, we offer reflections about what we learned that may be useful to other faculty developers who plan to gather data about the impact of programming on students' learning and on teaching effectiveness.

As Tennessee's flagship land-grant, research university, UT has many obligations to the state as well as to students and parents. One key obligation is to provide all possible support for student academic success. Therefore, the administration is tasked with asking various campus offices supporting the academic mission, such as the TLC, questions such as the following: How does the unit impact the success of students? How does the unit support the university teaching mission? How are programs aligned with the university strategic plan? The TILT program offers TLC staff and UT administrators a means to engage instructors, offer evidence-based teacher development, support improvements to student learning, and close the loop with data showing the effectiveness of the programming.

When UT's TLC joined TILT in 2015, the impetus was to bring a program of EBTS to instructors at UT. The TILT program appealed to TLC staff because it was an established program directed at higher education pedagogy, and TLC staff felt that the TILT program had the potential to guide cohesive faculty development that could be evaluated through the impact on students. TILT offered our center a clear structure to address questions of how to help instructors increase student engagement and retention and how to make the process of change clear and manageable for instructors. It also offered confidential individual reports to instructors based on data collected from students through survey questions about students' learning experiences at the beginning and end of term, so they benefited directly. Additional institutional review board (IRB) approvals internally allowed us to connect student survey data with information about grades and retention rates at UT. In other words, TILT appealed to administrators because of the potential to learn about and report on the impact of educational development in terms of student learning.

Program Overview

We brought training and survey tools from the TILT project to a new program designed by TLC staff called "Teaching for IMPACT." This program provided structured training about transparent instruction to instructors classified as the teacher-of-record, whether faculty or graduate students, with a focus on individual course unit design. Teaching for IMPACT incorporates key elements of TILT's purpose-task-criteria Transparency Framework:

- *IM*portance of the task that demonstrates student learning (e.g., test, project, or paper)
- *P*urpose and the *A*ctivities supporting that purpose, connecting the task to the course and unit goals

- *Criteria* for task assessment, such as a rubric or criteria sheet
- The *Task* itself, wherever it fits in the course structure, with instruction of course content and related activities leading up to the task required of students to demonstrate learning

In designing the IMPACT workshop for instructors, the TLC staff incorporated a "top 10" evidence-based teaching strategies list, drawn from the body of John Hattie's work (Shulruf, Hattie, & Tumen, 2008) as well as other literature such as research by Robert Marzano (2004). Six ideas from the TLC's top 10 list of evidence-based practices were emphasized in specific questions on the TILT end-of-term student survey:

1. State clear goals for each lesson. (TILT end-of-term-survey questions 36, 37, 38)
2. Tell students what they need to know and show them how to do the tasks you want them to be able to do. (39, 40, 41)
3. Provide students with feedback and solicit feedback from students in a feedback loop. (42, 43)
4. Check for student understanding. (33)
5. Nurture metacognitive knowledge and practices by students. (12, 44)
6. Teach learning strategies related to the course. (12) (TILT Higher Ed, 2014)

We incorporated these six practices in an IMPACT checklist that we used for instructor training. This checklist, discussed further in the chapter under "Programmatic Structure," prompted faculty to think about the importance of an instructional unit, the purpose and the criteria for the assessment at the end of the unit, and how the unit and its instructional strategies are structured.

Program Recruiting and Participants

Participants in the IMPACT program were selected from among those instructors who responded to a call for participants that offered small grant funding as an incentive. The grant call for participants was released in 2016 and 2017, following a limited pilot program in 2015. The call emphasized the connections between the program and UT's strategic plan (Vol Vision 2020). It explained the umbrella TILT program, the benefits of participating, and logistics of applying. It defined *teaching faculty* as faculty lecturers, clinical faculty, faculty-of-practice, and research faculty as well as graduate teaching assistants who were teachers-of-record for a course. Because instructors were not making curricular changes through the program, they could apply on their own without departmental approval. Following is the call for participation in the Teaching for IMPACT program:

> The Teaching for IMPACT program supports teaching faculty to create best practices to enhance undergraduate and graduate education, with a focus on supporting improved student learning. In this program, Teaching for IMPACT participants will explicitly incorporate small changes in active and engaged learning strategies, including accessibility strategies and embedded formative assessments, to promote student retention and enhance progression towards a degree, consistent with Vol Vision 2020 Strategic Priorities. Teaching for IMPACT Grants of $500 each enroll faculty in a program that will assist them—through a focused, one-time training workshop—in incorporating a few simple active learning and student learning strategies into their courses. (Teaching and Learning Center, 2016–2017)

Instructors were asked to submit their course syllabus and a letter of intent, which was to include their interest in the program, a "statement of learning outcomes you hope to improve and motivation to make changes," description of how any "course unit enhancement will address barriers to learning [and/or] provide further support for student retention and/or progression in learning and success" (Teaching and Learning Center, 2016–2017). They were also asked to describe any "formative feedback methods and summative (graded) assessments in use, if not listed in the syllabus." In this way, the call was aligned with the university's strategic plan to improve education, particularly undergraduate education, specifically where students routinely had trouble with the content. Although not stated explicitly, courses with high rates of withdrawals and grades of D and F were targeted. Many of the participants, although not all, in the IMPACT cohorts were teaching introductory science, technology, engineering, and math courses as well as language courses.

Programmatic Structure

Once enrolled, the instructors participated in a three-hour educational development workshop that occurred before the start of the course they identified for participation in IMPACT. The learning outcomes for participants were as follows:

1. Examine how to make improvements to teaching for student learning success.
2. Identify an early unit in your course and plan how to make small changes to increase transparency.

3. Adopt a small change that can then be applied throughout your whole course.
4. Learn and apply the goals and purposes of TILT, including the pre- and post-TILT surveys.
5. Fill out and submit the IMPACT checklist.

The workshop consisted of three main parts. The first part made use of TILT workshop slides and a TILT handout available on the TILT Higher Ed website. These materials are designed specifically for use by educational developers. Our staff introduced instructors to the use of transparency as an approach to teaching. TLC staff defined *transparency in learning and teaching* as using methods to help students understand how and why they are learning course content. Transparency methods promote goal-oriented, active, engaged learning and help students process information and retain it for deeper learning. Instructors were encouraged to focus on the three components of the Transparency Framework: (a) the purpose of knowledge and skills taught and how these connect to learning outcomes, (b) the tasks students would perform and how they would perform them, and (c) criteria for success—in advance of performing the tasks—with annotated examples so that students could see what excellence looks like and self-evaluate while performing the assigned tasks, before actual summative assessment. After explaining the Transparency Framework elements of purpose-task-criteria, staff reviewed TILT's national research findings as well as other evidence-based teaching literature.

Participants then began the second, interactive portion of the workshop. Instructors worked on prompts from the staff, individually and then in inter-disciplinary pairs. Staff provided faculty with examples of EBTS for each practice listed on the checklist. Each practice would allow them to imple-ment small changes in a unit of their course without the need to change the overall course plan and structure. Because the workshop was offered twice, each group numbered less than 20 participants, which enabled whole group discussion as well. First, they reviewed their own course outcomes (from the syllabus submitted as part of the application process). Instructors talked about how they divided their course into units, or "chunks" of learn-ing—whether they followed textbook chapters or their own concepts of units (from a week to several weeks). We found that how they divided courses into units depended in part on how they grouped individual lessons and saw logi-cal breaks, and where they placed assessments.

In the third part, instructors used the IMPACT checklist (Figure 7.1) to check off strategies they already used and to make note of others that they

Figure 7.1. IMPACT checklist.

Define the Importance of the Task

☐ Define for yourself how the unit task fits into the course learning objectives.

☐ Explain why the learning in this unit is important for the students.

☐ Explain how the learning process and outcome will be relevant and meaningful.

State the Purpose of the Task

☐ Share the rationale for the assessment task (e.g., test, assignment, or project) with students.

☐ Write and provide statement of student learning objective(s) for the unit, tied to expected course outcomes.

Start the Task

☐ Provide and review the instructions with students.

☐ Request and discuss student feedback to clarify understanding of the task.

☐ Create/organize the unit materials and activities leading up to the task.

Provide Criteria

☐ Provide grading criteria for students at the start of the unit (e.g., criteria list, rubric, checklist, rating system).

☐ Debrief the grade/score and feedback of the assessment task at the end of the unit. Use one method to debrief.

Suggested addition from the IMPACT research team: What activities and/or measures will you use to determine whether students achieved the desired learning goals?

Support the Task

☐ What activities lead up to the final assessment?

☐ Use one active learning strategy. _____

☐ Use one formative feedback mechanism. _____

☐ Use one metacognitive strategy. _____

could use to implement greater transparency in their instruction. Instructors discussed each other's plans in pairs and then as a whole group, which helped solidify the learning. Rarely did two faculty members use the same strategies or have the same gaps, even within the same discipline.

The checklist guided instructors through self-reflection and peer discussion because the statements prompted instructors to consider each unit of instruction through a forward design structure that mimicked outcomes design. Each statement on the IMPACT checklist began with an active verb directing the person's next step. Instructors were prompted to articulate the importance of learning in their course in a way that got them to reconsider what might be their own tacit knowledge (i.e., "knowing what to do" is based on their years of expertise and may need to be articulated clearly for novice learners). The act of defining the importance of an instructional unit and the learning required of students is unfamiliar in general to higher education instructors. Although instructors periodically articulate course purpose and goals to their departments, they rarely must explain individual units unless the course is under review. To see how focused these statements were in comparison to course goals and outcomes, here are some examples of the unit rationale ("purpose") statements produced by some of the faculty (answers are somewhat paraphrased):

- The "animation" assignment is designed to provide practice.
- [I want to] increase student technology-related vocabulary and cultural knowledge.
- The learning for this unit is a cornerstone for analyzing systems.

The checklist also prompted instructors to articulate how the learning process they designed for their course would be related to desired outcomes and assessments. This process allowed instructors to check for correct alignment between instruction planned for individual class sessions and instructor assessment of student learning at the end of the unit. For instance, instructors could talk about learning outcomes and preview grading criteria. In retrospect, we suggest asking instructors to record the specific assessment plan at this step, although the IMPACT project did not do so. Educational literature (Benassi, Overson, & Hakala, 2014; National Research Council, 2000) has shown that routine assessment reinforces student learning, yet what is *routine* is not defined in higher education overall. Some of the faculty in the IMPACT group decided to include many more opportunities for assessment than their courses originally contained. Some examples of the additional assessment steps they created include the following:

- Incorporating an extra quiz on the readings
- Adding a short assignment for more practice
- Adding questions on their [students'] learning habits

The checklist also prompted instructors to incorporate active learning, formative feedback, and metacognition. Under active learning, for example, the handouts given in the workshop suggested small group work, think-pair-share, and cognitive mapping. The active learning strategies that the IMPACT faculty planned also included the following:

- Student demonstrations for the whole class
- Discussion of animated models

Regarding formative feedback, for example, instructors might check for understanding through a feedback loop that includes instructors giving feedback to students on their work and instructors asking students for feedback on their learning in the course—on what helps and hinders their learning, including some of the following feedback loop activities planned by our IMPACT instructors:

- "Clearest point/Muddiest point" (questions on what was clear and what was muddy from that day's class session)
- Open-ended question and answer in a "one-minute paper"
- Initial background knowledge survey or pre- and postinstruction knowledge surveys

Active learning strategies are fairly common in higher education and the language is more familiar to instructors, but metacognition ideas are less so. For instance, the practice of using an exam wrapper was introduced in this session and adopted by several instructors. An exam wrapper is an exercise conducted after an exam in which students are asked questions about their study habits leading up to the exam and how they will improve their learning habits moving forward. Instructors were given resources on how to solicit student thinking as well as an excerpt on metacognition from the National Research Council (2000) e-publication *How People Learn.*

The workshop concluded with instructors completing and turning in a copy of their checklist planning tool (staff kept photos of each person's checklist). Follow-up contact was primarily by e-mail, as staff sent the workshop materials and additional resources as needed and sent reminders at the start, middle, and end of the semester. These reminders (a) prompted instructors to solicit student participation in the TILT surveys, (b) reminded instructors to consult their checklist plans, and (c) offered them support through consultation as desired by the participant instructors. The program was completed for instructors at the end of the semester in which they taught their course, upon receiving a confidential, individual instructor report from TILT's principal investigator, based on TILT postsurvey data. Staff concluded work with each cohort upon receiving a TILT report and studying the impact of the intervention on student succes. Although changes in staffing have interrupted some communication with faculty in the program, our interviews have recently opened up further dialogue.

Measuring the IMPACT: Data Collection

The IMPACT data-gathering process is important because it positions the team to link educational development practice with faculty and student learning outcomes—something that continues to be challenging in the field of educational development. As a unit under the provost's office, the TLC was asked to provide direct evidence of effectiveness of the IMPACT program as one of its reporting requirements. As noted in a report on *Institutional Commitment to Teaching Excellence*, by the American Council of Education (Sorcinelli, Berg, Bond, & Watson, 2017), many organizations want to "better understand the linkages between evidence-based teaching, student learning outcomes, and quality faculty development programs" (p. 13).

To further meet this requirement, we aimed to link objective data about students' actual achievement (including course grades, GPAs, and retention/persistence the following year) with data from the TILT survey, including student success predictors like confidence and sense of belonging as well as students' perceptions about their learning experiences. We used students' actual UT ID numbers to link the TILT data with information about grades, GPAs, and retention before immediately anonymizing and assigning randomized ID numbers. Cooperation between the IRBs of the University of Nevada, Las Vegas (UNLV) and UT made this possible by approving a protocol for the password-protected transmission of student data. The TILT project openly shares on its website all its current IRB approvals and documentation from UNLV as well as its past IRB documentation from the University of Illinois. For most institutions' IRBs, these reviews are adequate to allow the use of TILT surveys with their students. But when researchers at an institution join the TILT research team and plan to study their own students' data, additional IRB approval is sometimes needed. At UT, the IRB approved researchers from the UT staff and permitted their access to student data, while the IRB at UNLV also approved these staff members as new TILT research team members.

The data collected comprise the following:

- Campus-specific, objective measures of student success, including grades and retention data. These were shared by UT's institutional analysis office according to a careful and detailed protocol that allowed a very limited number of people to see actual student ID numbers before these data were linked to the students' TILT survey responses.

- Student survey data (subjective measures) about students' learning experiences, their academic confidence, and sense of belonging in college (predictors of student success) (Hausmann, Ye, Schofield, & Woods, 2009; Walton & Cohen, 2011). These came from the TILT presurvey and end-of-term survey. TILT's confidential, individual instructor reports use these (deidentified) data to show instructors how their students' views about their skills and their learning changed over time during the course.

- Interview data of faculty reflections about the impact of the experience on their teaching practice and their students' learning (to be finalized and coded in our next phase of research). These are gathered by one of the coresearchers from the TLC staff, tape-recorded and will be coded using NVivo following completion of all interviews. Excerpts discussed in this paper are chosen from a preliminary first impressions phase.

Student Data

Although the preliminary data indicate positive learning benefits for the students we surveyed with respect to predictors of student success including metacognitive awareness of skill development, confidence, and belonging, our sample size ($N = 58$) is currently too small to be certain.

One of the most important lessons learned in the data-collection process is that we must begin with a larger group of faculty and students to reach the 350-person sample size recommended by What Works Clearinghouse (WWC) standards (U.S. Department of Education, 2014). As we continue the IMPACT project and educational development efforts at UT, data collected from additional students will contribute to our database. We will continue to analyze these data over the next year for their significance regarding higher grades.

Instructor Data

To determine the benefits of the IMPACT project for instructors, we conducted interviews in person, using a semistructured interview protocol. Questions were grouped in the following categories: background information (about teaching experiences and professional training taken), the IMPACT training itself (e.g., How do you define *evidence-based teaching*? How do you define *transparency*?), the experience of implementing transparency (e.g., what changes they made or "describe some of the instances where you felt the changes made to the course had an impact on student learning"), and finally a few questions on their general views on faculty educational development. The instructors' comments identified several fundamental gains: they adopted the regular insertion of clear learning objectives in their courses, they intently examined their assessments, and they related their objectives and assessments to activities. In interviews, faculty recognized that the program would help "definitely improve [their] teaching" and give them a fresh look at their work on a course, "a reframing of it that I hadn't really thought before the IMPACT grant." Instructors found that offering students clear learning outcomes for their academic work correlated positively with transparency in teaching and learning transactions. Said one instructor,

> Another objective of the grant was communicating with the students what my expectations were. . . . To me transparency means that why keep this as a secret, why not tell the students exactly and be very straightforward about this as the most important things we need to learn from this section.

Another instructor noted that "it really work[ed] to be very upfront with them [on] the very first day and talk to them about their grades, how I looked at grades . . . the idea that it was based on." They believed this strategy of discussing objectives helped them communicate more comprehensively and effectively with the students in terms of making course activities transparent.

Instructors also looked at assessment more broadly to include many kinds of feedback situations. For one, it involved student peer-to-peer feedback: "Problems can be solved in many ways [and] we all learn from each other. . . . So the idea of feedback, of very immediate feedback is very viable." For another, it involved a lot of intermittent feedback: "What I really have done is give them more practice. A practice quiz before a quiz. Or a practice exam before an exam. I do that a lot more now, because . . . that helps them." The suggestion to incorporate more feedback through interval practice led the instructor to employ this evidence-based method.

Unexpectedly, instructors also connected the IMPACT program with big ideas for their courses and to their thinking about how to improve student learning. One instructor noted, "It is about making sure students are aware of . . . bigger goals than . . . what's happening on individual days." An arts professor used the opportunity to think more intentionally about how the highly interactive studio approach could be given structure to aid student learning—for this professor, the students' success with artistic production was key (and the professor sent the TLC examples of student work throughout the semester). As one instructor noted, "From the standpoint of students, it [transparency] implies a respectful learning environment." Another professor blended use of transparency methods with the introduction of a new assignment, in which undergraduates worked with graduate students to build an interactive model demonstrating a scientific process. They then demonstrated their new model at area high schools. In such ways, IMPACT served as a turning point in teacher practice, where they started to think of more changes in their course than what was required, so that the program facilitated new ways to teach. Concluded one instructor, "For me, the IMPACT grant was more [about] empowerment for students." This instructor saw the use of more transparent teaching methods as a way to give more agency to students.

In addition to examining student and faculty data, we also focused on the nine questions from the TILT end-of-term survey designed to measure the amount of transparency students perceive, triangulating around the concepts of purpose (questions 36–38), task (questions 39–41), and criteria (questions 42–44). Student response options included *never, sometimes, often,* or *always.* The mean responses from students in courses in the IMPACT cohort fell between *sometimes* and *often* on all but one measure. These results reinforce the connection between effective educational development and student experience as each instructor carried through, teaching their course using transparency. Their efforts were recognized by students, as shown in Figure 7.2.

One measure of transparency received lower responses from UT students, with most responses falling between *never* and *sometimes*: "My instructor provided students with annotated examples of past students' work." The question relates to transparency around the criteria for quality academic work. This is true of students' responses to this survey question nationally, across disciplines. As TILT's survey research indicates, many instructors do not regularly share examples of past students' work, and most do not usually obtain written permission from existing students to share examples of their work with future students. TILT Higher Ed now recommends that faculty instead share real-world examples of work that illustrate what it looks like when an instructor's criteria are met with varying degrees of success. When faculty bring such examples to class (i.e., published paragraphs from disciplinary research journals, photographs from local construction projects), students and faculty can discuss together the degree to which these examples

Figure 7.2. Excerpt from Chart B showing amount of transparency perceived by students.

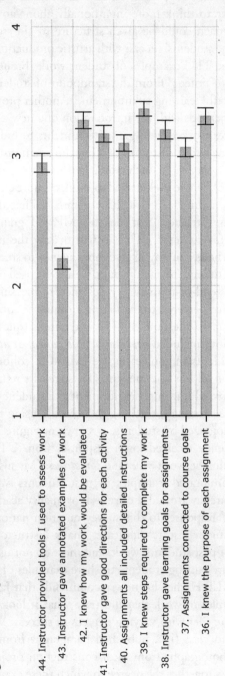

KEY	1	2	3	4	Transparency Survey Questions
Perceived Amount of Transparency in the Course CFA	Never	Sometimes	Often	Always	36 – 44

Number of students responding: 58

Error Bars Indicate +/- 1 SE

Confirmatory factor analysis verified a single factor underlying this group of survey questions.

Chart bar labels (left to right):
44. Instructor provided tools I used to assess work
43. Instructor gave annotated examples of work
42. I knew how my work would be evaluated
41. Instructor gave good directions for each activity
40. Assignments all included detailed instructions
39. I knew steps required to complete my work
38. Instructor gave learning goals for assignments
37. Assignments connected to course goals
36. I knew the purpose of each assignment

From TILT Higher Ed report for UT instructor team, fall 2016. Reproduced with permission of team members and Mary-Ann Winkelmes, director, TILT Higher Ed.

of work in the world satisfy the criteria the instructor has established for the students' work on a specific assignment. This gives students an opportunity to practice applying the criteria to multiple work samples before they must use them individually to monitor their own progress on an academic assignment. It also shows students how work like theirs is relevant in the world.

Further investigation of qualitative and quantitative data with larger groups of instructors and students should give a more complete picture. We are incorporating additional instructor interviews to assess more fully the program's impacts on instructors and their teaching practices.

Conclusion

The intention of Teaching for IMPACT was to align TILT principles with very specific evidence-based teaching strategies in a clearly scaffolded program in which instructors would make small changes in teaching for significant impact on student success and to link and measure the benefits of this faculty development offering for instructors and students. Because instructors themselves shared their own strategies, another intention of the IMPACT program was met—to provide a framework to bring teachers into dialogue about the process of teaching and learning with each other and with the staff at the TLC, who provide education and research expertise and support. As we noted previously, observations about some of the data will need further investigation.

However, we learned a few lessons and identified issues to be investigated by the research team and staff at the TLC. The following are areas where additional attention offers the potential to enhance workshop material or encourage continued participation by the instructors:

- In STEM disciplines, instructors do not usually provide students with examples of student work—student work is not archived to show to the next class, unlike in writing courses and courses with portfolio work. This barrier can be addressed at the start of the program. Educational developers can help STEM faculty and others give clear examples to students by suggesting they begin to archive student work to show to future students. In the meantime, the instructors could develop samples to illustrate where assessment criteria are met—or not—at differing levels.
- Instructors recommended a broader call for participants, to bring in more faculty than just a few adventurous people. In the program, we recommend that follow-up sessions be offered after a course is completed, so that instructors can share their experience with peers

and share effective practices they used throughout the process. In short, we recommend at least a second session for participants. It may also be effective to encourage participant instructors to advocate for transparency in their departments and encourage their department peers to participate.

- A pre- and postknowledge test for instructors about the concepts related to transparency would yield helpful information and could increase instructor metacognition. Educational developers could use the tests and share results with the instructors. In particular, the postknowledge test would reinforce what the instructors had learned through participating and could trigger metacognitive thought about the process to help them retain knowledge long term.
- We learned there is interest in continued support to the project participants. The TILT project has moved to a model of providing routine support through TILT webinars. Educational developers could incorporate the TILT webinars or similar types of online support into all educational development experiences. This information could also be available on demand for project participants and other instructors who become interested in using transparent methods in class.

On reflection, we have learned a great deal about our own practices as educational developers. The research project yielded not only further research questions but also invaluable information regarding the complex process of integrating data collection with educational development. We experienced the value of scaffolded learning in our workshop, which yielded intra- and interdisciplinary dialogue and instructor self-reflection. As instructors willingly share across disciplines, they enact the spirit of the larger TILT program.

EDITORS' HIGHLIGHTS

For educational developers considering engaging with the Transparency Framework as an opportunity to gather data or report on the impact of their work, consider the following points from these contributors:

- Draw connections between transparency and other evidence-based teaching practices in CTL programming.
- Use data derived from resources available through TILT Higher Ed as well as institutional data and/or instructor reflections efforts to demonstrate the significance of educational development.

References

Beach, A., Sorcinelli, M. D., Austin, A., & Rivard, J. (2016). *Faculty development in the age of evidence.* Sterling, VA: Stylus.

Benassi, V., Overson, C. E., & Hakala, C. M. (2014). Applying the science of learning in education: Infusing psychological science into the curriculum. *American Psychological Association, 37*(1), 1–303.

Brown, J., & Kurzweil, M. (2017). *Instructional quality, student outcomes, and institutional finances.* Washington DC: American Council on Education.

Hausmann, L. R., Ye, F., Schofield, J. W., & Woods, R. L. (2009). Sense of belonging and persistence in White and African American first-year students. *Research in Higher Education, 50*(7), 649–669.

Marzano, R. (2004). *Building background knowledge for academic achievement: Research on what works in schools.* Alexandria, VA: Association for Supervision and Curriculum Development.

National Research Council. (2000). *How people learn: Brain, mind, experience, and school* (expanded ed.). Washington DC: The National Academies Press.

Shulruf, B., Hattie, J., & Tumen, S. (2008). Individual and school factors affecting students' participation and success in higher education. *Higher Education: The International Journal of Higher Education and Educational Planning, 56*(5), 613–632.

Sorcinelli, M. D., Berg, J., Bond, H., & Watson, C. E. (2017). Why now is the time for evidence-based faculty development. In C. Haras, S. C. Taylor, M. D. Sorcinelli, and L. von Hoene (Eds.), *Institutional commitment to teaching excellence: Assessing the impacts and outcomes of faculty development* (5–16). Washington DC: American Council on Education.

Teaching and Learning Center. (2016-2017). Call for proposals: Teaching IMPACT grants [Internal document]. Knoxville: University of Tennessee.

TILT Higher Ed. (2014). Transparency in Learning and Teaching in Higher Education. Available from www.tilthighered.org

U.S. Department of Education. (2014). *WWC procedures and standards handbook* (Version 3.0). Washington DC: Institute of Educational Service.

Walton, G., & Cohen, G. (2011). A brief social-belonging intervention improves academic and health outcomes of minority students. *Science, 331*(6023), 1447–1451.

PART THREE

TRANSPARENT DESIGN
ACROSS HIGHER EDUCATION

8

TRANSPARENCY IN FACULTY DEVELOPMENT COLLABORATIONS AT A MINORITY-SERVING RESEARCH UNIVERSITY

Katie Humphreys, Mary-Ann Winkelmes, Dan Gianoutsos, Anne Mendenhall, Erin Farrar, Melissa Bowles-Terry, Gayle Juneau-Butler, Debi Cheek, Leeann Fields, Gina M. Sully, Celeste Calkins, Ke Yu, and Sunny Gittens

The Transparency Framework (see Figures I.2 and 1.3) has guided teachers, students, and faculty developers in designing teaching and learning materials that maximize equitable opportunities for students to succeed in college. This chapter examines how the framework can guide broader institutional practices to connect collaborators' educational development work, through shared language, resources, and goals, in support of an institution's strategic plan priorities. It introduces the idea of scaling applications of transparent design to increasingly larger contexts in higher education.

A group of over 30 staff, faculty, and students collaborate voluntarily to provide faculty development services at the University of Nevada, Las Vegas (UNLV). These collaborators represent every college and school and more than 10 administrative units, spanning academic affairs and student affairs. The Transparency Framework has helped the group address important challenges that any large team from across institutional units might face, such as the following:

- The need for a shared language that invites easy communication across disciplines and areas of expertise

135

- The codification of shared measures of success for the group, when each individual unit must also meet its own specific performance measures
- The adoption of a single, accessible planning tool for combining skills and resources across units in an equitable way and for assessing collective success

This chapter describes how the UNLV group applied the purpose-task-criteria Transparency Framework to their work in a variety of ways that enabled a robust faculty development program built by many contributors.

Context

UNLV is a large, urban, minority-serving institution (MSI) with the most diverse university undergraduate student population in the nation (*U.S. News & World Report*, 2018). Like many state institutions of higher education during the economic recession of 2008, UNLV experienced its share of state funding reductions, hiring freezes, furloughs, and closures or consolidations of programs and centers, including the closure of its teaching and learning center. Center staff and services then scattered across multiple units, including academic assessment, general education, online education, and the university libraries. In 2013, UNLV hired a faculty developer, Mary-Ann Winkelmes, who gathered leaders from 10 administrative units together to coordinate their efforts to offer teaching development services.

Shared Language to Support Collaboration

The group's initial meetings aimed to share information about each unit's faculty development goals and programming. Collaborators recognized the benefit of reducing redundancy and sharing the work. Multiple units, including academic assessment, the university libraries, academic advising and online education, student advising, the academic success center, campus life, civic engagement and diversity, the writing center, and the registrar's office, had been providing workshops for faculty that were specific to their unit's goals, without viewing campus-wide faculty development opportunities as a coherent curriculum. What stood in the way of easy collaboration initially was not a lack of will but rather a lack of shared vocabulary. Each unit had its own professional vocabulary, derived from the accrediting authority or other national organization that led that aspect of academic work. For example, librarians adopted Dee Fink's significant learning model (2013) and the language of information literacy, whereas online education staffers adopted guidelines from Quality Matters (2016–2018). Student advisers pursued aims of the National Academic Advising Association (NACADA), whereas campus life professionals spoke the language of the National Association of Student Personnel Administrators (NASPA). Colleagues who shared very similar goals for faculty development and student success did not understand the details of each other's descriptions.

A simple, shared language was desperately needed for the collaborators across units to communicate in any detail about their rationale and goals for faculty development programs they would build together. The purpose-task-criteria language of the Transparency Framework served this need. But simply adopting the words from the framework was not enough. Each unit mapped its own professional language and standards onto the Transparency Framework for all the other units to see. This exercise in cross-disciplinary translation enabled all the collaborators to understand each other's languages well enough to know that the words *purpose-task-criteria* would hold useful meaning for the whole cross-disciplinary group. Table 8.1 illustrates the translation exercise by integrating several units' views into one table.

The purpose-task-criteria language of the Transparency Framework helped the units in our collaborative working group to explain and understand the overall goals that each brought to the table. The faculty development collaborators began using the language of the Transparency Framework in contexts beyond group conversations, in the daily work of their individual units. As students and faculty across the campus become more familiar with the Transparency Framework, the language of purpose-task-criteria helps developers to clarify the support their units can offer for students and faculty. The following sections provide details regarding how each unit was able to adapt the Transparency Framework to meet its individual needs as well as relate to institution-wide goals.

University Libraries

The mission of UNLV libraries is to support learners as they discover, access, and use information effectively for academic success, research, and lifelong learning. Librarians work directly with students through a program of course-integrated library instruction, but they also work extensively with faculty on research assignment design and course preparation. Working with faculty is vital to the mission of the libraries, as it makes a long-term impact on how courses are planned and delivered, and how information competencies are taught to students across disciplines. For several years, librarians worked with faculty using the integrated course design approach created by Dee Fink

TABLE 8.1

TILT Framework Used to Facilitate Shared Language Across Units

Unit *Disciplinary guidelines*	Purpose *Skills practiced* *Knowledge gained*	Task *What to do* *How to do it*	Criteria *Measures for success* *Examples*
Libraries: Dee Fink (2013), Significant Learning Experiences	• Learning Goals	• Teaching/ learning activities	• Feedback and assessment • Number of students served • Number of faculty/staff served • Support for research productivity
Online Ed: Quality Matters (2014, 2017) rubric	2. Learning objectives, competencies* 4. Instructional materials* 6. Course technology* 8. Accessibility and usability*	1. Course overview and intro* 5. Course activities, learner interaction* 7. Learner support*	5. Assessment and measurement* • Number of online students • Number of student completions • Number of online courses • Number of hybrid courses
Registrar: Bennis (2009); Mahoney, Bates, & Striepeck (2016); Stark & Flaherty (2010); AACRAO (n.d.)	• Define how the office and the employee both benefit from a task that supports student success	• Actions that support the mission of student success • Employee annual reviews	• Evidence of impact and goal achievement • Smooth progression versus bottlenecks in students' path to completion • Student retention • Student completion
Writing Center: CWPA, NCTE, & NWP (2011)	• Coaches help students understand assignments and improve their writing	• Individual consultations	• Number of students served • Quality of service • Quality of training

(Continues)

TABLE 8.1 (*Continued*)

Unit *Disciplinary guidelines*	Purpose *Skills practiced* *Knowledge gained*	Task *What to do* *How to do it*	Criteria *Measures for success* *Examples*
Academic Success Center: CAS (2014)	• Goals • Education plan • Responsibility to meet requirements	• Articulate intent, curriculum • Use good intellectual habits	• Engage • Use complex info to assess goal achievement
Academic Advising: CAS (2014)	• Goal setting	• Identify desired courses, learning, GPA	• Goal progression • Self-monitoring, awareness
Campus Life & Recreation: ACPA & NASPA (2016)	• Outcomes of the programs and how those offer learning benefits for students	• What will students do? • How will they do it?	• Criteria, examples of successful work • Reflection on students' learning

Note. Numbered and asterisk entries correspond to Quality Matters principles (Quality Matters 2016–2018).

(2003). They altered that approach slightly in order to align the language with the Transparency Framework. By renaming learning goals as *purpose*, teaching and learning activities as *tasks*, and feedback and assessment as *criteria*, it was a simple matter to bring the libraries' course and assignment design efforts into close alignment with the collaborative group of faculty development providers. As the Transparency Framework has begun to pervade the UNLV campus, and many more instructors are using purpose-task-criteria to explain assignments to students, librarians have started to use the terms not only with faculty in an assignment design context but also in library instruction sessions to set up what students will be doing while in the library classroom. Increasingly, it is language students are familiar with and see in many of their courses, so it serves librarians well to adopt the same terms. Librarians' practice has been enriched by a careful consideration of how to make instruction transparent to students, and librarians' collaboration with faculty has been facilitated by this shared language and shared goal of transparency.

Online Education

Like many instructional designers and online education colleagues across the United States and internationally, UNLV's online education leaders and staff look to the national Quality Matters (2016–2018) rubric as a guide for best practices in online and/or blended courses. Applying this nationally accepted, research-based rubric to the improvement of existing courses or the development of new ones can help to ensure quality in online course development. Yet the extensive nature of the rubric (eight standards, each consisting of five to nine dimensions) and its somewhat specialized language required some translation across the disciplines represented in our UNLV instructional development group. The online education team mapped the Quality Matters standards onto the Transparency Framework in a manner that allowed easier communication about how the Quality Matters rubric informed the work of online education's designers and consultants who worked with faculty. The online education team also observed that the language of the Transparency Framework (purpose-task-criteria) is useful in communicating the main ideas from the Quality Matters rubric to faculty who had found the language of Quality Matters less accessible.

Registrar's Office: Enrollment Services

The registrar's office utilizes the Transparency Framework in several distinct ways. In 2015, the registrar's office adopted a strategic plan that aligned all the office's goals with student success measures identified in the university's Top Tier Plan, including retention of first-year students into the second year, availability of required classes to promote efficient time to degree, and graduation rates. The Transparent Framework aided the registrar's office in focusing staff members' work to achieve specific goals in support of student success, as in the following example:

> Purpose: Clear the Pathway to Degree Completion
> Task: Investigate roadblocks to retention progression and completion by (a) cutting down the turnaround time in supporting the students' pathways to graduation, (b) submitting three system modifications, (c) synthesizing curriculum updates with technical system adjustments and updates to the catalog, and (d) reducing frequency of substitutions, exceptions, and waivers.
> Criteria: The turnaround time for addressing student pathways roadblocks will be reduced to 48 hours and will be measured/monitored on a quarterly basis. System modifications will be submitted by the end of the semester with regular follow-up until implemented; a report will be developed and delivered to each advising center on an annual basis showing the frequency of substitutions, exceptions, and waivers

along with suggestions for curriculum changes that would reduce the volume. The graduation rate will continue to climb.

Using the purpose-task-criteria structure for evaluation, assessment, and planning increased the clarity of communication among registrar staff, facilitated faster goal completion, and improved outcomes. At the outset of a project, employees clarified their purpose (i.e., what they hoped to accomplish), how it fit with the office mission and vision, and its feasibility. They outlined the specific steps (tasks) they would undertake and how they would know they have been successful (criteria). In one case, a staff member indicated she wanted to enhance the reputation of the office which turned into the following:

Purpose: Sustain and expand the impact of the Registrar's Office through strategic public relations.

Task: (a) Continued presence at Advising Council, Faculty Senate, and Associate Deans' Council and introduction of annual meeting with each college dean (access deans through relationship with associate deans); (b) overhaul website and expand use of social media, (c) create an electronic newsletter, and (d) hold an annual open house.

Criteria: Hold 1 meeting with each dean by the end of the calendar year, leaving each meeting with an action item to be followed up on. Hold 4 focus groups and distribute a survey focused on the usability of the website, implementing at least 10 suggestions. Establish a baseline expectation for number of likes and followers across social media platforms and meet goals within specified time frames. Distribute newsletter on an annual basis and monitor feedback. Hold initial open house with a goal of 100 faculty/staff attendees across at least 20 departments and 250 student attendees.

The Registrar's Office could sometimes be inundated with research requests requiring data input, analysis, and extraction. The process for prioritizing these requests had been difficult, time-consuming, and occasionally inconsistent. The Transparency Framework was easy to adopt as a means for prioritizing requests, and it helped employees to better relate research requests with specific goals of the office.

Employees in the Registrar's Office regularly engage with students and offer advice. Staff knowledge of the Transparency Framework has resulted in conversations with students about how to seek clarity from their instructors about work assignments and the outcomes of the course. Registrar staff distribute the Transparency Framework for Students (Figure I.3) to all incoming UNLV students. The framework is also promoted to a specific group of at-risk students whom the staff serves in a mentor/mentee capacity.

Writing Center

UNLV's Writing Center employs 40 consultants including undergraduates, graduate students, and professional staff, who serve about 9,000 students in consultations and workshops each academic year. One of the biggest challenges novice academic writers face is understanding the instructions for assignments, projects, and writing tasks. About 37% of the students who use the Writing Center come from rhetorical traditions quite different from those familiar to the academy, including first-generation U.S. students, Generation 1.5 students, and international students. Additionally, UNLV has a large population of working, low-income students, a population that is often reluctant or unable to visit instructors and professors during office hours.

The Writing Center's main purpose is to help students understand and succeed with their writing assignments. Individual in-person or online consultations are the methods with which this is accomplished. Consultants use the Transparency Framework to help students parse and better understand their assignment prompts, to guide them in seeking clarification about assignments, and to encourage students' metacognition when working on writing assignments. Consultants foster students' engagement, persistence, and self-awareness, all of which are part of the *Framework for Success in Post-Secondary Writing* (CWPA, NCTE, & NWP, 2011). The Writing Center has also incorporated the framework into its "Understanding Writing Assignments" workshop for students.

The Transparency Framework also helped the Writing Center to clarify internal roles and training processes for consultants. The director has adapted the framework as a template for composing work assignment and project instructions, and this template is used for all training assignments. Moreover, because approximately 30% of the Writing Center's consultants are first-semester graduate students teaching courses for the first time, many have adopted the transparent assignment design template for composing their own instructions in addition to using it during consultations. Consultants also report using the framework to ask questions about unclear instructions in the graduate classes they take.

Finally, the Transparency Framework helps the Writing Center demonstrate how its work is linked to its goals for success, as in the following example:

Purpose: Greater writer independence in the planning stages of writing, increased confidence in understanding assignments, and use of the purpose-task-criteria template to ask questions about assignments during instructors' office hours.

Tasks: Workshops, consultations, meetings, invitations, public outreach to departments and colleges, and feedback from director to consultants.

Criteria: Periodic surveys and evaluation forms that gauge confidence and gather information about contexts where writers use the purpose-task-criteria framework. Consultants use the purpose-task-criteria framework to conduct reflective self-evaluations, and the director uses the purpose-task-criteria framework to offer formative evaluation to consultants.

Measures of Success

As much as the Transparency Framework helped units to understand shared similarities in efforts to support faculty and student success, it also highlighted and clarified differences—particularly differences in how each unit measured its own success. For example, Online Education was specifically interested in the number of online students and their course completion rates, as well as the number of new online courses, whereas the University Libraries looked at numbers of students and faculty served, as well as the support that librarians and databases provided for research productivity. The Registrar's Office used smooth progression through required courses in degree programs and adequate availability of required courses as measures of their success, along with student retention and graduation rates. Examples from the Academic Success Center, Academic Advising, and Student Affairs further illustrate such differences.

The Academic Success Center

The UNLV Academic Success Center partners across campus to provide academic programs and services designed to support student retention, progression, and completion. The center's various offerings include campus-wide tutoring, supplemental instruction, math bridge programs, academic success coaching, services for student-athletes, first- and second-year seminars for exploring majors, academic advising for exploring majors and non-degree-seeking students, scholarship programs, and others. The center collectively found that the Transparency Framework served as an effective tool for communicating with students. The primary variation across operations related to the scale of the perspective, which ranged from an individual student (micro) to an entire group of students (macro). For instance, Student-Athlete Academic Services utilized the framework to help student-athletes develop a weekly time management plan that determined the purpose-task-criteria for success regarding their usage of time. Alternatively, the Math Bridge Program used the design on their syllabi to better articulate the purpose of the program, what was required to successfully complete the program, and how students' success would be measured. Student Success Coaching focuses the Transparency Framework on the micro (individual student) level. The framework allows each coach to ensure the individual needs of students are met based on each student's unique situations. Although the Transparency Framework is one-size-fits-all, it allows for multiple solutions. Whether used through a micro or macro lens, each program and service agreed that the framework was an effective tool for communicating imperative information to students in a more focused format. Table 8.2 illustrates multiple ways the Academic Success Center applies the TILT framework.

Academic Advising

UNLV's student support infrastructure also includes 11 discipline-specific, college-based academic advising centers housed on campus, each with its own unique approach to working with its majors. As a method of connecting academic advising work with relational academic support projects and faculty initiatives on campus, the academic advising units have been applying the Transparency Framework to their work. The focus on purposes, tasks, and criteria is helpful in two main ways: (a) communication between advisers and faculty about the focus of courses and how courses fulfill requirements for the major and (b) communication between advisers and students about course selection, course work, and course learning outcomes.

As faculty increasingly use the purpose-task-criteria framework in their assignments and syllabi, advisers and students benefit from the increased transparency. Information about these three elements are equipping academic advisers and students with more information about what particular courses entail, how student work will be evaluated, and what learning outcomes can be generally expected. Focusing with students on purpose-task-criteria provides information about what will be required to successfully complete course work. Advisers help students to balance their course selections and academic goals with complex and sometimes competing personal lived experiences outside of the classroom. The purpose-task-criteria framework helps to clarify the information necessary for decision-making. Advisers aim to capitalize on the increased confidence and belonging the Transparent Framework can provide for students by helping students apply it in the broader context of

TABLE 8.2
Multiple Uses of TILT Framework by the Academic Success Center

Context *Academic* *Success Center*	Purpose *Skills practiced* *Knowledge gained*	Task *What to do* *How to do it*	Criteria *Measures for success* *Examples*
Student-athlete weekly meeting	• Effective time management • Task completion for progression	• Review of syllabi and course schedule • Review of upcoming assignments, readings, tests, athletic obligations	• Grades and athletic performance • Successful balance of academic and athletic obligations • Evaluate and adjust time management
Student time management	• Successful time management	• Complete a "Time Block" worksheet • Attend a time management workshop	• Completes assignments on time • Self-report on successful school/life balance
Know and use campus resources	• Students use campus resources	• Teach/learn about available resources	• Visit and use the recommended resources
Improve study skills	• Students learn and adopt good study skills	• Understand the study cycle • Practice SQ3R • Practice note-taking strategies	• Attends three or more coaching sessions • Maintains above the minimum GPA for degree program

course selection and planning the path to their degree. Table 8.3 summarizes multiple ways advisers use the TILT framework with students.

Student Affairs (Campus Life and Recreation)

In *Learning Reconsidered: A Campus-Wide Focus on the Student Experience* (Keeling, 2004), student affairs national associations redefine *learning* as "a comprehensive, holistic, transformative activity that integrates academic learning and student development" (p. 2). Grounded in this framework,

TABLE 8.3

Multiple Uses of the TILT Framework by Academic Advising

Context *Academic* *Advising*	Purpose *Skills practiced* *Knowledge gained*	Task *What to do* *How to do it*	Criteria *Measures for success* *Examples*
Major selection	Identify and declare a major	• Understand strengths and weaknesses • Locate information • Use resources	• Declare a major before 48 credits • Develop self-reliance, confidence
Retention, progression, completion	Graduation/ completion	• Course planning • Pursue undergraduate learning outcomes • Fulfill General Ed requirements	• 30 requirement-fulfilling credits per year

the UNLV Division of Student Affairs has a cocurricular agenda defining intended student learning outcomes for student life activities that align with university undergraduate learning outcomes. But students were not seeing the connections between their campus life activities and the learning outcomes. The Office of Student Affairs is using the Transparency Framework to rewrite student job descriptions to emphasize how the jobs offer learning experiences to student workers that are aligned with university undergraduate learning outcomes, including communication skills, citizenship and ethics, inquiry and critical thinking, and global/multicultural knowledge and awareness (Figure 8.1) (UNLV Campus Recreational Services, n.d.). Further, the revised job descriptions make the student staff evaluation process simpler by aligning the tasks with stated criteria for success. This has been a valuable process, creating enriching dialogues about the purpose of student staff training and development, and mechanisms are in place to assist students in reflective learning by asking students to articulate how their student employment experience relates to their academic and career goals.

Planning Shared Work and Assessing Collective Success

Once the faculty development team could anchor their collaboration in the Transparency Framework, the balance between the group's goals and each

Figure 8.1. Campus recreation, building manager job description.

Building Manager Position, 10–15 hours per week

PURPOSE:
This position is responsible for daily operations of the Student Recreation and Wellness Center (SRWC). . . . University Undergraduate Learning Outcomes practiced on the job include: communication skills, citizenship and ethics, inquiry and critical thinking, global/multicultural knowledge and awareness. This person will enforce all building policies and be able to communicate to a diverse group of patrons why the policies are in place. The building manager is responsible for the supervision of all student employees and will act as an effective leader and mentor. Preferred qualifications include: one year of student employment experience within campus recreation at the SRWC. . . .

TASKS:
Duties and Responsibilities include, but are not limited to:
- Act in the role of a supervisor on duty for the facility. . . .
- Assist any and all SWRC staff when needed.
- Responsible for the opening and closing of the SRWC facility.
- Cash handling and backup to the cash drawer attendant. . . .
- Knowledge of all programs, services, and facilities of the SRWC including Rebel Wellness Zone, fitness, intramurals, sport clubs and aquatics.
- Provide tours of the facility upon request of potential members, students, etc.
- Knowledge of computer software, including Rec Trac, When-to-Work, Time Clock Plus, Google Docs, Gmail.
- Knowledge of all equipment and equipment set-up and tear-down throughout building for special events, tournaments and open recreation requests (volleyball, badminton, floor hockey, table tennis).
- First responder to all SRWC emergencies, including preparation of follow-up paper work.
- Act in a professional manner by upholding SRWC policy when involved in conflict management with patrons, students and staff.
- Proper radio protocol and response in a timely manner, includes radio communication to SRWC, wellness and custodial staff. . . .
- Act as a role model for fellow staff members. . . .
- Communicate clear and concise information as needed to patrons, students, emergency medical service personnel and police services.
- Practice peer education to develop student staff growth and success.
- Assist with hiring and training of all new building managers. . . .

CRITERIA FOR SUCCESS:
Building managers will be evaluated on their performance each semester. The staff evaluation process consists of a self-evaluation, peer evaluation, and supervisor evaluation that address the following:
- Ability to display a positive leadership model for all patrons and CRS staff (UULOs: communication skills, citizenship and ethics).
- Ability to prioritize tasks, manage time and balance professional and personal commitments for self and staff (UULOs: inquiry and critical thinking, global/multicultural knowledge and awareness).

collaborating unit's unique goals required careful attention. If sharing information about the topics and schedules of teaching development workshops being offered by various units was a mutually beneficial purpose that brought a leader from each unit to the table, the need for equitable balance became paramount immediately. Each participating unit needed to contribute to the shared tasks in ways that benefited the criteria for success for the collaboration while also making progress toward the unit's own strategic plan metrics for success.

Purpose

With a shared language in place, the group discussed their shared purpose: to plan a sequence of faculty development events that would provide teaching development support in a logical sequence, particularly targeting moments in the academic calendar when faculty would most need advice on particular topics. With this purpose in mind, planning the tasks required identifying needs and arranging them in a sequence. Course design workshops would take place late in a term or over break, whereas assignment design help or advice about active learning and discussion leading might happen early in a term. To fill in discipline-specific gaps where staff members lacked the needed expertise, a team of faculty development fellows was appointed to help. Nominated by their deans and funded partially by the provost and partially by their deans, the fellows brought disciplinary expertise and credibility to the team of providers.

Tasks

Sustaining the tasks for our faculty development work was a bit more difficult. Careful planning was necessary to ensure the multiple collaborating units contributed resources equitably. Each unit had different numbers of staff with varied expertise. The group explicitly incorporated these concerns into the planning. Units contributed based on the availability of staff, expertise, and funds available for a variety of faculty development events, activities, and resources. For example, staff members from the Office of Information Technology and Online Education contributed to sessions for faculty receiving training in a new learning management platform for online courses, whereas University Libraries and Assessment Office staff, along with Student Life staff, often collaborated on workshops and institutes about best teaching practices for faculty and instructors. When more discipline-based support was needed, the faculty development fellow contributed. Staff members from many units, along with the fellows, faculty, and instructors, contributed to faculty development events (e.g., the campus-wide Best Teaching Practices Expo) and services (e.g., peer observation of teaching and individual teaching consultations, as well as faculty mentoring). Balancing the time commitments of the fellows as well as staff from various campus units has required careful attention.

In cases where our faculty development programming required funding to support space reservations, equipment, materials, or catering costs, the task of balancing contributions became a shared exercise in equitable budgeting. Several of the larger units, including the Academic Success Center, University Libraries, and the Office of Undergraduate Education, were able to make contributions approximately proportionate to the unit's resources for cosponsored campus events like a guest speaker or the campus-wide Best Teaching Practices Expo. Such events directly contributed to increasing the measures of success for those individual units as well as the measures of success for the group's collaboration. Some of the faculty development programming did not benefit all the units equally. Workshops focusing on science, technology, engineering, or mathematics (STEM) instruction, or training sessions designed to support online-only courses, for example, were more difficult for all our collaborators to justify supporting financially. Regardless of an event's focus, in-kind contributions of staff suggestions or time were more readily available than financial contributions.

Criteria

All the faculty development team members agreed that student success and faculty satisfaction were important long-term goals for the collaboration, and these have been reflected in the group's strategic plan (Table 8.4). The criteria for success provided the group with a tangible way to demonstrate that each unit's contribution has accomplished something of value. Yet each unit also had its own set of short-term goals and disciplinary best practices defined in the unit's office mission, strategic plan, or by the unit's accrediting or professional organizations. Their faculty development work served a variety of unit-specific purposes in addition to the shared purposes that we identified for the group. How could the collaboration address all of those separate, smaller goals in a way that would satisfy each unit enough to maintain active collaboration in the faculty development providers' group? This seemed an almost impossible task. It was a shift in the university's strategic plan that provided a solution. While the teaching development group from across units was developing its strategic plan, its coordinator, Mary-Ann Winkelmes, was serving on the executive committee for UNLV's Top Tier strategic plan. As metrics of success for the university's plan developed, the teaching development team incorporated some of these into its own strategic plan—mainly in the areas of student success and faculty satisfaction, both of which were

TABLE 8.4

Abbreviated Strategic Plan* (Goal 1 of 3) for Instructional Development Working Group, UNLV, Fall 2017

PURPOSE	< --------------------- TASKS --------------------- >			CRITERIA
Address emerging needs	*Resources to Address Needs*	*Partners*	*Outreach to Stakeholders*	*Assessment: Measures of Success*
Increased support for faculty development services	Events (single) connected through a "curriculum" for faculty development • January Expo: Best Teaching Practices • May General Ed symposium • Winter/Summer institutes • Fall Orientations: Faculty, Undergrads, GAs • Post-orientation Series: o Teaching o Research o Technology o Faculty Mentoring o Admin Fac Connections o Grad Student Certificates	• Provost • President • Faculty Affairs • Undergrad Education • Assessment • Library • Office of Info Tech • General Education • Diversity/Intersection • Service-Learning • Academic Success Center	• Deans and/or department chairs nominate Faculty Fellows • Provost appoints (honorific) • Units and provost share $ support • Visits to colleges, deans' councils, faculty senate, to invite focus areas including: – high DFW courses, – large intro courses, – General Education	Increases in: **Faculty Satisfaction/ Outcomes** • National COACHE survey • Faculty diversity • Faculty retention/ progression • Internal assessment (in-house climate surveys, Hurney 2016 model/ Kirkpatrick: reaction, learning, behavior, results) • Use of best/equitable teaching practices

Programs (ongoing)			Student Success:
Programs (ongoing)	• Student Life (Campus Recreation, etc.)	• Provost announcements	**Student Success:**
• Curricular Coherence project (funded by the Association of American Colleges & Universities)	• Online Education	• Monthly e-mail with services/events	• National NSSE engagement survey
Services and Resources:	• Advising	• Professional Development Calendar shared/developed online	• National SSI satisfaction index
• Faculty Mentoring Fellows	• Writing Center	• Research funds to Faculty Mentoring Fellows, Teaching Academy Fellows	• 1st–2nd year retention rates
• Teaching Academy Fellows	• Deans	• Hourly pay to student observers	• Graduation rates: 4yr, 6yr
• Student observers	• Departments		• Teacher evaluation scores (overall course/instructor)
• Funds for hosting, research, awards, fellows, student observers			• GPAs
• Online resources:			• Student self-ratings of confidence, belonging, skills
o Asynchronous communities			• Student exit surveys
o Archive of events/ materials			**Support for Faculty Development**
o Shared Professional Development calendar			• Structural support for faculty development: unit or center
			• Renewing budget for faculty development
			• Grant application assistance

*Main criteria for success (aligned with UNLV's Top Tier Initiative): faculty satisfaction/success and faculty outcomes; student success; ongoing support for faculty development.

emerging as important goals in the university's new Top Tier plan. Each collaborating unit saw in the group's strategic plan that the contributions helped to achieve a Top Tier goal, at a time when units across the university were defining contributions to match Top Tier goals.

Even where the collaborating units' strategic plan goals differed around particular aspects of student success, every unit benefited from demonstrating the whole group's contributions toward an institutional goal like higher student retention rates. The University Libraries, for example, aimed to improve students' information literacy, whereas Online Education sought to increase the number of students enrolled in online courses, and Student Life sought to increase student engagement. Higher student retention rates benefit all three units' individual goals. For example, in 2014–2015, the faculty development group collaborated to provide programming that engaged instructors of large, introductory-level courses and also small, writing-heavy, first-year seminar courses in adopting transparently designed assignments. The retention rate (percentage of students still registered the following fall) for 870 first-time, full-time, first-year students who received the transparent assignments was significantly higher than the average retention rate for the first-year, first-time cohort. And 2 years later, the higher retention effects persisted for those students (Introduction, this volume; Winkelmes, Calkins, & Yu, forthcoming). All the collaborating units that contributed to this faculty development program were responsible for this improvement and may claim credit for supporting this increase in student success. The effect is so significant that UNLV now introduces all incoming students to the Transparent Assignment Framework for Students (see Figure I.3) and UNLV syllabi are required to include language that encourages students to seek transparent instruction: "Transparency in Learning and Teaching—The University encourages students to use a transparency template [Figure I.3] to discuss with their instructors how assignments and course activities benefit student success" (UNLV, 2017).

Conclusion

The Transparency Framework of purpose-task-criteria is a useful and adaptable tool that now infuses the work of many units at UNLV. The framework has helped to bridge communication gaps and establish a thriving collaboration among units that provide a coherent, intentional program of faculty development services, even when UNLV's organizational structure did not require, incentivize, or even reward the collaboration. Each unit continues to see the value of its contributions as a sustainable piece of the whole. One of the long-term criteria for success in the teaching development group's strategic plan (in addition to improved student success and faculty satisfaction) is the sustained, long-term support of teaching development efforts by the university, including dedicated staff and an eventual faculty development center. If such resources are provided, the purpose-task-criteria format of the strategic plan for faculty development will be essential to balancing new resources with existing units' and colleges' voluntary contributions in order to maintain the success of faculty development work at UNLV.

For many institutions where cross-unit collaboration is desired or already underway, the Transparency Framework may help to support the ways that units negotiate shared work, shared resources, and shared measures of success. Practitioners in the areas of institutional assessment, student support, and faculty development at conferences across the United States have suggested partners that might use the Transparency Framework to connect work around goals including student success, faculty satisfaction, equity, diversity, or other major institutional and national aims (Figure 8.2).

In addition, collaborators from across the country have suggested possible measures of success to monitor in conjunction with a TILT project. For example, these might include student success predictors such as academic

Figure 8.2. Examples of campus and cross-institutional partners.

Campus Partners

- Academic unit administrators
- Advisers
- Athletics staff
- Diversity officers
- Faculty development staff and teaching/learning center staff
- Institutional analysis staff
- Online education staff
- Registrars and staff

- Accessibility and disability officers
- Assessment staff
- Campus life staff
- Faculty and instructors
- Graduate student instructors
- Librarians
- Peer mentors
- Tutoring/supplemental instruction staff

Cross-Institutional Partners

- Consortia: regional, national
- Cross-institutional networks united by region or size
- Discipline-based professional organizations
- Higher ed interest groups
- Institutional types (minority-serving institutions, small colleges, community colleges, universities, state system schools)
- Transfer-connected institutions and feeder schools

confidence and sense of belonging; metacognitive awareness of skill development; objectively scored student work samples; rates of D/F grades or withdrawals from courses; retention rates in school and/or in a major; persistence of ethnically underrepresented students in STEM; graduation rates; increased diversity of students and/or faculty and staff; and increased student/faculty/staff satisfaction. Broader measurements of success for the implementation of a TILT project might include community engagement, postgraduation employment rates for alumni, research productivity, the scholarship of teaching and learning, and/or alumni engagement.

The example of the UNLV faculty development strategic plan illustrates how a collection of units turned the Transparency Framework into a plan that guides collaboration. Similar cross-unit collaborations in the service of various institutional goals may also benefit from using the Transparency Framework to establish a shared language, identify shared goals, clarify unit-specific goals, negotiate sharing of resources across units, and establish a collaborative strategic plan.

EDITORS' HIGHLIGHTS

For collaborators from a variety of units across an institution who are considering how to achieve faculty development goals or other institutional priorities, consider the following points from these contributors:

- The purpose-task-criteria Transparency Framework can improve collaboration across multiple campus units by establishing a shared, common language and by clarifying contributions and expectations.
- Strategic planning among multiple partners with both distinct and shared goals can be facilitated by using the Transparency Framework to map out collaborators' purposes, tasks, and criteria to find an equitable balance that benefits their unit-specific goals *and* the group's shared goals.

References

ACPA–College Student Educators International & NASPA–Student Affairs Administrators in Higher Education. (2016). *ACPA-NASPA professional competencies rubrics*. Washington DC: ACPA-NASPA.

American Association of Collegiate Registrars and Admissions Officers (AACRAO). (n.d.). Staffing leadership. In *Resources: Professional competencies*. Available from https://www.aacrao.org/resources/core-competencies/professional-proficiences/enrollment-management/staffing-leadership

Bennis, W. (2009). *On becoming a leader*. New York, NY: Basic Books.

Council for the Advancement of Standards in Higher Education (CAS). (2014). *CAS standards for academic advising programs*. Manhattan, KS: National Academic Advising Association Clearinghouse (NACADA). Available from http://standards.cas.edu/getpdf.cfm?PDF=E864D2C4-D655-8F74-2E647CD-ECD29B7D0

Council of Writing Program Administrators (CWPA), National Council of Teachers of English (NCTE), & National Writing Project (NWP). (2011). *Framework for success in post-secondary writing*. Available from http://wpacouncil.org/files/framework-for-success-postsecondary-writing.pdf

Fink, D. L. (2013). *Creating significant learning experiences: An integrated approach to designing college courses*. San Francisco, CA: Jossey-Bass.

Hurney, C. A. Brantmeier, E. J., Good, M. R., Harrison, D. & Meixner, C. (2016). The faculty learning outcome assessment framework. *The Journal of Faculty Development, 30*(2), pp. 69–77.

Kirkpatrick, J. D. & Kirkpatrick, W. K. (2016). Kirkpatrick's four levels of training evaluation. Alexandria, VA: ATD Press

Keeling, R. P. (Ed.). (2004). *Learning reconsidered: A campus-wide focus on the student experience*. Washington DC: American College Personnel Association (ACPA)/National Association of Student Personnel Administrators (NASPA).

Mahoney, L., Bates, M., & Striepeck, S. (2016). The evidence behind evidence-based leadership. *Articles & Whitepapers*. Pensacola, FL: Studer Group/NACADA Clearing House. Available from https://www.studergroup.com/resources/articles-and-industry-updates/articles-and-whitepapers/the-evidence-behind-evidence-based-leadership

Quality Matters. (2016–2018). *Non-annotated standards from the QM Higher Education Rubric* (5th ed.). Annapolis, MD: MarylandOnline, Inc. Available from https://www.qualitymatters.org/qa-resources/rubric-standards/higher-ed-rubric

Stark, P. B., & Flaherty, J. (2010). *The only leadership book you'll ever need*. Newburyport, MA: Career Press.

University of Nevada, Las Vegas (UNLV). (2017). *Minimum criteria for syllabi—Academic year 2017–2018*. Las Vegas, NV: University of Nevada, Las Vegas. Available from https://www.unlv.edu/sites/default/files/page_files/27/SyllabiContent-MinimumCriteria-2017-2018.doc

University of Nevada, Las Vegas Campus Recreational Services. (n.d.). *Building manager position description*. Available from https://www.unlv.edu/sites/default/files/page_files/27/SRWC-StudentEmployment-BuildingManager.pdf

U.S. News & World Report. (2018). *Campus ethnic diversity: National universities*. Available from https://www.usnews.com/best-colleges/rankings/national-universities/campus-ethnic-diversity

Winkelmes, M. A., Calkins, C., & Yu, K. (forthcoming). Transparent instruction increases students' long-term persistence and success.

9

TRANSPARENCY AND THE GUIDED PATHWAYS MODEL

Ensuring Equitable Learning Opportunities for Students in Community and Technical Colleges

Jennifer Whetham, Jill Darley-Vanis, Sally Heilstedt,
Allison Boye, Suzanne Tapp, and Mary-Ann Winkelmes

Like many community college systems across the United States, the Washington State Community and Technical College (CTC) system has set two ambitious and interrelated goals around the larger umbrella of student success—the first goal is to increase completion by all students and the second goal is to direct a rigorous and sustained focus of our collective attention to close equity gaps. To achieve these two goals, the Washington State CTC system is currently engaged in a statewide Guided Pathways Initiative. However, many faculty perceive the work they perform at the classroom level as disconnected from the holistic success outcomes (sometimes referred to as "30,000 foot" or "money" outcomes) that drive educational policy at the institutional, state, and national levels. In a recent survey conducted in the fall of 2017, many faculty members in our system reported feeling alone, isolated, and unsupported in overcoming the obstacles and challenges that prevent them from being successful in their classrooms, including how to best support students who, for whatever reason, end up in their classrooms without adequate academic preparation. This chapter describes how a group of faculty developers from a community college system (Washington State CTC) use the Transparency in Learning and Teaching (TILT) framework to engage faculty in applying and adopting a Guided Pathways model. We share the methods used and some lessons learned that may be useful for other states' efforts and for considering how TILT can serve as a method for advancing big picture reform efforts.

A Guided Pathways approach simplifies the options for college students. This approach groups courses together

> to form clear paths through college and into careers, whether students enter those careers directly after graduation or transfer to a university for more study in their chosen fields. Students get intensive, targeted advising to choose a path, stay on the path, learn what they need to know and graduate. (Washington State Board for Community and Technical Colleges, 2018)

As a model, Guided Pathways challenges those of us who work in higher education to commit to a new way of making change—to approach educational reform through the lens of systems thinking. A Guided Pathways redesign means carefully scaffolding and structuring how our students experience us from the beginning to the end—from their first moments (what the Community College Research Center calls "initial connection to college") to their completion of a high-quality credential that has prepared them to enter the workforce and take advantage of future educational opportunities (Bailey, Jaggars, & Jenkins, 2015b, p. 2). The four design principles for the Guided Pathway model, summarized by the Washington State Board for Community and Technical Colleges (Washington State Board for Community and Technical Colleges, 2017b), are noted in Figure 9.1.

In Washington State, where 40% of public baccalaureate graduates start at one of our CTCs and faculty members comprise 53% of employees in our 34 CTCs (Washington State Board for Community and Technical Colleges, 2017a), we know that none of this is possible without engaging large numbers of faculty in ways that are meaningful to them as practitioners. Faculty engagement is critical to the success of Guided Pathways programs (Bailey, Jaggars, & Jenkins, 2015a). To build a robust foundation for our faculty to engage with the vital role they play in increasing completions, eliminating equity gaps, and creating transparent, flexible pathways for students, we used the Transparency Framework and other TILT materials in our state-level efforts to provide faculty with professional development opportunities that connect directly to their role in improving student learning in ways that affirm their already substantial contributions. As one of our faculty developers memorably phrased it, "You can't talk about student success without talking about faculty success."

Faculty define learning outcomes in the context of an individual course or a department. It can be difficult for faculty to find opportunities to work across departments with colleagues to identify connections across various disciplines around the shared work of supporting student learning constructively (i.e., not blaming or finger-pointing at the students, other faculty members, departments, or even other stakeholders such as K–12). A

Figure 9.1. The four design principles of Guided Pathways.

Clarify the paths

Clearly mapping out every program, indicating which courses students should take in what sequence and highlighting courses that are critical to success, along with "cocurricular" requirements and progress milestones. For each program, detailed information is provided on the employment opportunities targeted by the program and the transfer requirements for bachelor's programs in related fields.

Help students get on a path

From the moment of entry, students are shown all the career and program options within their metamajor and, with guidance, develop an individual educational plan. Courses are redesigned and supports are put in place to enable students to complete college-level math and English courses appropriate to their intended field of study, ideally within their first year of study.

Help students stay on the path

Through intensive advising, student progress is closely monitored in order to keep them on their path, assist them if they want to choose another path, intervene when they go off the path. Assistance is provided to students who are unlikely to be accepted into limited-access programs to redirect them to a more viable path to credentials and a career.

Ensure students are learning

Program learning outcomes are aligned with the requirements for success in further education and employment in a related field. Faculty use the results of learning outcomes assessments to improve the effectiveness of instruction in their programs. A key focus of teaching in the pathways model is attention to collaborative, active learning that is relevant to the student's field of interest. This includes teaching and learning in the classroom as well as learning that takes place outside the classroom, such as through internships or service-learning.

Note. Adapted by Washington State Board for Community and Technical Colleges from Jenkins, Lahr, & Fink (2017).

Guided Pathways redesign has the potential to offer faculty continuous and ongoing opportunities to collaborate as they define and assess how learning outcomes for their courses connect with those at the campus and state levels in ways that improve instruction to directly impact student learning. This kind of work requires large groups of faculty, administrators, and other stakeholders, often across institutions, to communicate and agree on a set of assessment practices and standards. However, these conversations must be structured carefully, as some faculty hesitate to adopt cross-disciplinary learning outcomes and/or standards of assessment that seem different from their own course-specific and discipline-specific goals for student learning. Furthermore, cross-disciplinary and cross-institutional conversations about assessment can be easily stymied by a lack of shared language, a lack of shared assessment practices, and a reluctance to accept one standard method. The TILT framework offers an excellent vehicle for these conversations as faculty members think about cross-disciplinary learning outcomes and their own course-specific or discipline-specific outcomes, how they communicate these outcomes transparently to students, and what they expect students to do to achieve these outcomes.

The Washington Program

In our Washington system, our intention was to introduce the essential practices of ensuring student learning (Guided Pathways Principle 4) in ways that would engage our faculty rather than trigger their resistance. The Transparency Framework and materials that were found in the TILT resources were invaluable. Over a 2-year period, a statewide group of faculty developers created, implemented, tested, and refined a core workshop that has been delivered to large groups of faculty members with the goal of bringing our faculty together around a tangible task such as assignment redesign within the framework of the bigger Guided Pathways reform effort. For example, during our system-level New Faculty Institute (held every fall) and on system-wide professional development days, we used the TILT core workshop. All materials were openly licensed with a Creative Commons CC BY license, which allows modifications of the original source materials with citation. This workshop could be facilitated in 50 minutes (if that is all the time allocated) or over a period of several hours. We designed the content and activities with a full range of potential faculty concerns in mind, particularly concerns that an emphasis on closing equity gaps and increasing the number of students completing degrees would equate to less rigorous academic achievement by students, or as one faculty member put it, "dumbing down" the curriculum.

Because conversation about specific goals for student learning can almost instantly feel unwieldy at the scale of an institution, to say nothing of a state system, we wanted to get really concrete at the classroom level—in other words, the instructor's individual assignments. The transparent assignment template allowed us to focus faculty conversation on the purposes, tasks, and criteria for assignments. We find faculty are continually intrigued by the notion that assignment design is an equity strategy and that making small tweaks to their assignments (from "less" transparent to "more" transparent) ensures rigor and improves student learning both at the classroom level *and* at the level of large-scale student success outcomes such as retention and workplace readiness—both of which are important goals for the community college system and population.

Workshop Overview

Our workshop asked faculty to reflect on their own assignments that failed to yield the desired results and then work in pairs to compare and contrast assignments from diverse disciplines that have been revised using the Transparency Framework (UNLV Office of the Executive Vice President and Provost, n.d.). The workshop also introduced faculty to the research behind the TILT project regarding its benefits for students and equitable learning and then concluded with an informal peer review process, during which participants worked in cross-disciplinary pairs to share information about an assignment they regularly teach and receive feedback to help make it more transparent.

   During the small group discussions, faculty noticed important differences between the less and more transparent example assignments. The more transparent ones explicated rationale, provided examples and criteria that students could use to judge their own progress while doing the work, and offered a sequence of scaffolded opportunities for students to acquire discipline-based skills. Invariably, at least one participant noticed that the more transparent examples still have room for improvement—they could be further revised using the transparent assignment template. This was an excellent opportunity for the facilitators to contextualize a capacity-based notion of continuous improvement, not only as part of a Guided Pathways redesign but also in a way that conveyed a deep respect for the challenge of faculty work. In addition, faculty quickly understood that although an assignment will never reach a platonic ideal, small tweaks, made continuously over time, will result in better and better assignments, and thus an evolution in faculty practice and in student learning. Finally, as student populations change, faculty will continue to have opportunity to test the assignment; the assignment will change along with the changing student body, as does the instructor.

Transparency and Equity for Community College Students

The Washington faculty in these workshops also responded favorably to the research that demonstrated the equitable learning provided by transparent instruction and appreciated the tangible opportunity to provide greater equity of learning opportunities in their own courses by making strategic revisions to just two assignments. One faculty member wrote, "Providing a long assignment prompt that is well designed is an equitable solution. At community colleges we need to meet students where they are at and help them get to where they want to be." Indeed, the demographic data on community college enrollment in the United States show that such institutions serve a large proportion of minority, first-generation, low-income, and adult students (Ma & Baum, 2016). The need for equitable learning opportunities in this context is compelling.

Further, as our faculty began to see more clearly the connections between students' mastery of specific discipline-based skills and the urgent need for equitable opportunities to develop those skills, their desire for equity increased as they recognized that equity enables *greater* (not lesser) mastery for all students. Our faculty see in TILT's research that it is possible to close the equity gap between low-income, underrepresented, and first-generation students, on the one hand, and White and Asian students, on the other, by elevating the achievement of *all* students. As one faculty member observed, "Educators still need to have more discussions about equity, social justice and rigor. Being equitable and social justice driven does not mean there is no rigor, it is the opposite." Equity in pursuit of improved student success likewise aligns directly with the fourth principle of the Guided Pathways model—ensuring students are learning.

Translating Outcomes Horizontally Across Disciplines

When faculty have an opportunity to talk in structured yet generative ways with colleagues outside of their own disciplines, they see how a particular learning outcome, such as critical thinking, translates across the disciplines. That translation happens as faculty members talk to each other about their assignments using the shared language provided by the transparent assignment template with clear roles (i.e., the novice to the discipline but the expert learner).

It is this exercise of translation that gives learning outcomes meaning. One of the problems is that "assessment talk" is foreign to practitioners: it uses labels that come from rubrics and do not make sense to faculty members consumed and inspired by the concrete day-to-day work of teaching. "Critical thinking," for example, is too broad. After this workshop, the biology professor now knows what "critical thinking" means in the literature class; the communications professor knows what it means in the sociology class. This changes instruction by translating teachers' goals for students' learning across disciplines. As one faculty member wrote, "Students' success depends mostly on the connections we are able to establish with one another," and student success is the ultimate goal of the Guided Pathways model. This one conversation about assignment-level learning goals that faculty themselves define also helped them to pivot toward state system-level goals from Guided Pathways as they began to gain a broader awareness of the importance of interdisciplinary thinking and higher order objectives.

Translating Outcomes Vertically From Assignments to Programs, Institutions, and Systems

Our version of the TILT workshop, as it has evolved, provides faculty with a contextualized foundation for a functional assessment literacy and a shared language to talk about increasing completions, eliminating equity gaps, and ensuring student learning in ways that translate across departments, disciplines, and programs. This workshop and the Transparency Framework invite faculty to align the learning goals from several of their own assignments with those for a department and/or major or degree program. Working from the specifics of an assignment toward the general language of institutional learning outcomes catalyzes several important aspects of our statewide conversations in the following ways:

- Voicing and addressing faculty fears about relaxed academic standards of achievement
- Providing space for conversations about broad assessment goals and institutional learning outcomes
- Offering a structure and a shared language for connecting discipline-specific and assignment-specific learning outcomes to learning goals at the program, institution, and state levels

Faculty skepticism about the dangers of "dumbing down" the curriculum is allayed when faculty identify the learning outcomes for their own assignments and courses and give their own meaning to the terminology they have encountered in program- and institution-level learning outcomes statements. At one of our system colleges that used this approach, a faculty member wrote,

> It is important to be clear about the purpose, task, rationale, expectations [, and so on] for increased chance of student success. Also, it was an eye-opener to see the connections across disciplines of college-wide desired student abilities and scaffolding that occurs with pre-req[uisite]s.

As this faculty member suggests, the Transparency Framework can be instrumental in helping faculty recognize how their own work in the classroom, at the ground level, plugs into and supports larger institutional goals. Once faculty members are acquainted with the shared language that the Transparency Framework enables, they can begin to appreciate how they share similar goals with other disciplines and how success toward those course-level goals facilitates greater student success moving up the institutional ladder, at the departmental, institutional, and system-wide levels. This simple start with faculty thus has much broader implications, and this pilot program is preparing for implementation at a larger group of institutions within the Washington State CTC system.

The Transparency Framework offers benefits that are particularly meaningful for the needs of community colleges, in terms of equitable learning for their distinctive student populations as well as institution-wide goals for retention and job readiness in a relatively condensed period of time. As Pat Hutchings (1996) has explained, what we need is a culture of teaching and learning where approaches to fostering student success can take hold. Fostering a culture of assessment that drives the continuous improvement of teaching and learning is an enormous task that becomes more possible when the starting point is a specific assignment where faculty can concretely focus on specific learning outcomes.

Cross-institutional discussions among faculty and administrators around abstract, generalized learning outcomes often break down when participants recognize that the vocabulary means different things to different people. The Transparency Framework's simple language of purpose (skills, knowledge), tasks, and criteria can help by providing a shared language that administrators and faculty can use, much like the collaboration and shared understanding seen through the Transparency Framework among academic units at UNLV (see chapter 8). Further, grounding faculty conversations about Guided Pathways in the concrete context of assignments and discipline-specific learning goals has aided our effort to work across institutions in our state system. Once learning outcomes and measures of learning mastery are explicitly identified for assignments, those assignments become effective tools for assessment, and larger conversations about assessment at the course level, program level, and institutional level became possible. TILT's aligning and assessing outcomes model (Figure 12.3) can help to frame such conversations.

Conclusion

The change management literature is clear on two things: the value of transparent communication during large-scale initiatives such as Guided Pathways and the necessity of engaging large numbers of faculty. Whereas the "what" and the "why" are obvious, the "how" remains largely elusive. However, here in Washington State, TILT has given us a framework and the tools to do both.

EDITORS' HIGHLIGHTS

For educational developers considering implementing transparency-based programming within a community college system, consider the following points from these contributors:

- The Transparency Framework can be beneficial for engaging faculty in system-wide educational goals and helping them translate horizontally across disciplines and vertically from assignments to departmental, program, institutional, and state-level learning goals.
- The Transparency Framework can help support goals of student equity and success for community and technical colleges.

References

Bailey, T., Jaggars, S. S., & Jenkins, D. (2015a). *Redesigning America's community colleges: A clearer path to student success.* Cambridge, MA: Harvard University Press.

Bailey, T., Jaggars, S. S., & Jenkins, D. (2015b). *What we know about Guided Pathways.* New York, NY: Columbia University, Teachers College, Community College Research Center. Available from https://ccrc.tc.columbia.edu/media/k2/attachments/What-We-Know-Guided-Pathways.pdf

Hutchings, P. (1996). Building a new culture of teaching & learning. *About Campus: Enriching the Student Learning Experience, 1*(5), 4–8.

Jenkins, D., Lahr, H., & Fink, J. (2017). *Implementing Guided Pathways: Early insights from the AACC Pathways colleges.* New York: Community College Research Center (CCRC), Teachers College, Columbia University. Available from https://www.sbctc.edu/colleges-staff/programs-services/student-success-center/guided-pathways.aspx

Ma, J., & Baum, S. (2016). Trends in community colleges: Enrollment, prices, student debt, and completion. *College Board Research: Research Brief.* Available from https://trends.collegeboard.org/sites/default/files/trends-in-community-colleges-research-brief.pdf

UNLV Office of the Executive Vice President and Provost. (n.d.). *TILT higher ed examples and resources.* Available from www.unlv.edu/provost/transparency/tilt-higher-ed-examples-and-resources

Washington State Board for Community and Technical Colleges. (2017a). *Community and technical colleges at a glance.* Available from https://www.sbctc.edu/

resources/documents/about/facts-pubs/community-and-technical-colleges-at-a-glance.pdf

Washington State Board for Community and Technical Colleges. (2017b). *Four design principles of Guided Pathways* (Adapted from Jenkins, Lahr, & Fink, 2017). Available from https://www.sbctc.edu/colleges-staff/programs-services/student-success-center/guided-pathways.aspx

Washington State Board for Community and Technical Colleges. (2018). *What is Guided Pathways?* Available from https://www.sbctc.edu/colleges-staff/programs-services/student-success-center/guided-pathways.aspx

10

TRANSPARENCY TO CLOSE OPPORTUNITY GAPS IN THE LARGEST STATE SYSTEM

A Pilot Experiment

Emily Daniell Magruder, Whitney Scott,
Michael Willard, Kristina Ruiz-Mesa, and Stefanie Drew

W hat if the country's largest state university system, with an initiative to double graduation rates while closing equity gaps, adopted transparent assignment design across institutions? That is the question 4 faculty developers (1 in the system office and 3 on campuses), asked in late 2016, a few months after the California State University (CSU) announced targets for Graduation Initiative 2025: Increase 4-year graduation rates for first-time, full-time, first-year students from 19% to 40% and 2-year rates for transfer students from 31% to 45%, while completely eliminating equity gaps. We wanted to demonstrate that faculty development produces changes in faculty teaching practices that in turn lead to improved student outcomes. We needed a scalable teaching and learning intervention that could contribute to the CSU's completion goals *and* its equity goals while allaying concerns that the graduation initiative would reduce academic rigor and increase faculty workload. This chapter offers an overview of our pilot implementation at 2 institutions and its impact on students, faculty, and faculty developers. It concludes with our insights about how other state systems or cohorts of institutions might benefit from adopting transparent assignment design.

System-Wide/Cross-Institutional Context

We turned to the Transparency in Learning and Teaching (TILT) initiative, because it offered a simple, easily replicable teaching intervention that has been shown to increase student success. We were interested in data showing that transparent assignment design affords first-generation, low-income, and historically underrepresented college students, in particular, a more equitable educational experience (Winkelmes, Bernacki, Butler, Zochowski, Golanics, & Harriss Weavil, 2016). Moreover, TILT principles had already been introduced and well received in our system at multiple campuses including Los Angeles, Dominguez Hills, and Northridge. A team of faculty at California State University, Los Angeles, participated in the AAC&U Transparency and Problem-Centered Learning project in 2014–2015; TILT's Transparency Framework was incorporated into the General Education civic-learning requirement adopted as the campus converted from quarters to semesters (Fisher, Kouyoumdjian, Roy, Talavera-Bustillos, & Willard, 2016). Faculty who attended a transparent assignment design session at a system-wide teaching institute indicated a desire to explore transparency within their courses. We were attracted by transparent assignment design's low cost and low threshold for implementation. Because those involved with the TILT project share materials and implementation supports via online resources, the primary cost for training would be faculty stipends. Because faculty can redesign assignments without cutting content or making changes that require curriculum committee approval, faculty perceive transparent assignment design as straightforward and beneficial for students.

Although all four faculty developers had seen faculty achieve modest results after redesigning courses with low completion rates, we aimed to scale a simple, effective intervention by shifting the unit of change from individuals to cohorts of faculty positioned to institutionalize and sustain improvement. It will be difficult to expand effective teaching practices if "innovation continues to be seen as an individual trait of charismatic innovators rather than as a normative requirement of good teaching" (Kezar, 2011, p. 238).

Thus, we created the CSU Transparency Project with the following goals: (a) to create momentum for innovative teaching by linking faculty at two institutions, (b) to learn how faculty developers motivate communities of instructors to adopt effective teaching practices, and (c) to build capacity for facilitating faculty development that increases student success. In the process, we hoped to learn why proven teaching practices find fertile ground in some higher education contexts but not others.

Implementation

Like Graduation Initiative 2025, our plan for the CSU Transparency Project was ambitious. The student cohort against which the six-year targets for the system-wide graduation initiative will be measured in 2025 enters in fall 2019. We planned to implement transparency strategically in spring 2017 within the context of entry-level gateway courses on two campuses and replicate results achieved by TILT at the University of Nevada, Las Vegas (UNLV), including higher retention rates for first-time, full-time, first-year students. In the first phase, we provided training in transparent assignment design on two campuses, asked faculty to redesign two assignments using the transparent assignment design template, and fostered intracampus collaboration among faculty as they administered the assignments and reflected on their effect on student attitudes and learning. In the second phase, we collected and analyzed similar data and prepared dissemination of results within the CSU and beyond. In addition to having faculty invite students to take the TILT survey, we gathered additional evidence of impact on student learning by inviting faculty to track scores on relevant questions on student evaluations of teaching. We gathered evidence of impact on faculty by having them reflect on the process of implementing transparent assignment design.

Faculty developers, who see themselves as change agents leading from the middle, are often challenged with persuading faculty to participate voluntarily in professional development focused on instruction. To position our work as integral to achieving the goals of our system-wide Graduation Initiative, we needed to be strategic. Rather than fill seats with willing volunteers, we wanted to reach faculty teaching critical courses and to transform entire courses, not just individual sections. Creating motivation for faculty meeting our criteria to participate was our first challenge.

At CSU Los Angeles conditions for scaling effective practice across all sections of an entry-level course existed. COMM 1110: Oral Communication, which fulfills a lower division general education requirement, enrolls 3,700 to 4,000 students annually. It is taught by graduate teaching associates (GTAs) currently enrolled in the communications studies master's program and non-tenure-track faculty, most of them graduates of the master of arts program. All sections are overseen by a course director who fosters a strong culture of communication through weekly meetings, e-mails, and mentoring sessions. COMM 1110 was redesigned in 2016 as part of a system-wide grant program to improve completion rates in bottleneck courses. To build students' social capital by strengthening oral communication skills, the course director created a syllabus and custom textbook with materials reflective of students' lived experiences, added assignments relevant to their professional goals, incorporated an interactive video platform for self and peer feedback, and enhanced pedagogical training for instructors with instructional communication methods. Although the recent redesign meant that we did not have a clean "before" sample for comparison, this coordinated course presented a unique opportunity to work with a hard-to-reach instructor population. Moreover, the course director had previous successful collaborations with a faculty developer.

For the Transparency Project in spring 2017, the course director and COMM 1100 instructors (N = 23 of 27 who attended an initial 1-hour workshop) participated in a three-hour transparent assignment design workshop. The faculty developer reviewed transparent teaching techniques, the transparent assignment template, and sample assignments from the TILT Higher Ed website. Instructors used the transparent assignment design template to evaluate less and more transparent versions of an assignment and discussed, with the course director and the faculty developer, how transparent assignment design practices could be implemented into the COMM 1100 course. The faculty developer and the course director then revised two assignments and incorporated them into the custom textbook. Prior to transparent assignment design training, the course assignments included some transparent elements, such as purpose and criteria for success, but they did not specify skills or knowledge associated with the assignment. The revised assignments now include the purpose, knowledge, skills, tasks, and criteria for success for each major course assignment. Although the instructors did not create the tasks or detailed assignment guides, they learned to explicate the purpose of each assignment transparently; to lead students in rich discussion of skills they would obtain or sharpen; to create examples of A, B, and C work; and to use rubrics to evaluate student work.

Following the three-hour workshop, transparent assignment design was reinforced in weekly meetings led by the course director. The teaching team discussed upcoming assignments and course material and shared ideas and best practices for communicating the value, purpose, and learning involved with each lesson and assessment. These meetings afforded instructors the opportunity to practice framings and explanations with peers and receive feedback on transparency. The faculty developer offered one-on-one consulting for faculty following the workshop, although few sought this assistance.

Recruiting at CSU Northridge was more challenging. The faculty developer leveraged a strong relationship with institutional research to access approximately 100 e-mail addresses of faculty planning to teach courses in the upcoming semester with low completion rates and significant equity gaps. Private invitations (Figure 10.1) resulted in only 2 RSVP responses. The program was then opened to all 2,500 faculty (tenure-track and lecturers), with

Figure 10.1. Recruitment message to selected faculty at CSU Northridge.

Subject line: Pre-Invitation-$200 Transparent Assignments Workshop.

Message: Hello, I have a pre-invitation for you to attend a paid Faculty Development workshop to discover how a simple change to your assignment guidelines could impact student learning and sense of belonging at [CSU Northridge]. [CSU Northridge] has partnered with colleagues from Cal State LA, UNLV (i.e., Dr. Mary-Ann Winkelmes) and the Institute for Teaching and Learning in the CSU Chancellor's Office to <u>empirically investigate what happens when we increase transparency</u> in course assignments for students. Interested in joining this small fun project? See details:

When: Tuesday February 7th, 2017
Time: 10:45am–12:30pm (see note about alternative times)
Room: EU101
RSVP: Space is very limited.
Stipend: $200 for full participation (see details)
Eligibility: You must have a course assignment other than exams (e.g., homework, paper, project, poster, etc.) that you can distribute to students on or after Tues Feb 7th.

What are the easy steps involved?
1) Attend the Feb 7th Faculty Development workshop ($100)
2) Modify the guidelines of your course assignments for your course using our easy template
3) Invite your students in one of your spring courses to take an online pre-survey now and post-survey at the end of the semester
4) Complete a follow-up faculty assessment (an additional $100 for steps 2–4)

If you are interested in joining, but unable to attend Feb 7th, indicate alternative availability in the RSVP form. If enough interest results, we may offer a 2nd workshop.

E-mail me if you have questions and have a great week!

Note. Reproduced with permission of Whitney Scott.

unprecedented results. Registration filled within 2 hours, and the waiting list grew to over 70 interested faculty. We thus ended up with contrasting cases. At CSU Los Angeles, the project involved a cohort of non-tenure-track instructors teaching sections of a coordinated course. At CSU Northridge, the project involved a heterogeneous group of faculty across ranks (on and off the tenure track) teaching courses across disciplines and levels.

How faculty learned about and implemented transparent assignment design at CSU Northridge varied slightly from the CSU Los Angeles project. Faculty attended a two-hour workshop based on slides and handouts provided by TILT structured to (a) contextualize transparent assignment design within the graduation initiative and equity-minded teaching, (b) build rapport by sharing participants' existing teaching strengths and challenges (collected in a presurvey during registration), (c) demonstrate that cognitive performance decreases when cues needed to navigate a task are absent via three perception games, (d) generate buy-in by examining TILT data graphs, (e) provide TILT examples of more and less transparently designed assignments, and (f) build empathy through paired role-plays of teachers explaining to students how to do an assignment using TILT prompts. At the end of this chapter we discuss how and why these role-play activities are critical for faculty buy-in. The workshop concluded with instructions on how student and faculty data would be collected. There was no formal follow-up to the workshop. A few faculty sought one-on-one consultation from the faculty developer.

Results

We adopted a multilayered approach to understand the impact of this inter-campus collaboration. First, we share how students were impacted by their perceptions and performance. Second, we examine how faculty responded to implementing transparent assignment design. Third, we reflect as faculty developers on our lessons learned.

Impact on Students

To investigate the student impact of transparent assignment design, we partnered with UNLV's TILT research team to facilitate data collection from students at both campuses. The TILT survey gauges student perceptions in the areas of sense of belonging, academic confidence, employer-valued skills, and perceptions of transparency in the course. Faculty who redesigned assignments invited their students to complete an online survey hosted by TILT at the end of the term. This resulted in 583 student responses across both campuses from various disciplines (e.g., humanities, sciences, social sciences, business, engineering, arts), with approximately 45% who identified as female, 36% who identified as male, and 19% who did not identify as male or female. A large number of students described their race as other than White (78%), with 45% of the entire group identifying as first-generation college students. This sample reflects the diversity of CSU students.

Figure 10.2. Chart A: Students in your course and in similar more transparent courses.

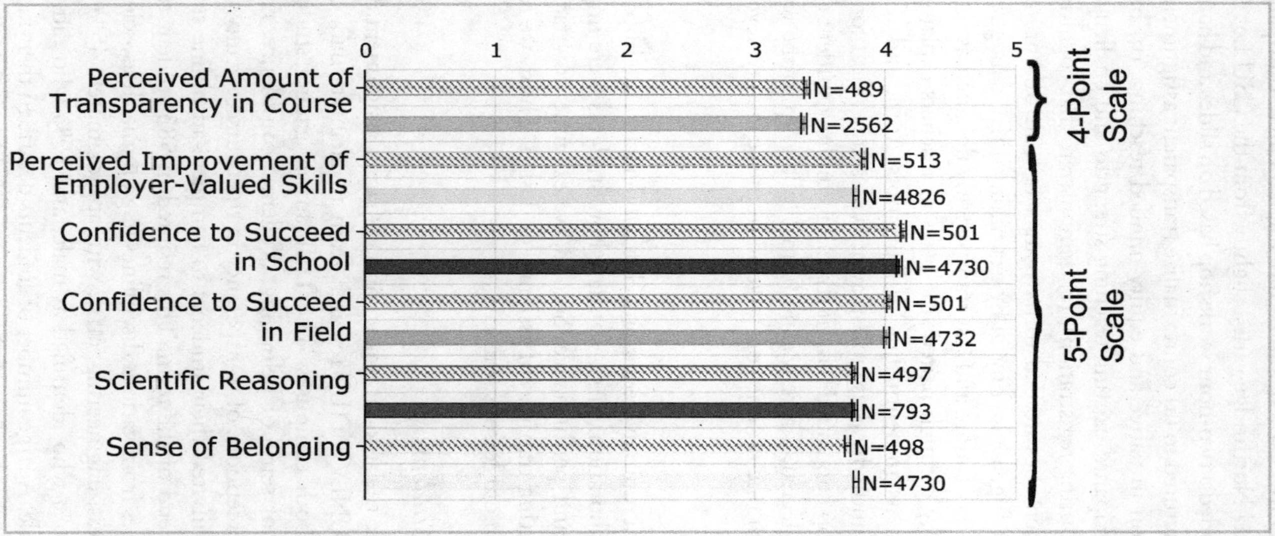

Perceived Amount of Transparency in Course — N=489, N=2562

Perceived Improvement of Employer-Valued Skills — N=513, N=4826

Confidence to Succeed in School — N=501, N=4730

Confidence to Succeed in Field — N=501, N=4732

Scientific Reasoning — N=497, N=793

Sense of Belonging — N=498, N=4730

4-Point Scale

5-Point Scale

KEY	1	2	3	4	5	Transparency Survey Questions
Perceived Amount of Transparency in the Course	Never	Sometimes	Often	Always	-----	36–44
Perceived Improvement of Employer-Valued Skills	Not at all	A little	Moderate	A lot	A great deal	4–6, 8–12
						21, 22, 24
Confidence to Succeed In School	Much less	Somewhat less	No difference	Somewhat more	Much more	25
Confidence to Succeed In Field						26
Scientific Reasoning	Not at all	A little	Moderate	A lot	A great deal	45–47
Sense of Belonging						33–35, 48–49

Error Bars Indicate +/- 1 SE

N: number of students responding

Less Transparent: mean perceived transparency < 3.3/4

More Transparent: mean perceived transparency ≥ 3.3/4

ES: effect size (Hedges' G). Effect size of 0.25 for standard deviations or larger are "substantively important." [U.S. Department of Education, *What Works Clearinghouse Procedure and Standards Handbook*, version 3.0. Web. March 2014, p .23.]

*Hart Research Associate employer surveys. *Falling Short?* (2015), *It Takes More than a Major* (2013), *Raising the Bar* (2009).

Hashed bars = Your students   Solid bars = Students in similar courses

From TILT Higher Ed report for UT instructor team, fall 2016. Reproduced with permission of team members and Mary-Ann Winkelmes, director, TILT Higher Ed.

Note. From TILT Higher Ed report for CSU multi-institution instructor team, spring 2017. Reproduced with permission of team members and Mary-Ann Winkelmes, director, TILT Higher Ed.

Overall, the TILT report revealed that students from transparent assignment design courses shared similar experiences and beliefs as students from the larger national TILT project. In every area of the TILT survey, our students reported similar perceptions as TILT's experimental group (Figure 10.2). For instance, in the area of academic confidence (i.e., confidence to succeed in school and in the field) students at both campuses rated themselves relatively similarly to the large number of students in courses who had also received transparent instruction at other campuses. The same was true for sense of belonging, employer-valued skills, and actual degree of transparency in the course. This leads us to believe that our faculty were able to implement this teaching intervention just as effectively as other faculty with whom TILT has worked.

Given this positive and consistent TILT finding, we were curious if examining student responses by individual question within the four subcategories would reveal outliers. The results for three questions are worth noting. In the subcategory of *perceived amount of transparency in the course*, one question was rated on average by all students lower than the rest of the questions in this category (i.e., *Instructor gave annotated examples of work*). According to Winkelmes, this is a trend in many TILT reports generated for other campuses (M. Winkelmes, personal communication, spring 2017). This corroborates a common tension faculty developers experience during transparent assignment design workshops: some faculty are highly resistant to the idea of giving students sample work. They worry students will mimic or plagiarize examples or that showing sample work will stunt creative or critical thinking. However, during the workshop when faculty play the role of student attempting to figure out how to complete an assignment, many agree that having some work samples would guide the learning process. Yet these data illuminate that in implementation on both campuses, students did not perceive that they received annotated examples. Perhaps this attitudinal change, key to transparent teaching, takes longer to implement. This tells us that our next step as faculty developers is to provide greater support in this aspect of transparent assignment design.

Another subcategory, *sense of belonging*, also contains an interesting story when individual questions are examined. The two lowest rated questions in this category focused on sense of belonging within the greater campus community. In fact, the second to lowest rated category of the entire survey was *I feel that I am a member of my school's community*. In addition, *How much has this course helped you to feel that you are a member of your school's community* was also markedly low. Taken together, these data align with much of the research aimed at attempting to bolster student connection on campuses (Pike & Kuh, 2005; Tovar, Simon, & Lee, 2009; Walton & Cohen, 2011).

However, in contrast, the question that received the highest mean score across the entire TILT survey was also in this category: *How much did the instructor value you as a student?* Sense of belonging is complex because it spans microlevel interactions (e.g., student-professor dynamics of value and caring) and macrolevel experiences across contexts, many of which are outside the control of a single instructor. How can we leverage the importance of this highly rated question by students? Can we assume that transparent assignment design is a vehicle for demonstrating student value? If so, this finding should be a beacon for faculty developers to highlight that bolstering students' sense of belonging is not only within faculty control but also easy to accomplish through instructional routines like assignment design.

Although the TILT survey data are powerful in aiding our understanding of the student perspective, we also wanted to investigate observable change in student performance as evidenced by GPA and nonpass rates such as D, F, W (Withdrawal), or WU (Unofficial Withdrawal) grades. To accomplish this type of analysis, we worked with institutional research offices to receive data sets that would allow statistical comparisons to be made. This analysis was focused on CSU Los Angeles, the campus that implemented transparent assignment design across sections of a single course. We looked retrospectively at aggregated student performance data from a COMM 150 course taught in a prior academic quarter when transparency was not incorporated and compared that to an equivalent COMM 1100 course in the new semester system after transparent assignment design was implemented. Frequencies of D, F, W, and WU grades were 9.82% in COMM 150 in spring 2016 and 12.48% in COMM 1100 in spring 2017. Statistical comparison of the average GPAs in the 2016 course (N = 33, M = 2.73, SD = .32) and the 2017 course (N = 55, M = 2.76, SD = .34) were performed. Levene's test for equality of variances was not significant, allowing equal variances to be assumed, and $t(86)$ = -0.520, p = .604. These results indicate there were no significant differences between the spring 2016 and 2017 courses.

Although we were hopeful these data would show great strides in student performance, we must appreciate a macrolevel confounding variable the year transparent assignment design was implemented. This campus was converting from quarters to semesters; therefore, analyses comparing these courses becomes noisy. COMM 150 was taught on the quarter calendar in spring 2016, and COMM 1100 was the first time the course was taught on the semester system in spring 2017. It is difficult to assess student performance during campus transitions of this magnitude.

Impact on Faculty

To prompt deep learning about transparency while assessing impact on faculty, both institutions incorporated the critically important practice of reflection (Brookfield, 1998). Instructors at CSU Los Angeles, trained to use transparently designed assignments in the custom COMM 1100 textbook, completed an online survey with three questions about (a) how their teaching practices changed, (b) how students responded, and (c) how the team could incorporate more transparent practices in subsequent terms. Faculty at CSU Northridge completed a longer online survey (Figure 10.3) with questions to determine if they implemented transparent assignment design and their perception of the effect on student learning. Stipends were processed ($100 for participating in the transparent assignment design workshop and an additional $100 for actually redesigning assignments) upon completion of the survey, which included a reminder to motivate their own students to complete the TILT survey.

In aggregate, the surveys confirmed that faculty found a positive impact of transparent assignment design in their courses. For example, in response to a survey question, a science, technology, engineering, and math (STEM) faculty member reflected on student performance on homework, saying, "It was very successful and I didn't expect it to be so effective." Over 75% of faculty at an institution indicated on the online survey that they perceived an increase in student work quality. The faculty surveys were most important for what they revealed about designing and implementing effective professional development. Proponents of improvement science emphasize that context determines the effectiveness of interventions (Berwick, 2008). Through qualitative assessment, we hoped to find evidence of change in practice, evidence of transformation of instructors' identities in relationship to their students, and an increasing sense of teaching self-efficacy, because it is easy to believe that equity gaps result from social issues beyond faculty control. The following sections note the promising instructional effectiveness themes that emerged from faculty reflections (recorded on the surveys) that have promised to augment faculty development programming outcomes.

Small Changes Can Lead to Larger Change

Several COMM 1100 instructors found that training on the transparent assignment design framework resulted in broad changes in teaching practices. A second-year instructor wrote, "The transparency training had a profound impact on the way I approach my classrooms. It helped elevate my teaching style and has been a good compass on how I engage my students in their in-class and take-home assignments." Another second-year instructor wrote, "The transparency training we participated in made me much more

Figure 10.3. Transparent assignments final assessment at CSU Northridge.

1. Did you revise any of your assignments to be more transparent this semester?
2. Elaborate your response to the previous questions. If no, why not? If yes, how many assignments did you revise; what primary changes did you make to the assignment(s); did you end up changing the assignment as a result?
3. Did you detect any of the following differences this semester using the more transparent assignments, compared to past semesters when you used this same exact assignment? (Quicker or easier for me to explain to students; Longer or harder for me to explain to students; Fewer student questions; More student questions; Fewer students in my office hours; More students in my office hours; Greater student engagement/motivation with the assignment(s); Less student engagement/motivation with the assignment(s); Other)
4. Did revising your assignments lead you to make other changes in your class beyond that assignment? Elaborate if yes.
5. Were there any challenges to implementing this Transparent Assignment Framework in your assignment or course?
6. Let's investigate if student performance and learning was different using transparently designed assignments. Do you have a sense that the quality of student work you received was different this semester?
7. What was the average grade on your transparent assignments this semester compared to previous semesters? Share any additional data (quantitative or qualitative) that reveal differences or similarities noticed. (If you are not done grading the assignment yet, you can send us the results later).
8. Before drawing any conclusions, are there any unique course or student characteristics this semester we should know about that could confound any findings (e.g., smaller class size; more freshmen than usual; new prerequisites; more time allotted to do the assignment, etc.)?
9. Do you plan to continue using the transparent assignment template in the future?
10. Is there anything you want to share about your experience using the transparent assignment template?
11. You should have received an e-mail from Mary-Ann Winkelmes (UNLV TILT project) with instructions on how you should invite students to complete a survey. To optimize response rates, if possible use the last 10–15 minutes of a class session so they may complete it. If that is not possible, please give students a specific deadline and send email reminders. What is your plan to optimize student responses?
12. Will you send Faculty Development's Coordinator an e-mail right now and attach your transparently designed assignment(s) AND previous less transparent version(s)? It would be helpful if you could name the documents using this format: (your last name); (pre or post); (short name of assignment). Once she receives this and your e-mail with attachments, she will process your $200 stipend.

Note. Reproduced with permission of Whitney Scott.

aware of the need for equity in my lesson plans. I incorporated the practice of asking and posing questions to the class during my lectures to get a better understanding of their level of knowledge and build from there." Such attitudinal shifts are as important as reports of change in practice.

Redesigning Assignments for Greater Transparency Produces Deeper Understanding of Being Student Centered

Acknowledging responsibility to search continually for methods conducive to student learning signals that the threshold concept identified by Barr and Tagg as a shift from focusing on the teacher to focusing on the learner has been mastered (King & Felten, 2012). A second-year COMM 1100 instructor evidenced grasp of the learning paradigm:

> The transparency training had an impact on my teaching style because it forced me to become much more reflective. It became very important for me to deliver information to my students in a way where they not only understood how to do an assignment but also why they are doing it and how they can . . . apply concepts to their everyday lives.

Transparent Assignment Design Transformed Faculty Identities

Some faculty expressed increased teaching self-efficacy by, somewhat paradoxically, sharing responsibility for learning with students. Another second-year instructor wrote,

> It was no longer on me to produce students who knew the material, nor was it on them to learn the material, instead, it was on us to reach the goal together. Transparency training gave me the confidence to ask students directly: I need to get you here and you need to get here, what do you think is the best way to get us there?'

Impact on Faculty Developers

Just as we aimed to shift the unit of change from individual faculty to courses by leveraging peer learning within faculty cohorts, we aimed to boost our own professional growth by functioning as a small community of practice for faculty developers (Lave & Wenger, 1998). Throughout the process of facilitating the workshop, consulting with faculty, and collecting and analyzing data, we reflected on three questions:

1. Do faculty find better student learning with transparent assignment design?
2. How do faculty developers motivate instructors with the greatest impact?
3. How does system-level collaboration among faculty developers augment the implementation of transparent assignment design?

Do Faculty Find Better Student Learning With Transparent Assignment Design?

As faculty developers, it was important for us to know how faculty conceive of the relationship between using transparent assignment design and impact on student learning. How would they go about drawing conclusions and how would this impact their future plans? Conversations with students about their learning—a key feature of student-centered practice—can change faculty perceptions. One faculty member indicated that transparent assignment design did not appear to result in any significant change in student performance as assessed by her own statistical analyses comparing mean scores from multiple assignments in previously taught courses. However, before the next term began, this faculty member was observed strongly advocating for transparent assignment design. On the last day of class, after completing the program survey, she had discovered from the students themselves how much they valued her assignment guidelines. In that informal, impromptu dialogue with students, they expressed that transparent assignment design was critically important for their success, a finding that suggests she may have missed a deeper understanding about her own teaching practice. In future programs, we will prompt faculty to solicit student feedback.

Similarly, the reflective surveys functioned as conversations with faculty about their learning, a key feature of faculty-centered programming. When prompted to examine if student learning deepened using transparent assignment design, the faculty developer discovered that faculty used various kinds of data to investigate if transparent assignment design improved learning: (a) comparing assignment averages (e.g., previous semester's nontransparent assignment average score of 79.5% versus the current transparently designed assignment average of 86.1%), (b) comparing work within the same semester (e.g., beginning homework average scores of 81.5% versus subsequent homework averages of 91.2%, 90%, and 93.6%), and (c) reflecting qualitatively (e.g., noticing deeper levels of critical thinking and greater excitement about assignments). Although faculty offered possible confounding or contextual variables that could explain improvement (e.g., smaller class size, more time given to complete the assignment), all expressed a willingness to try this approach in the future, even those who did not detect improvement in student performance.

How Do Faculty Developers Motivate Instructors With the Greatest Impact?

One of the most important lessons learned is that enticing faculty to make small changes to their practice depends on two elements: the content of the professional development program (e.g., transparent assignment design) and the facilitation of that content.

The first element appeals to the faculty developer with an understaffed office, who is overwhelmed, or who is new to the position. Transparent assignment design is ideal because it is a free, open-source, prepackaged evidence-based curriculum that can be easily absorbed into a center. Furthermore, its intuitive name turned out to be an unexpectedly powerful public relations tool for recruitment efforts. For example, faculty and administrators at one institution, who never attended a transparent assignment design workshop or read about it, were observed advocating for transparent assignment design based on the workshop announcement alone. The name *transparent assignment design* invites the audience to know the content and sparks high interest. It would be absurd to argue that opaque assignments are better for students. In today's higher education climate, where everyone is hungry for data-driven innovations, transparent assignment design is attractive. It leverages the existing strengths of faculty and provides concrete examples that can be quickly applied. With a modest faculty stipend, a little time, and the possibility of increasing teaching enjoyment, the workshop TILT has designed satisfies these important conditions.

The second element of motivating faculty to improve practice centers on a less studied topic, the faculty developer's facilitation skills. Two faculty developers could use the freely shared TILT materials very differently, impacting faculty motivation to implement. Not having to develop workshop content allowed us to focus on common moments in transparent assignment design training that require expert facilitation skills.

For example, the most engaging and yet riskiest element of the transparent assignment design workshop is the role-play activity. Faculty listen while a peer from another discipline pretends to be a student making sense of an assignment they have described. The role-play is then flipped, with the first faculty member making sense of the partner's assignment. Role-playing a student's view of their own and peers' courses can propel faculty to take action, but it can also arouse resistance. When faculty must adopt the learner/ novice position, especially in another discipline, they quickly remember the emotional and cognitive dynamics that occur with being an uncertain student (e.g., a STEM faculty member became nervous when making sense of a humanities assignment). It can also be a challenging and vulnerable realization to admit that one's carefully crafted assignments lack clarity. Although the activity is playful and fun, facilitators must recognize when faculty become vulnerable and improvise to meet them where they are in their own process of change. This is a critical skill for a facilitator, and our cross-campus collaboration propelled learning this skill set.

Another facilitator skill to be mastered entails responding to faculty who disagree with the recommendation to provide multiple work examples. This kind of objection, commonly raised about alternative pedagogies, derives from a belief about rigor—that students learn less when they are pampered

(Nelson, 2010). We realized that inviting faculty to see parallels in their own lives motivates learning, just as it does for students. Instead of debating with faculty who object, or even citing research, facilitators can ask questions that evoke situations where transparency produces better outcomes: when is the last time you found yourself unclear how to navigate a task (e.g., operating a new phone or getting through the DMV) or achieve a high-stakes professional milestone (e.g., navigating the tenure and promotion process)? Once faculty realize that they are holding higher standards for students (e.g., no late work, no missing class, no assignment revisions), they are willing to revise beliefs about academic rigor and adjust assignments to facilitate deeper learning.

In moments of vulnerability and resistance, facilitators should maintain a neutral, inquiry-based demeanor with their communication (e.g., "Tell me more." "What makes you think that?"). The temptation to pour expert knowledge about how people learn into participants' minds can be strong. Yet that same knowledge holds that for deeper learning to happen, engagement through dialogue is paramount. Facilitators must keep participants engaged with peers so that alternative viewpoints, including misconceptions and inaccuracies, surface. Otherwise, faculty are unlikely to change their teaching practices after the workshop. Attunement with the audience and restraint are skills facilitators develop through practice over time. Peer feedback within a faculty developer learning community aids the development of these capacities. The communications among developers in our state project and their interactions with TILT's founder, Mary-Ann Winkelmes, offered us such a community.

How Does System-Level Collaboration Among Faculty Developers Augment the Implementation of Transparent Assignment Design?

Our small community of practice afforded us the benefits of peer learning we sought to create for faculty and student learners. Checking in with faculty as we planned the project and prepared workshops and as they introduced transparent assignments expedited our own professional growth. We learned more about faculty concerns (e.g., that transparent assignment design might encourage a superficial, checklist approach to completing assignments) and experiences (e.g., that presenting redesigned assignments required more class time, that seeing the need to make deeper changes is overwhelming) by collaborating across institutions than we would have implementing on our own. This brought to light how common it is for faculty developers to work in isolation as one-person centers. It would have been difficult to do this project alone, so this collaboration freed bandwidth to focus on the finer nuances of effective implementing and refining our craft as facilitators.

Cross-institutional collaboration also increased accountability. Regular check-ins reminded us to follow up with faculty after the hard work of recruitment and training was completed. Perhaps most importantly, collaboration boosted confidence. Although we might have gathered stronger data if we had delayed implementation, we learned that we can motivate faculty to make small, significant changes, and we now have data and adopters from our own institutions to counter skepticism and promote implementation.

Conclusion

Although any cross-institutional project involves challenges, overall we found great success with the implementation of transparent assignment design at both institutions. The boldest findings came from the faculty themselves. Transparent assignment design inspired them to integrate a deeper understanding of student-focused teaching. It challenged some to reconsider their pedagogical decisions with their assignments, including providing sample exemplars. In summary, transparent assignment design invited faculty to adopt students' perspectives and we believe this is a powerful way to motivate faculty to positively change their teaching.

As faculty developers, the single biggest challenge for our team was balancing our scholar-practitioner roles. Facilitating quality professional learning with new content while simultaneously evaluating the implementation proved to be overly ambitious. Inconclusive student performance results (e.g., nonsignificant differences in student GPA) remind us that slow, intentional planning can result in larger sample sizes and comparison groups that emulate controlled experiments. We decided not to think of the CSU Transparency Project as a classic social science intervention but instead as an incremental change in *our* practice as professional developers. Faculty development centers, like ours, not already engaged in research need time and assistance from administrators to build relationships with institutional research staff to ensure access to data critical for analysis.

Our cross-institutional collaboration positively fueled efforts to build these relationships and prompted us to invite a colleague who could conduct statistical analysis to join the team. We needed each other to navigate this process, and we benefited tremendously from Mary-Ann Winkelmes's mentorship and data-collection resources from TILT Higher Ed. Within our state system, it is still the norm that faculty move into faculty development midcareer for time-limited terms, and few campuses allocate much more than one full-time equivalent for center direction and staffing. Often faculty development directors straddle a faculty appointment and attend to their faculty duties (e.g., conducting research, teaching, service) while attempting to conduct their director tasks; it is overwhelming. But from the perspective of the system office, a project like this builds capacity by distributing leadership for effective instruction.

Furthermore, transparent assignment design is affordable professional development, especially in relation to the explosion of for-profit faculty development programming. For those in a position to make funding decisions about faculty development programming, we found transparent assignment design to be relatively low-cost and sustainable. The costs included travel to learn transparent assignment design (e.g., attending a Professional and Organizational Development [POD] conference) and modest faculty stipends. Because the TILT project freely distributed all training materials, collected faculty and student data, and engaged with us in ongoing Zoom meetings to fine-tune implementation, we were able to elevate our combined ability to scale this practice across campuses.

What are our next steps? At one institution, the faculty developer is repeating the process but with an enhanced layer of support. One lesson learned from faculty reflections and examining some of their assignments is that faculty need more guidance and accountability while redesigning assignments. Although some faculty made significant revisions, others made miniscule changes. As a result, in the next phase all faculty will be required to collaborate with a faculty librarian who will serve as a coach while revising their assignments. Because faculty librarians are often on the front lines as students seek help to complete their assignments, they are an untapped resource for teaching faculty.

Another direction for transparent assignment design is eliciting assistance from administrators to target specific courses where student success is critical. For instance, the initial recruitment hurdles experienced at CSU Northridge shine light on the fact that transparent assignment design may be most effectively deployed in lower-division courses where students most benefit from clear expectations and faculty have least access to professional development. A question left unanswered for us through this project is why more faculty teaching lower-division courses do not participate in our faculty development programming.

In conclusion, assessing the impact of faculty development is difficult when universities regularly change variables that can affect our work. An important lesson learned is that faculty developers should change their practice incrementally, just as we recommend faculty do. At the beginning of our project we asked ourselves numerous times if we should have waited to implement to ensure all moving pieces were in place. But we decided this question was like asking if someone new to teaching should wait until they are ready. As we know, at some point you have to dive in to discover what needs to be learned and enhanced. Thus we are thrilled with our decision to move forward given all that we have learned and now can share with others.

EDITORS' HIGHLIGHTS

For faculty developers working to implement TILT programming across multiple institutions, consider the following points from these contributors:

- Gathering and sharing data across institutions, including TILT survey data, faculty reflections, and institutional student success data, can provide convincing evidence to encourage broader adoption of transparent instructional practices, especially when faculty describe the transformative impact of TILT on their teaching practice.
- For understaffed faculty development offices, TILT Higher Ed offers a free, open-source, evidence-based curriculum that is easy to adopt. This allows more time for focusing on the quality of delivery and facilitation.
- Cross-institutional collaboration provides collegial support for small faculty development offices and increased accountability for implementation, data gathering, and follow-up activity.

References

Berwick, D. (2008). The Science of improvement. *JAMA The Journal of the American Medical Association, 299*(10): 1182–1184.

Brookfield, S. D. (1998). Critically reflective practice. *Journal of Continuing Education in the Health Professions, 18*(4), 197–205.

Fisher, K., Kouyoumdjian, C., Roy, B., Talavera-Bustillos, V., & Willard, M. (2016). Building a culture of transparency. *Peer Review, 18*(1/2), 8.

Kezar, A. (2011). What is the best way to achieve broader reach of improved practices in higher education? *Innovative Higher Education, 36*(4), 235–247.

King, C., & Felten, P. (2012). Threshold concepts in educational development: An introduction. *Journal of Faculty Development, 28*(3), 5–7.

Lave, J., & Wenger, E. (1998). *Communities of practice: Learning, meaning, and identity.* Cambridge, UK: Cambridge University Press.

Nelson, C. E. (2010). Dysfunctional illusions of rigor: Lessons from the scholarship of teaching and learning. *To Improve the Academy, 28*, 177–192.

Pike, G. R., & Kuh, G. D. (2005). First- and second-generation college students: A comparison of their engagement and intellectual development. *The Journal of Higher Education, 76*, 276–300.

Tovar, E., Simon, M. A., & Lee, H. B. (2009). Development and validation of the college mattering inventory with diverse urban college students. *Measurement and Evaluation in Counseling and Development, 42*, 154–178.

Walton, G. M., & Cohen, G. L. (2011). A brief social-belonging intervention improves academic and health outcomes of minority students. *Science, 331*, 1447–1451.

Winkelmes, M. A., Bernacki, M., Butler, J. V., Zochowski, M., Golanics, J., & Harriss Weavil, K. (2016). A teaching intervention that increases underserved college students' success. *Peer Review, 18*(1–2), 31–36.

11

TRANSPARENT INSTRUCTION IN A STATEWIDE HIGHER EDUCATION NETWORK

Terri A. Tarr, Russell D. Baker, and Kathy E. Johnson

The Transparency in Learning and Teaching (TILT) initiative made its way to our state through a serendipitous webinar, introduced at a time when faculty leaders of our fledgling Liberal Education and America's Promise (LEAP) Indiana network (LEAP Indiana, n.d.) were primed to notice teaching initiatives aligned with themes of equity, belonging, and the retention and success of first-generation students. LEAP Indiana seeks to create and support connections among diverse faculty from across all Indiana colleges and universities who are passionate about teaching and the exploration of innovative pedagogies aligned with the Association of American Colleges & Universities (AAC&U) LEAP States Initiative. This chapter shares strategies used to spread TILT through networks spanning multiple campuses of two- and four-year public institutions. It is a story still very much in a fledgling state, but we hope that this narrative and the lessons we have learned thus far might provide insights regarding how TILT could be introduced across a large network or an entire state to scale its effects to the benefit of thousands of students.

This chapter also examines the consequences of the strategies we have used to expand faculty members' understanding and implementation of transparent assignment design through the creation of two statewide networks. First, a network of directors of teaching centers has met regularly to plan programming and faculty workshops that enable TILT to be taught, assessed, scaled, and sustained across multiple four-year institutions. Second, a course-based network of faculty from Ivy Tech Community College of Indiana campuses has emerged. This network has cultivated support for utilizing TILT in introductory writing courses by establishing a digital community in the Canvas Learning Management System that enables resources to be shared throughout the state. In the remainder of the chapter, we share strategies used across both contexts to launch, expand, and prepare to evaluate the effectiveness of these networks, followed by lessons learned along the way. However, we first need to provide a bit of background regarding these networks.

Ivy Tech Network

More than 150,000 students take courses through Ivy Tech each year, making it one of the largest institutions in the country under a single accreditation. Ivy Tech has 19 campuses, with numerous additional site locations. Ivy Tech Community College offers more than 150 programs designed to prepare graduates for immediate workforce entry or to successfully transfer to a 4-year degree program.

Like most other community colleges in the United States, Ivy Tech attracts an exceptionally diverse student population. For example, more than half of the African American college students in Indiana are enrolled at Ivy Tech campuses. Ivy Tech attracts a significant percentage of students from lower income households, with many students returning to school after several years in the workforce. A significant majority of students are working, with many holding full-time jobs. In short, the Ivy Tech student profile strongly matches the goal of the 2014–2015 national project of "promoting learning, particularly integrative learning across general education courses, for underserved students" (AAC&U, 2014). More than any other single outcome, the profound improvement on student success metrics for higher risk students, as reported by Winkelmes, Bernacki, Butler, Zochowski, Golanics, and Harriss Weavil (2016) for seven minority-serving institutions, is what compelled Ivy Tech to join the LEAP Indiana initiative and encourage our campuses to consider participating.

Teaching Center Director Network

Particularly at four-year institutions, teaching centers offer a natural home and strong potential for scaling and sustaining TILT professional development offerings. Bringing together a group of teaching center directors to learn about the TILT approach and to support each other in developing TILT faculty development programming can be an effective way to disseminate, scale, and sustain TILT practices to a wide faculty audience across institutions.

Strategies for Launching Effective Networks

The development of one such network of teaching center directors across Indiana higher education institutions is currently underway across Indiana University, a multicampus university with a flagship campus (Bloomington) and an urban research campus (Indiana University–Purdue University Indianapolis [IUPUI]) along with 5 regional comprehensive campuses and an IUPUI extension in Columbus, Indiana. Campuses are separately accredited through the Higher Learning Commission and collectively enroll more than 114,000 students.

Convene Task Forces Focusing on a Unified Goal

A task force consisting of Ivy Tech English program chairs and faculty was formed to identify strategies for improving student success and completion in English composition (ENGL 111). Many of these faculty and academic administrators attended the LEAP Indiana Conference during which Mary-Ann Winkelmes conducted a TILT workshop. It quickly became apparent to the English composition faculty task force that the goals of the TILT initiative were consistent with the strategies already being identified to improve ENGL 111 student outcomes. Enthusiasm began to build among these faculty around the potential of this initiative to positively impact student success. Winkelmes returned to Ivy Tech to meet with a group of Ivy Tech English Composition faculty who investigated the TILT initiative and potential benefits of implementation for English Composition. We fully expect the TILT initiative to play a significant role in the final strategic recommendations of this task force.

Following the LEAP conference, the chief academic officer at IUPUI convened a task force of teaching center directors from institutions associated with LEAP Indiana work to explore how to best encourage broad dissemination and implementation of the TILT transparent assignment approach and to inform faculty about scholarship of teaching and learning (SoTL) opportunities associated with the work.

Build on Existing Meetings

Teaching center task force cochairs took advantage of an already scheduled meeting with other Indiana University (IU) teaching center directors to share information about the TILT approach, determine center directors' interest in

TILT, and discuss possible approaches to incorporate TILT into center work. Interest in promoting the TILT approach on their campuses was high and directors agreed to meet again virtually to begin work together on bringing TILT to their campuses.

Use Support and Resources Already Provided by TILT Higher Ed Augmented by Locally Developed Resources

Once teaching center directors' interest in TILT was established, a group of nine teaching center directors met with Winkelmes by videoconference to talk about how TILT faculty development offerings have been structured in other institutions and what support she might continue to provide for TILT professional development programming. During the meeting, Winkelmes discussed a variety of ways that campuses could introduce faculty to TILT, including having faculty watch a fully recorded workshop or webinar, providing workshop materials for centers to offer during their own introductory workshop, or having Winkelmes facilitate the workshop in person or through a webinar. She recommended that TILT workshops or webinars be cofacilitated by the teaching center director in order to enhance sustainability and to establish a campus-based project leader. Directors are also in an ideal position to adapt and contextualize the approach to make it work well for faculty at their own institutions.

A securely shared online folder was created for directors to use for TILT-related sharing. Directors identified the following as valuable support and resources:

- General feedback about faculty adoption of practices, especially for common courses
- Dedicated time with faculty across campuses to share ideas on how to be transparent and to exchange even anecdotal information about successes and obstacles
- Conversation among campuses about their TILT activities and what works versus what doesn't
- Examples of calls for applications, workshop modifications, incentives for faculty; culminating event(s) to share faculty products and experiences with transparent assignments; a shared research project across campuses; a shared grant proposal; a shared Box site; course materials such as syllabi

Ivy Tech faculty members have expressed a strong sentiment that there is no substitution for in-the-room professional development. However, the availability of resources associated with TILT enables faculty to work on their own materials at their own pace and empowers department chairs throughout the state to make resources available to faculty recognized as innovators in composition instructional design and theory.

Since Ivy Tech faculty teaching English composition met with Winkelmes, the transparent assignment process has been disseminated through a centrally located digital community established in the Canvas Learning Management System to share resources with all faculty teaching English Composition. In addition, several English program chairs have led professional development workshops with their faculty, using materials publicly available on the TILT Higher Ed Examples and Materials webpage (TILT Higher Ed, n.d.).

Ivy Tech's efforts to incorporate TILT have not been limited to English courses. On our Kokomo campus, half of the August faculty development in-service day was devoted to training faculty from several program areas on implementing transparent assignment design. The Ivy Tech Muncie campus also is spearheading an effort to bring TILT workshops to additional faculty members, including part-time faculty.

Strategies for Post-Launch Expansion and Scaling of Work Across Networks

During our spring 2018 faculty in-service week, Winkelmes facilitated a Zoom webinar for faculty representing more than half of the Ivy Tech campuses across the state. She met with facilitators prior to the workshop, enabling each local campus to have a trained workshop facilitator who led a follow-up workshop after the initial presentation from Winkelmes.

Incorporate TILT Into Teaching Center Workshops or Other Existing Faculty Training Activities

To prepare teaching centers to disseminate the approach among faculty, it was necessary to train teaching center staff. Winkelmes provided the teaching center directors with access to a 33-minute "Train the Trainers" webinar recording. Directors watched the recording on their own and then met once again via videoconference with Winkelmes to discuss questions about the workshop (Figure 11.1).

Another opportunity to provide training was at an IU teaching centers meeting attended by approximately 60 teaching center directors, faculty, and staff. All directors at the meeting were familiar with TILT, and some had implemented it with faculty, but most center personnel

Figure 11.1. Teaching Center director questions about Train-the-Trainer workshop.

1. How comfortable does everyone feel about presenting the content in the training video?
2. What additional information do you/we need?
3. What ways, if any, might we want to modify the training?
4. How much time does Mary-Ann spend on the workshop?
5. How are the follow-up workshops run? What is the content?
6. How can we support each other in developing and offering our own versions of the workshop?
7. How much time must be allocated for the research portion of the workshop versus the application portion of the workshop?
8. In the workshop descriptions, there is a reference to a two-question survey for participants to complete prior to the workshop. What are the questions?
9. What can we do to collaborate with other centers and faculty who have modified their assignments to clarify purpose, tasks, and criteria?
10. What kinds of pre- and postchange measures can be used?
11. How have control groups been used?
12. What can be done to ensure that faculty implement the assignments?
13. If funds are not provided to faculty, what other incentives might be used to get faculty interested?

Note. Reproduced with permission of Terri Tarr.

were less familiar with the approach and hadn't yet attended a TILT workshop. At the meeting, two teaching center directors led an introductory TILT workshop, which everyone at the meeting attended. Workshop slides were drawn from resources provided on the TILT project website. Center directors also updated each other on the status of TILT implementation on their campuses.

One of the strategies teaching centers have shared is to use TILT not only for faculty-designed assignments but also as an approach that can strengthen teaching center workshops and other activities. Gwendolyn Mettetal, IU South Bend, has TILTed an advisory board meeting, course goals workshop, assessment workshop, teaching strategies and high-impact practices workshop, associate faculty orientation, network mentoring workshop, and peer review of teaching workshop (Figures 11.2 and 11.3).

Figure 11.2. TILT for assessment workshop.

- Purpose
    - Identify multiple ways to assess the course goals
    - Develop and use rubric
- Task
    - Learn about grading
    - Work as a group on developing assessments for an example course
    - Begin to determine assessments for their own course
- Criteria
    - Identify two to four appropriate assessments of course goals
    - Be able to develop and use a rubric

Note. Reproduced with permission of Gwendolyn Mettetal, IU South Bend.

Figure 11.3. TILT for advisory board meeting.

- Purpose
    - Share what we have been doing and what we are planning
    - Get your input on priorities
    - Ask you to volunteer
- Task
    - Participate in Kahoot!
    - Share UCET news and plans with others
- Criteria
    - We get data on priorities
    - We get some volunteers

Note. Reproduced with permission of Gwendolyn Mettetal, IU South Bend.

After attending the TILT workshop at the IU teaching centers meeting, IUPUI Center for Teaching and Learning (CTL) faculty and staff members decided to TILT the Journal Club held internally at their center (Figure 11.4).

The TILT initiative is being implemented at Ivy Tech's largest campus in Indianapolis, which is also the most diverse campus in the system. The assistant department chair of English presented the workshop to approximately 25 full- and part-time faculty at the fall in-service training session and participants each completed 4 TILT-modeled assignment sheets. Figure 11.5, for example, demonstrates how an assignment identifies course learning goals that are also described in the syllabus.

The collection of assignments is now available online to all English faculty. Evaluation of the project will be conducted at the end of the fall term with plans for expansion in the spring.

Figure 11.4. TILTed CTL journal club.

Purpose

- To discover new ideas about teaching and learning
- To ensure that the CTL consultants and fellows stay current in what is the best research available and what are the current best practices
- To explore applications of theory to CTL practice
- To identify the common content and characteristics of the field that undergird the IUPUI CTL curriculum
- To build a community of scholarly practitioners to enhance the conversation about teaching at IUPUI

Tasks

Convener:

1. Arrange the schedule and remind participants of the goals for the Journal Club (JC) in general and the specific questions at issue with the current reading
2. Keep the conversation on schedule, especially ensuring that the JC has time to gather the wisdom of the discussion into a recommendation for CTL practice
3. Record final take-aways and suggested follow-up activities based on the discussion
4. Give an end-of-semester update of discussion outcomes, if any

Discussion Leader:

1. Choose a reading that addresses an issue or question central to the mission and values of the CTL practice and general field
2. Provide the focal questions for the reading and the discussion
3. Initiate the conversation and ensure that all JC members have an opportunity to respond to the questions posed and are invited to raise questions or issues of their own

JC Members

1. Read carefully and critically the chosen reading
2. Prepare to engage fully with questions posed prior to the meeting and to raise other issues or questions
3. Identify themes and patterns in the discussion that may contribute to an overview of the topic at hand and create steps toward an application to CTL theory and practice
4. Develop collaboratively the new ideas that emerge from the discussion, new ideas for CTL staff, the CTL, the campus, or the field
5. Report out to the CTL subsequent occasions when the insights and developments of the JC have informed specific CTL practices

Criteria

- Successful attendance and participation by all CTL consultants and fellows
- Significant additions to the repertoire of strategies available to consultants and fellows in working with faculty
- Significant additions to the programs and resources offered by the CTL

Note. Reproduced by permission of Anusha S. Rao, Douglas Jerolimov, and Richard Turner, IUPUI.

Figure 11.5. Excerpt from comparative analysis essay assignment prompt.

Skills:

English 111 helps you develop and practice writing and thinking skills essential to your success in college and in your professional life beyond school. . . . This assignment will ask you to practice the following skills: . . .

(1) Understand communication theory and the roles audiences play in the writing process.

(2) Apply critical reading and thinking skills to the writing process.

(4) Develop strategies for making independent, critical evaluations of . . . texts.

(7) Write well-organized essays with a firm thesis and a clear introduction, body, and conclusion.

Note. Reproduced with permission of Heather King, Ivy Tech Community College.

Implementing an initiative across a complex system such as Ivy Tech is complicated. Rather than mandating that all campuses incorporate the TILT initiative, the institution has chosen to allow voluntary participation and to give faculty opportunities to participate in a training workshop before they commit to being involved. If the fall pilot initiatives demonstrate positive results on student success, momentum and enthusiasm are expected to spread quickly.

Each IU teaching center director is developing a plan for campus faculty professional development activities related to transparent assignments. Campuses vary in terms of whether they plan to incorporate the approach into back-to-school workshops, general workshops open to all faculty, workshops targeting specific groups, existing groups (e.g., student success academy faculty fellows, first-year experience faculty, communities of practice, coalitions of gateway course instructors, academic departments), or newly formed short-term faculty learning communities. At IUPUI, the CTL is collaborating with the Gateway to Graduation Program, Learning Communities, and First Year Programs to offer a TILT pilot for instructors teaching first-year students who are interested in modifying or creating student assignments using the TILT approach.

Emphasize Research Findings Regarding Impact on Students

Perhaps in contrast to four-year institutions, expanding TILT across a community college is not as heavily motivated by faculty opportunities to engage in scholarly research on TILT. The primary expectation for community college faculty is to focus on teaching excellence. Engagement in SoTL research is not required of faculty. Rather, community college faculty are eager to pursue TILT as it has a clear evidence base for helping to reduce achievement gaps, is logically focused on good assignment design (which few faculty receive formal training in), and is something that can be implemented immediately, regardless of when during a semester it is learned.

Explore Connections With Other Initiatives or Additional Campus Partners

The teaching center directors learned from Winkelmes about other ongoing national initiatives to which directors (and faculty) could connect, such as the John N. Gardner Institute's Gateway to Completion (G2C) program and TILT's collaboration with the National Institute for Learning Outcomes Assessment (NILOA) on efforts to improve student success by focusing on assignments and then scaling up to the syllabus, course, department, school, and finally the institutional level. (See chapter 12 in this book for a description of NILOA's approach.)

Other professionals on campus, such as academic advisers and supplemental instruction staff, may be integrated into campus TILT work given its clear impact on student success and retention. For example, academic advisers at IUPUI have formulated learning outcomes for their advising work and frequently ask students to engage in activities that are intended to help demonstrate achievement of these learning outcomes, such as the development of a two- or a four-year ePortfolio-based academic plan that includes written reflections on engagement in high-impact practices such as internships, undergraduate research, service-learning, and global/international learning experiences. Adopting a TILT framework for these advising-related assignments would provide an innovative approach that could be impactful for students on campus and that might generalize well to other institutions. (See chapter 8 for a description of how advisers at UNLV adopted the Transparency Framework.)

The leaders of Ivy Tech's statewide faculty professional development initiative, the Master Teacher Academy, are considering incorporating TILT training into their curriculum for the next cohort of faculty participants. The spring professional development opportunity will be a crucial next step as the institution seeks to expand the Transparency Framework.

Explore Shared Research Interests

The TILT approach can provide faculty members with SoTL opportunities related to their TILT work. Teaching center directors gain an opportunity to demonstrate the impact that faculty development can have on campuses by helping to improve student retention, persistence, and graduation rates. Pre- and post-TILT student surveys are available for faculty to administer to their students, and the TILT project will provide confidential, individual instructor reports that summarize the student survey data.

Research interests among the teaching center directors are still emerging and varied. They include reduction of DFIW rates (the number of students in a course who received a final grade of D, F, Incomplete, or Withdraw), improvements in student retention, student feelings of belonging, and student confidence among first-year and transfer students. There is also an interest in cocurricular partnerships between academic affairs and student affairs as well as analyses of the faculty experience related to using the transparent assignment approach. Directors would like to provide opportunities for faculty to develop their own SoTL projects and have information to share with faculty about administering a pre- and posttransparency survey to students.

Engage Administrative Leadership

Russell D. Baker, a cocontributor of this chapter, fulfills the role of vice president of the School of Arts, Sciences and Education and has been in a position to provide strategic leadership and encouragement to campuses who are considering implementation of TILT. With assessment functions at Ivy Tech and development of strong transfer pathways to the four-year institutions also under his direction, faculty have been working for some time on ensuring that assignments in our gateway courses are comparable to those in similar courses at four-year schools. The TILT initiative shows promise for integrating these alignment efforts across the LEAP Indiana network. (Chapter 9 describes a similar effort in the Washington State Community College system.)

Evaluating Success

Ivy Tech is tagging TILTed courses for evaluation purposes. Each course section in which the faculty member is incorporating TILT has been identified with a unique course identifier in the Banner Student Information System. This will facilitate evaluation of this initiative on student completion and success. Ivy Tech plans to compare student success metrics in course sections utilizing TILT with those from courses taught by the same faculty in the previous year.

Though the work led by teaching center directors is still in its nascent phase and will be broadened to include more center directors from LEAP member institutions, many criteria for success have been identified that will serve as a framework for assessing our efforts. These include the following:

- Number of campuses offering TILT faculty development programs
- Number of TILT faculty development programs offered
- Number of faculty attending TILT faculty development programs
- Number of faculty who have TILTed their assignments
- Number of students in courses with TILTed assignments
- TILT pre- and postsurvey results showing impact on student confidence and sense of belonging
- Impact on retention and graduation rates of students in courses with TILTed assignments (overall impact and disaggregated by student demographic groups)
- Presentations and publications resulting from directors and faculty involved with TILT initiatives
- Impact of TILTing on faculty teaching strategies, attitudes, or beliefs

Lessons Learned: The Earliest Days

Although most faculty naturally gravitate toward opportunities to collaborate with other faculty and share a desire to continuously improve the effectiveness of their teaching, it can be daunting to lead a teaching initiative across institutional borders. Indiana does not share California's system-based organization of two- and four-year institutions described in chapter 10, and LEAP Indiana, by design, has been a faculty-owned and faculty-led network. We share some reflections on lessons that we have learned in these early days in hopes that they might be useful to college and university leaders in other states or to coordinating boards.

Leadership Is Critically Important

It is tremendously helpful that leaders across Ivy Tech Community College and Indiana University have committed to sustaining this work, and in some cases have made considerable resource investments to incentivize faculty participation. LEAP Indiana has been incorporated into one senior leader's position description at IU, but most of the individuals working in this area (including this chapter's contributors) are balancing this work on top of many other competing job responsibilities. Dedication to the work and a true commitment to LEAP principles as essential to undergraduate education are key. We have struggled to communicate continuously about the work through a statewide electronic mailing list, Twitter account, and website and still find that many faculty are unaware of what LEAP truly means. The need for leaders to continuously communicate about the work will likely never diminish. Strong leadership is necessary to maintaining a coalition of champions across a network of private and public institutions.

Networking Directors of Teaching Centers Benefits TILT and Beyond

Although faculty naturally are attracted to the logic behind TILT, it is unlikely that TILT could ever be expanded and sustained purely through faculty word of mouth. Faculty reside within departments and programs nested within schools and campuses. The locus of support for initiatives such as TILT should naturally be campus centers for supporting teaching and other aspects of faculty professional development. We found that there was no statewide network of center directors in our state. By forming this network, directors gain a supportive group of peers beyond their own home campus, as well as the opportunity to collaborate on cross-institutional SoTL research. Nevertheless, we are mindful that many faculty on our campuses seldom choose to engage with teaching and learning centers, or do so only when directed by a dean or chair because improvements in teaching are desired. Ultimately, we need to create multiple on-ramps for helping faculty to engage with initiatives such as TILT—one approach will never fit all.

Identify Faculty Leaders and Spotlight Their Work

Faculty generally are highly motivated to improve student learning and care deeply about reducing disparities in educational outcomes. Yet TILT requires additional time, particularly if faculty have inherited long-untouched assignments from course coordinators, textbook ancillaries, or even graduate school advisers. We have found that it is important to try to let the work evolve somewhat organically, even if that takes more time, while also taking every opportunity to publicly recognize faculty engaged in the work through newsletters, speeches, and social media. Though this assumption has not yet been supported empirically, we assume that faculty motivation is increased through such public forms of recognition and that it also helps to spawn peer networks by identifying current implementers of TILT on particular campuses.

Don't Underestimate the Importance of Institutional Research Infrastructure

TILT is a powerful means of promoting excellent assignment design while also making clear to students why and how they should engage with their course work. However its real impact is on eliminating achievement gaps that are frequently evidenced among students from diverse backgrounds. Although faculty are well-positioned to examine the effects of TILT within a semester, they do not have access to institutional data that enable examination of the effects of TILT on students from different demographic groups or that permit longitudinal analyses of the impact that transparent assignment design might have beyond the semester in which the course is taken. Institutional researchers are critically important to engage in order to develop a comprehensive analysis of TILT's impact on students as well as the return on investment for the institution.

SoTL Is Optional, Particularly at Two-Year Institutions

One of the hallmarks of the TILT initiative has been the support for faculty engagement in related scholarship. We have been surprised that relatively few faculty have expressed interest in this dimension of the work, preferring instead to focus on the more concrete and pragmatic aspects of syllabus and assignment redesign. Indeed, faculty at Ivy Tech Community College are not expected to engage in SoTL work on top of their already high teaching loads. Faculty at four-year institutions have anecdotally shared concerns that this type of research may not be valued as highly as research or creative activity within the discipline. Thus we conclude, at least at this early phase of the initiative, that the opportunity to engage in SoTL is not a powerful motivator for faculty participation. That said, we are eager to follow the research agenda currently under development by the network of CTL directors.

Capture Student Perspectives

We are increasingly mindful that TILT has not had a significant "student voice" across campuses—either from the perspective of undergraduate students we teach or from the perspective of graduate students who may be supporting the instructional mission of four-year institutions as teaching assistants. This is an important priority for our future work, though it will likely need to be based on individual campuses, given the absence of statewide networks for students.

Conclusion

Even though our efforts to help TILT become a signature element of LEAP Indiana are still in their earliest days, we believe that we have learned a great deal and are fully convinced that the work has been worthwhile. We are pleased that TILT has galvanized broad faculty engagement across two- and four-year institutions, and our collection of shared resources aimed at boosting student success is growing. A robust network of teaching center directors will help ensure that the work is sustained and improved over time. At the time of this writing, the LEAP Indiana steering committee has appointed its first faculty fellows to focus on assessment efforts related to TILT, and we are eager to engage them in helping to conceptualize and enact the future phases of this important endeavor.

EDITORS' HIGHLIGHTS

For educational developers and administrators considering implementing transparency-based programming in a statewide network, consider the following points from these contributors:

- Draw on existing infrastructure, such as established meetings or training activities, and take advantage of resources provided by TILT to build a network.
- Engage administrative leadership and other campus partners.
- Emphasize research findings that illustrate the impact of transparency on student success.

References

Association of American Colleges & Universities (AAC&U). (2014). *Call for applications from minority-serving institutions to participate in an AAC&U LEAP project.* Available from https://www.aacu.org/problemcenteredlearning

LEAP Indiana. (n.d.). *LEAP.* Available from www.leapindiana.org

TILT Higher Ed. (n.d.). *TILT Higher Ed examples and resources.* Available from TILTHigherEd.org

Winkelmes, M. A., Bernacki, M., Butler, J. V., Zochowski, M., Golanics, J., & Harriss Weavil, K. H. (2016). A teaching intervention that increases underserved college students' success. *Peer Review, 18*(1/2), 31–36.

12

ASSIGNMENT DESIGN AS A SITE FOR PROFESSIONAL DEVELOPMENT AND IMPROVED ASSESSMENT OF STUDENT LEARNING OUTCOMES

Jillian Kinzie and Pat Hutchings

Over the past several years, the National Institute for Learning Outcomes Assessment (NILOA) has worked with faculty around the country on assignment design, and the Transparency Framework has been central to that effort. As we reflect on that work in the context of other efforts featured in this volume, what comes to mind is the image of a fractal, "a never-ending pattern that repeats itself at different scales" (Fractal Foundation, n.d.). We see the Transparency Framework's principles of purpose, task, and criteria as a fractal-like pattern that repeatedly promotes student success at different scales. It encourages more effective, transparent assignments in the many course and cocurricular settings that constitute students' journeys through their educational experience. It can also help to connect the many and diverse improvement efforts being undertaken across the country by campuses and larger organizations committed to enhancing undergraduate education. Such connections are sorely needed in the face of restricted resources, over-busy schedules, and competing calls on the attention of faculty and other institutional leaders. If higher education is to provide coherent pathways to learning for all students, we need the kind of shared frameworks and language featured in this volume that can help to make teaching a communal and transparent enterprise, something we build together, in ways that support learning for all students.

This chapter traces the history of NILOA's assignment-focused professional development work and underlines the importance of transparent assignments and transparent language for engaging faculty in assessment. It offers a set of guiding principles for using transparent assignment design as a route toward more effective, improvement-focused assessment on a broad scale. Additionally, as the fractal image suggests, it considers how a focus on transparent assignments can open onto a much larger set of conversations about the purposes of higher education and our responsibility as educators to bring all students to high levels of achievement.

History and Context

Documenting what students know and can do is of growing interest to colleges and universities, accrediting groups, higher education organizations, disciplinary associations, foundations, and others beyond campus, including students, their families, employers, and policymakers. This interest propelled the formation of NILOA, established in 2008 to discover and disseminate how academic programs and institutions can productively use assessment data to improve the experience of students. This goal, in turn, called for heightened attention to the role of faculty in the assessment process. NILOA's many resources include a Transparency Framework for institutional assessment of students' learning (NILOA, n.d.). Accordingly, in 2013, NILOA launched an ambitious initiative to work with faculty on the design and use of assignments. We entered this work with a big-picture hypothesis—that using the tasks that faculty design and require of students as a source of evidence about student learning outcomes could help shift assessment from an add-on activity, undertaken primarily for compliance and reporting purposes, to a process at the heart of effective teaching and equitable learning.

Within this larger context, the focus on assignments has gathered significant momentum. In NILOA's 2017 survey of provosts, about 65% reported that "classroom-based performance on assessments such as simulations, comprehensive exams, critiques, assignments, etc." were used on their campus to assess or represent undergraduate student learning (Kinzie & Kuh, 2017). The use of assignments was, in fact, the third most popular assessment method, just behind national student surveys and rubrics. Further, when asked which assessment approach was most useful to inform decisions, provosts pointed to classroom-based assessments as their number one response (Kuh, Jankowski, Ikenberry, & Kinzie, 2014).

Indeed, faculty engagement has long been recognized as a central element in successful assessment programs (Cain & Hutchings, 2015; Gray, 2002). Advocates argue that it allows for more authentic assessment work; ties assessment more directly to course-based experiences; increases the likelihood that assessment will inform improvement; and, importantly, puts faculty ownership of learning at the heart of assessment. In short, institutional leaders and the assessment community more broadly have been looking for new ways to meaningfully engage faculty. Yet NILOA's research points to several perceived impediments to greater faculty engagement in assessment: a sense that it is a passing fad, a compliance activity disrespectful of faculty expertise, or a bad match with the academic reward system. Not surprisingly, provosts see a need for greater faculty involvement in assessment (Kuh & Ikenberry, 2009; Kuh et al., 2014).

Compelled by the need to meaningfully involve faculty in assessment and intrigued by the potential of assignment design to do so, NILOA set about both to learn from campus work on assignments and to support it. Beginning in 2011, NILOA began tracking campus experience with the Degree Qualifications Profile (DQP), a framework of degree-level proficiencies in five domains (Lumina Foundation, 2011). Our findings pointed to the power of the DQP to catalyze powerful campus conversations about outcomes; to prompt curricular mapping, review, and revision; and to rethink assessment (Jankowski & Giffin, 2016). But we also found a growing number of DQP-engaged campuses that were turning their attention to the design of assignments, seeking to bring them into closer, more intentional and transparent alignment with DQP (or DQP-like) proficiencies (Hutchings, Jankowski, & Ewell, 2014).

Assignments as a Focus for Professional Development

To explore the alignment between an outcomes-based quality framework like the DQP and what faculty ask students to do in the assignments they pose, in October 2013 NILOA began hosting a series of events for faculty interested in working together to design or redesign assignments that both document and advance student learning around the DQP proficiencies. Our aim, with funding from Lumina Foundation, was to create an online repository—a library—of peer-reviewed assignments that others could adapt and be inspired by.

The faculty we worked with, over 100 of them across the 4 events, applied to participate and were selected based on the draft assignment they submitted. In advance of the face-to-face meeting, they read one another's draft assignments. At the meeting, they met in facilitated groups of 4 or 5, which we called *charrettes*, a term from architecture used to denote a process of collaborative design (Hutchings et al., 2014). Each charrette followed a simple protocol:

- Framing, in which the assignment author briefly reviews the focus and purpose of the assignment—5 minutes.
- Facilitated question-and-answer sessions, focusing on ideas for strengthening the assignment—15 minutes
- Written feedback from each participant to the assignment author—5 minutes

The goal of the charrette is for participants to help one another revise their assignments to make them clearer and more transparent about the outcome students will demonstrate and how the assignment's purpose, task, and evaluation criteria align with shared program and institutional outcomes. Figure 12.1 is the original NILOA charrette process guide, adapted (in italics) to reflect the principles of the Transparency Framework.

Several elements contributed to the success of this process. First, participants *wanted* to participate in the event; they applied to the program and saw it as an honor (though a somewhat daunting one, some of them told us). Second, the process was facilitated; each small group had a facilitator whose job it was to keep the discussion moving, on target, and constructive. Third, discussion was concrete—focusing not on assignments in general but on the particular assignment in front of the group. Fourth, each person left with feedback about how to improve her or his assignment, organized around a small number of simple prompts. Figure 12.2 illustrates how those prompts can be expanded (in italics) to more explicitly reflect the principles of the Transparency Framework.

After participating in the charrette, faculty returned to campus and worked to improve their assignments based on the feedback they received. The "final" version ("final" because assignments are always a work in progress) was then submitted to NILOA and posted to the NILOA Assignment Library, which, as of this writing, contains approximately 80 assignments, each accompanied by a reflective memo in which the faculty member explains the context and purpose of the assignment, how well it is working, and possible next steps in its design and use. Additionally, each entry in the library is given a title, a scholarly citation, and a Creative Commons license.

Stimulated (we believe) by the NILOA and Transparency in Learning and Teaching (TILT) initiatives, many campuses have begun organizing their own assignment-focused professional development events, using open access resources to support their efforts that NILOA, through the NILOA Assignment Charrette Toolkit (NILOA, 2012), and TILT, through TILT Higher Ed Examples and Resources (TILT Higher Ed, n.d.), provide.

Figure 12.1. NILOA's assignment design charrette process, adapted to reflect the principles of the Transparency Framework.

Assignment-Design Charrette Process
with Transparent Assignment Design Notes (from Mary-Ann Winkelmes) in italics

In groups of five, each person/team will have an opportunity to share their assignment and receive suggestions and feedback from the group. In order for everyone to have an opportunity to give and receive feedback, we will use a timed carousel process. There will be five rounds. You will be a "presenter" for one round and a "participant" for the other four rounds.

Each round is 25 minutes.

Introduce assignment (5 min):
Presenters will introduce the assignment and provide background information such as: in what course the assignment is used, at what point in the course, pertinent information about the students in the course (majors versus nonmajors), what they find most challenging about the assignment, how it builds on earlier work and/or prepares students for more advanced work in later courses (or success beyond graduation), your experience with the assignment to date, how you hope to strengthen it, and what kinds of feedback and suggestions you would like from others.
Listeners: jot down thoughts and questions but please do not interrupt the presenter, let them have their full five minutes. ***Consider what the presenter says or implies about the purposes (knowledge to be gained, skills to be practiced), tasks, and criteria for this assignment.***

Discussion (15 min):
Listeners will respond to what they have heard, taking turns asking questions, sharing thoughts, feedback, and so on. The purpose of the discussion is to help your colleague strengthen their assignment so please be constructive and collegial. Also, please mind the time and allow each participant the opportunity to contribute to the discussion. Discussion should address the four questions on the feedback sheet. Presenters: listen carefully and respond to the inquiries. Think about alignment, but also think creatively about possible solutions. ***Would the assignment benefit from additional clarity about its purposes, tasks, and criteria? Is this information equitably accessible so that all students begin the assignment from the same starting line?***

Feedback (5 min):
Everyone: Based on the discussion, use the feedback form to give the presenter written feedback and suggestions. The presenter can use this time to write down notes about the assignment, based on what they just heard, ***to consider how accessibly the assignment communicates an intentional rationale about the purposes, tasks, and criteria for students' learning so that students can monitor their success while they are working on the assignment*** and to outline next steps for revision or additional feedback.

Note. Reproduced with permission of NILOA and Mary-Ann Winkelmes.

Figure 12.2. NILOA's charrette feedback template, adapted to reflect the principles of the Transparency Framework.

Assignment-Design Charrette Feedback Sheet
with Transparent Assignment Design Notes (from Mary-Ann Winkelmes) in italics

Assignment _____

Comments From _____

1. What outcomes do you think students will be able to demonstrate with this assignment? *How will the knowledge and/or skills learned from doing this assignment benefit the students' long-term learning?*

2. What are the main strengths of this assignment for assessing the identified outcomes? *Do students understand what the criteria look like in multiple examples of real-world practice?*

3. Thinking about the assignment from the point of view of students, what questions or suggestions do you have? Do students understand the purpose (how the outcomes from this assignment will benefit their long-term learning)? Do students understand how to approach the tasks involved in this assignment? *Do students understand how to apply the criteria for success to their own progress while they are working on the assignment?*

4. Other suggestions and possibilities—especially in response to the author's questions about the assignment. *Do the author's purposes, tasks, and criteria for this assignment inform all parts of the assignment in a way that is equitably accessible to students?*

Note. Reproduced with permission of the National Institute for Learning Outcomes Assessment and Mary-Ann Winkelmes.

Guiding Principles for Assignment Design Work

The insight that the tasks designed by faculty and required of students could be grist for broader institutional student learning outcomes assessment is not new. Historically, a handful of campuses (e.g., Alverno College and King's College) have embedded assessment in the regular work of the classroom. Having watched and learned from such work over the years, NILOA has identified four principles that guide our work on assignment design.

Outcomes Across All Levels

It is difficult to improve if you do not know what you are aiming for, and all of NILOA's work, including the Assignment Library Initiative, begins with and is driven by the need to be clear and explicit about what students are expected to know and be able to do. The good news is that 84% of campuses have now formulated a set of learning outcomes required of all students (Kuh et al., 2014). In many cases those outcomes have been shaped by national frameworks like the DQP or the Association of American Colleges & Universities (AAC&U) Essential Learning Outcomes, which provide common language and standards for student learning outcomes.

This widespread adoption of learning outcomes represents real progress, but it is only a beginning. To be more than merely aspirational, institutional outcomes—which are almost by definition at a high level of abstraction—must be aligned with and enacted through program outcomes, course goals, and the design of assignments (Hutchings, 2016; Jankowski & Marshall, 2017). This large-scale alignment for an institution can be summarized using the Transparency Framework. At a transparent institution, the work of aligning learning outcomes might look like the following:

- *Purpose:* Explicate institution-level outcomes for all students, aligned at every level
- *Tasks:* Alignment of tasks through levels of the institution, all aimed at equitable student learning
- *Criteria:* Agreement about indicators and what success looks like

Indeed, one of the most compelling arguments for a focus on assignment design is that it is at the level of the assignment that high-level outcomes are translated into the tasks that actually drive student learning. Biggs (2014) refers to this translation as "constructive alignment of teaching," in which "what it is intended students should learn, and how they should express their learning, is clearly stated before teaching takes place" (p. 5). Constructive alignment ensures that learning activities, including assignments and assessments, are intentionally linked across the institution, department, and course level in ways that give students opportunities to demonstrate their learning and make it possible for the institution to judge how well outcomes have been attained. The Transparency Framework can be a helpful tool in this regard, posing questions about purpose, tasks, and criteria that support conversations about the alignment of learning outcomes at every level. Figure 12.3 illustrates how this can work around a learning outcome like the development and mastery of "Intellectual and Practical Skills," one of the major outcomes supported by both Lumina's DQP and the AAC&U's Essential Learning Outcomes.

Faculty Engagement

One of the enduring challenges of assessment is to engage faculty (Hutchings, 2010; Kuh et al., 2014), who have tended to see such work as an add-on and an imposition—and for good reason. From its earliest days, assessment was deliberately distanced from the work of the classroom and especially from faculty judgments of student work through grading. Unfortunately, this distancing from the classroom also separated assessment from the very action it most sought to influence—the work of teachers and students (Ewell, 2009).

In contrast, a focus on assignments sends a signal that it is, in fact, the faculty who are most distinctly qualified to make judgments about the quality of student work. Assessment embedded in course assignments thus invites faculty engagement by valuing the work that educators already do as designers of effective assignments. Accordingly, one of the most compelling arguments for work on the design and use of assignments is that it integrates assessment into the ongoing, regular work between educators and students, where it is most likely to make a difference.

More Actionable Data

Alas, as study after study has shown, making a difference—using assessment findings to drive improvements—is very much a work in progress. Campuses are now generating a good deal of evidence about what students know and can do, but that evidence is often put on a shelf, quite literally, where it is not seen or engaged by those who might benefit from it (Banta & Blaich, 2011; Blaich & Wise, 2011; Maki, 2017). There are reasons for this shortfall. Much of the early work on assessment focused on issues of instrumentation, with testing companies turning out one tool after another designed to measure student achievement and institutional effectiveness. Unfortunately, the findings from such "exoskeletal" approaches (Ewell, 2013, p. 8)—typically

Figure 12.3. Aligning/assessing outcomes for intellectual and practical skills.

Aligning & Assessing Outcomes	Purpose	Tasks	Criteria
National Outcomes	Intellectual and Practical Skills (DQP, AAC&U)	Demonstrate, exemplify through artifacts	National leaders' consensus, approval
Institutional Outcomes	Intellectual Reasoning / Critical Thinking	Accreditation report provides evidence, examples	Accreditors' approval
Program Outcomes	Disciplinary inquiry and analysis	Students work exemplifies outcomes	Program leaders, faculty, students see outcomes in student work
Department Outcomes	Inquiry and analysis in the subdiscipline	Compare/assess student work samples from all courses	Department faculty and students see outcomes mastered in student work from all courses
Course Outcomes	Topic-area inquiry	Individual and group assignments build students' skills	Students and Instructor see how student work samples demonstrate mastery. Course grades indicate mastery level
Assignment Outcomes	Students judge reliability of information from several sources	Prescribed activities help students practice this skill	Students understand how criteria apply, can self-evaluate while working

reported as summative scores for very broad outcomes (e.g., critical thinking)—were often not a match with the questions educators cared about or the information they needed to implement improvements. Knowing that the majority of the institution's students score at the 50th percentile on critical thinking might signal a concern, but it provides relatively weak clues about what to do to improve student performance.

In contrast to the early model of assessment employing external instruments, many campuses today have recognized the value of approaches that draw from what students do in the classroom (Kinzie & Kuh, 2017; Kuh et al., 2014) and that reflect "our students' best work" (AAC&U Board of Directors, 2008). These approaches move beyond traditional psychometric features to increase what Messick (1989) calls "consequential validity," (p. 8), the power of assessment to bring improvements where they are most wanted—in this case, in actually advancing the learning of all students. A focus on assignment design meets this important test of consequential validity and actionability.

More Equitable Learning

Finally, assignments are not only a source of rich evidence about student learning but also powerful pedagogical engines, sending signals to students about what faculty value and expect. This point is dramatically underscored by findings from the TILT initiative, which show that well-constructed, transparent assignments can improve the performance of all students and that the gains are even larger for those who are underserved (Winkelmes et al., 2016).

The concern for equity and for closing the opportunity gap also drives Maki's (2017) vision of real-time assessment. Too often, she argues, assessment focuses on only a sample of students, and its timing means that results come too late to help the students whose performance has been documented. Thus she argues for assessment as a "nonstop longitudinal commitment to students' academic success" (Maki, 2017, p. 79), which necessarily means focusing on the work of every student, in all of their educational experiences. This commitment to the learning and success of all students is central to the DQP (Ewell, 2013), and it is one that motivates the NILOA work we are describing here.

Assignments as a Foundation for Building a Wider Community of Practice and Expertise

Assignments can be an integrative force, helping to connect and strengthen larger institutional and even national initiatives aimed at improving undergraduate education. As we have come increasingly to understand, the most important reason for a focus on assignments is not to improve assessment; it is to transform the way faculty (and students) think about learning and teaching. NILOA's 2017 survey of provosts confirmed that institutions are undertaking multiple reform initiatives (e.g., revising general education or scaling up high-impact practices), but that the two most frequently reported initiatives were facilitating faculty work on the design of assignments and curriculum mapping (Kinzie & Kuh, 2017). Given the realities of initiative fatigue, we wondered how these efforts could be connected in ways that make all of them more powerful. The Transparency Framework of purpose-task-criteria offers a simple tool that is helpful for framing such conversations because it can be applied to assignments, courses, departments, programs, and even institutional or national learning outcomes. Two campus examples, from Utah State University and the University of Central Oklahoma, illustrate how attention to transparent assignments can be connected to larger efforts to improve teaching and learning across the institution.

Utah State University

Utah State University has effectively integrated a variety of faculty-led initiatives, including the Utah Tuning project, the use of the DQP with various programs and colleges, AAC&U's Quality Collaboratives project (also focused on the DQP), and the Multi-State Collaborative (MSC), among others (Jankowski & Jones, 2016). Their involvement in Tuning best illustrates the connection between transparent assignments and broader institutional and program goals to advance institutional transformation. The Tuning project focused attention on how faculty in several disciplines prepare students for the capstone experience. To answer this question, the institution undertook a backward mapping exercise, looking course by course at individual student learning artifacts and course assignments in relation to students' journey to the capstone and their degree outcomes. This approach was then reinforced by involvement in the MSC, which focused on using authentic student work as evidence of learning, the articulation of shared standards for student learning, and the use of faculty expertise as the arbiter of quality. The institution has now effectively integrated a focus on assignments and aligned outcomes in its Tuning, DQP, and MSC processes to change the way it thinks and talks about students and curriculum (Jankowski & Jones, 2016).

The University of Central Oklahoma

The University of Central Oklahoma created the Student Transformative Learning Record (STLR) as a tool and process to capture, assess, and document students' transformative learning in important employability, communication, and citizenship skills (Hynes, Pope, Loughlin, & Watkins, 2015). Faculty and professional staff trained in STLR assessment create learning activities and assignments (curricular and cocurricular) associated with one or more of the institution's six tenets (discipline knowledge, leadership, etc.). Students participate in the STLR-tagged assignments, events, or projects, and then STLR-trained faculty and staff assess students' progression in the related tenet(s) using a common STLR rubric. The STLR dashboard and ePortfolio allow students to capture their participation and catalog learning across the spectrum of their educational experiences. STLR has provided a unified platform for bringing faculty and student affairs staff together in the creation of assignments and activities tied to outcomes, while also giving students a way to reflect on and better integrate their learning in and outside the classroom.

These two institutional examples offer quick but powerful illustrations of the role that attention to transparent assignment design can play in larger improvement efforts, bringing a laser-like focus on student learning and optimizing overlaps and complementarity among initiatives in transparent ways. And they are not alone. We are now seeing the development of additional projects and communities of practice around the creation of transparent assignments. These include, of course, the work described by this volume's authors. They also include several AAC&U initiatives mentioned earlier: the Faculty Collaboratives project (AAC&U, n.d.a) focused on strengthening alignment between assignments used in two and four-year institutions; the MSC (AAC&U, n.d.b), in which AAC&U's Valid Assessment of Learning in Undergraduate Education (VALUE) rubrics are used to judge student performance on faculty-designed assignments and assessments of several critical student proficiencies; and the newly formed VALUE Institute (VALUE Institute, n.d.).

In turn, these efforts bring us back to the widespread interest in the quality of student learning introduced at the beginning of this chapter. Motivated by concerns about quality, cost, and student success rates, higher education has been challenged to improve through greater accountability for student outcomes and expanded institutional assessment and improvement projects. NILOA, TILT and other initiatives including Lumina's DQP and the AAC&U's Essential Learning Outcomes, are examples of such projects, as is the Measuring College Learning project that defined a discipline-specific vision of assessment and explicated insights from faculty about outcomes across six fields (Arum, Roksa, & Cook, 2016).

What all of these projects have in common is a commitment to the central leadership role that faculty must play in the definition and assessment of what students should know and be able to do. We submit that thoughtful, collaborative work on the design and use of assignments, which sit at the intersection of faculty members' role in assessment and students' demonstration of learning outcomes, provides a natural opportunity for all colleges and universities to engage with national concerns about and initiatives on quality in undergraduate education.

EDITORS' HIGHLIGHTS

For leaders at the institutional, regional, or national levels interested in employing the Transparency Framework, consider the following points from these contributors:

- Higher education leaders surveyed across the United States agree it is essential to involve faculty in meaningful conversations about assessment. Engaging faculty is most easily accomplished by starting with a focus on their teaching practices and materials. The Transparency Framework can help engage faculty in conversations about students' learning at the level of assignments, courses, programs, institutions, and national higher education outcomes.
- The Transparency Framework offers many opportunities to transform undergraduate education and link it with broader national higher education goals. Online resources such as those provided by TILT Higher Ed and the NILOA Assignment Design Toolkit can support communication among faculty and administrative leaders about making learning goals transparent, relevant, and accessible for students.

References

Arum, R., Roksa, J., & Cook, A. (2016). *Improving quality in American higher education: Learning outcomes and assessments for the 21st century.* Hoboken, NJ: Wiley.

Association of American Colleges & Universities (AAC&U). (n.d.a). *Faculty Collaboratives Project.* Available from aacu.org/faculty

Association of American Colleges & Universities (AAC&U). (n.d.b). *Current VALUE Project: Multi-State Collaborative to advance quality student learning and SHEEQ.* Available from aacu.org/value/msc

Association of American Colleges & Universities (AAC&U) Board of Directors. (2008). *Our students' best work: A framework for accountability worthy of our mission* (2nd ed.). Washington DC: Author.

Banta, T. W., & Blaich, C. F. (2011). Closing the assessment loop. *Change, 43*(1), 22–27.

Biggs, J. (2014). Constructive alignment in university teaching. *Higher Education Research and Development Society of Australasia (HERDSA) Review of Higher Education, 1,* 5–22.

Blaich, C. F., & Wise, K. S. (2011). *From gathering to using assessment results: Lessons from the Wabash National Study* (NILOA Occasional Paper No. 8). Urbana, IL: University of Illinois and Indiana University, National Institute for Learning Outcomes Assessment (NILOA).

Cain, T., & Hutchings, P. (2015). Faculty and students: Assessment at the intersection of teaching and learning. In Kuh, G. H., Ikenberry, S. O. Jankowski, N. A. Cain, T. R., Ewell, P. T., Hutchings, P., & Kinzie, J. (Eds.), *Using evidence of student learning to improve higher education.* (pp. 95–116.) San Francisco, CA: Jossey-Bass.

Ewell, P. T. (2009, November). *Assessment, accountability, and improvement: Revisiting the tension* (NILOA Occasional Paper No. 1). Urbana, IL: University of Illinois and Indiana University, National Institute for Learning Outcomes Assessment (NILOA).

Ewell, P. (2013, January). *The Lumina Degree Qualifications Profile (DQP): Implications for assessment* (NILOA Occasional Paper No. 16). Urbana, IL: University of Illinois and Indiana University, National Institute for Learning Outcomes Assessment (NILOA).

Fractal Foundation. (n.d.). *What is a fractal?* Retrieved from http://fractalfoundation.org/fractivities/WhatIsaFractal-1pager.pdf

Gray, P. (2002). The roots of assessment: Tensions, solutions, and research directions. In T. W. Banta & Associates (Eds.), *Building a scholarship of assessment* (pp. 49–66). San Francisco, CA: Jossey-Bass.

Hutchings, P. (2010, April). *Opening doors to faculty involvement in assessment* (NILOA Occasional Paper No. 4). Urbana, IL: University of Illinois and Indiana University, National Institute for Learning Outcomes Assessment (NILOA).

Hutchings, P. (2016, January). *Aligning educational outcomes and practices* (NILOA Occasional Paper No. 26). Urbana, IL: University of Illinois and Indiana University, National Institute for Learning Outcomes Assessment (NILOA).

Hutchings, P., Jankowski, N. A., & Ewell, P. T. (2014). *Catalyzing assignment design activity on your campus: Lessons from NILOA's Assignment Library Initiative.* Urbana, IL: University of Illinois and Indiana University, National Institute for Learning Outcomes Assessment (NILOA).

Hynes, S., Pope, M., Loughlin, P., & Watkins, S. (2015, October). *The student transformative learning record at the University of Central Oklahoma: A commitment to improving student learning.* Urbana, IL: University of Illinois and Indiana University, National Institute for Learning Outcomes Assessment (NILOA).

Jankowski, N., & Jones, N. (2016, September). *Utah State University: Bringing it all together to foster intentional learners* (DQP/Tuning Case Study). Urbana, IL: University of Illinois and Indiana University, National Institute for Learning Outcomes Assessment (NILOA).

Jankowski, N. A., & Giffin, L. (2016, June). *Degree Qualifications Profile impact study: Framing and connecting initiatives to strengthen student learning.* Urbana, IL: National Institute for Learning Outcomes Assessment (NILOA).

Jankowski, N. A., & Marshall, D. W. (2017). *Degrees that matter: Moving higher education to a learning systems paradigm.* Sterling, VA: Stylus.

Kinzie, J., & Kuh, G. D. (2017, October 23). *National view of the field: 2017 NILOA Provost Survey results.* Presentation at the Assessment Institute, Indianapolis, Indiana.

Kuh, G., & Ikenberry, S. (2009). *More than you think, less than we need: Learning outcomes assessment in American higher education.* Urbana, IL: University of Illinois and Indiana University, National Institute for Learning Outcomes Assessment (NILOA).

Kuh, G. D., Jankowski, N., Ikenberry, S. O., & Kinzie, J. (2014). *Knowing what students know and can do: The current state of student learning outcomes assessment in US colleges and universities.* Urbana, IL: University of Illinois and Indiana University, National Institute for Learning Outcomes Assessment (NILOA).

Lumina Foundation for Education. (2011). *The degree qualifications profile.* Indianapolis, IN: Author.

Maki, P. L. (2017). *Real-time student assessment: Meeting the imperative for improved time to degree, closing the opportunity gap, and assuring student competencies for 21st-century needs.* Sterling, VA: Stylus.

Messick, S. (1989). Meaning and values in test validation: The science and ethics of assessment. *Educational Researcher, 18*(2), 5–11.

National Institute for Learning Outcomes Assessment (NILOA). (n.d.). *Providing evidence of student learning: A Transparency Framework.* Retrieved from http://www.learningoutcomesassessment.org/TFcomponents.htm

National Institute for Learning Outcomes Assessment (NILOA). (2012). *Assignment charrette toolkit.* Available from learningoutcomeassessment.org/assignment-toolkit.html

Transparency in Learning and Teaching in Higher Education (TILT Higher Ed). (n.d.). *TILT Higher Ed examples and resources.* Retrieved from TILTHigherEd.org

VALUE Institute. (n.d.). *Learning outcomes assessment at its best.* Available from valueinstituteassessment.org

Winkelmes, M. A., Bernacki, M., Butler, J. V., Zochowski, M., Golanics, J., & Harriss Weavil, K. (2016, Winter/Spring). A teaching intervention that increases underserved college students' success. *Peer Review, 18*(1/2), 31–36.

Final Thoughts

Allison Boye, Suzanne Tapp, and Mary-Ann Winkelmes

This collection has aimed to tell the story of the Transparency in Learning and Teaching in Higher Education (TILT Higher Ed) project and the Transparency Framework it promotes, and thus to offer readers a look at the wide variety of possible applications the framework offers, along with practical suggestions for making those implementations successful. Although the framework had its beginnings in assignment design, it quickly demonstrated its utility for bigger reforms in curricular design, assessment, strategic planning, cross-institutional initiatives, and beyond— all toward the goal of improved student learning and success. As this collection reveals, the Transparency Framework has much to offer individual faculty members, students, faculty developers, centers for teaching and learning, and other higher education leaders alike.

The Transparency Framework has foundations that are firmly rooted in educational research about best practices in teaching and learning. Ongoing research further illustrates the impact it can have for student success and equity. The scholarship surrounding the TILT project confirms that students, particularly those who are underserved (first-generation, ethnically underrepresented, and/or low-income), consistently show gains in their academic confidence, sense of belonging, and metacognitive awareness of their skill development when they receive transparent instruction. As emerging research investigates the implications of transparent assignment design in particular contexts (e.g., science, technology, engineering, and math classes or large gateway courses), we anticipate continued adoption of transparency in instruction and increased understanding of its benefits for students' learning. We also look forward to new scholarship and avenues for TILT Higher Ed, including its potential as a strategic planning tool, multi-institutional student success initiative, or possibilities that have yet to be imagined.

If readers take nothing else away from this collection, we hope that it is the realization that transparency is a simple change that can wield powerful and positive influence, whether in the form of individual student success on a single assignment or institution-wide student retention and performance. The Transparency Framework can encourage faculty to improve their communication with students as well as students' understanding about how they learn, deepen faculty reflection about teaching and learning, help centers for teaching and learning find new ways to extend their reach and support campus change, allow diverse units to speak the same language, or assist higher education administrators in pursuing critical campus goals and national learning outcomes with direct contributions from faculty. Instructors and campus stakeholders can engage with TILT Higher Ed or implement the Transparency Framework on a small or large scale according to their needs and capabilities. It is our hope that this collection provides readers with valuable insights into the process and practical advice for implementing transparency across a variety of contexts.

LIST OF ACRONYMS

Higher education is known for collecting acronyms and many appear throughout this book. The following list may be helpful to readers.

AACRAO	= American Association of Collegiate Registrars and Admissions Officers
AAC&U	= Association of American Colleges & Universities
AAWG	= Assignment Alignment Working Group
ACPA	= American College Personnel Association
CATL	= Center for the Advancement of Teaching and Learning
COACHE	= Collaborative on Academic Careers in Higher Education
CSU	= California State University
CSULA	= California State University, Los Angeles
CSUN	= California State University, Northridge
CTC	= Community and Technical College
CTE	= Center for Teaching Excellence
CTL	= Center for Teaching and Learning
CWPA	= Council of Writing Program Administrators
D	= Grade of D
DF	= Grade of D or F
DFIW	= Grade of D or F or Incomplete or Withdrawal
DFW	= Grade of D or F or Withdrawal
DQP	= Degree Qualifications Profile
EBTS	= Evidence-Based Teaching Strategies
FLC	= Faculty Learning Community
G2C	= Gateways to Completion (an initiative of the John N. Gardner Institute for Excellence in Undergraduate Education)
GPA	= Grade Point Average
GTA	= Graduate Teaching Associate
IRB	= Institutional Review Board
IU	= Indiana University
IUPUI	= Indiana University–Purdue University Indianapolis
LEAP	= Liberal Education and America's Promise (an initiative of the Association of American Colleges & Universities)

MSC   = Multi-State Collaborative (an initiative of the Association of American Colleges & Universities)

MSI   = Minority-Serving Institution

NACADA = National Academic Advising Association

NASPA   = National Association of Student Personnel Administrators

NCTE   = National Council of Teachers of English

NILOA   = National Institute for Learning Outcomes Assessment

NWP   = National Writing Project

POD   = Professional and Organizational Development Network in Higher Education

QEP   = Quality Enhancement Plan

QM   = Quality Matters

SCALE   = Small Changes Advance Learning

SES   = Socioeconomic Status

SoTL   = Scholarship of Teaching and Learning

STEM   = Science, Technology, Engineering, and/or Mathematics

STLR   = Student Transformative Learning Record

TAD   = Transparent Assignment Design

TILT   = Transparency in Learning and Teaching

TILT Higher Ed   = Transparency in Learning and Teaching in Higher Education project

TLC   = Teaching and Learning Center

TLPDC   = Teaching, Learning, and Professional Development Center

TTU   = Texas Tech University

UNLV   = University of Nevada, Las Vegas

UT (sometimes UTK)   = University of Tennessee, Knoxville

UULO   = University Undergraduate Learning Outcomes

VALUE   = Valid Assessment of Learning in Undergraduate Education

W   = Withdrawal

WU   = Unofficial Withdrawal

WWC   = What Works Clearinghouse

EDITORS AND CONTRIBUTORS

Editors

Mary-Ann Winkelmes, PhD, is executive director of the Center for Teaching and Learning at Brandeis University and the founder and principal investigator of the Transparency in Learning and Teaching in Higher Education project (TILT HigherEd). From 2013 to 2018 she was a senior fellow at the Association of American Colleges & Universities, and she was director of instructional development and research and an associate graduate faculty member in the department of history at the University of Nevada, Las Vegas. She has also served in leadership roles in teaching and learning centers and faculty development programs at the University of Illinois at Urbana-Champaign, the University of Chicago, and Harvard University.

Allison Boye, PhD, is associate director for academic and pedagogical development in the Teaching, Learning, and Professional Development Center at Texas Tech University.

Suzanne Tapp, MA, is the executive director of the Teaching, Learning, and Professional Development Center at Texas Tech University.

Contributors

Russell D. Baker, EdD, is vice president for the Office of Academic Affairs at Ivy Tech Community College.

Melissa Bowles-Terry, MLIS, is head of educational initiatives for the University Libraries at the University of Nevada, Las Vegas.

Celeste Calkins, PhD, is a postdoctoral scholar and institutional research data analyst at the University of Nevada, Las Vegas.

Debi Cheek, EdD, is the coaching coordinator for the Academic Success Center at the University of Nevada, Las Vegas.

Robert D. Cox, PhD, is an associate professor of habitat restoration ecology in the Department of Natural Resources Management at Texas Tech University.

Jill Darley-Vanis, MA, is a professor of English and adjunct faculty coordinator at Clark College in Vancouver, Washington.

Stefanie Drew, PhD, is an associate professor of psychology and the associate director of faculty development at California State University, Northridge.

Erin Farrar, MS, is director of campus recreational services and student recreation and wellness center facilities at the University of Nevada, Las Vegas.

Peter Felten, PhD, is an assistant provost for teaching and learning, executive director of the Center for Engaged Learning, and professor of history at Elon University.

Leeann Fields, MA, is assistant director of professional development and compliance at the University of Nevada, Las Vegas.

Ashley Finley, PhD, is senior adviser to the president, vice president for civic engagement and community, and secretary to the board at the Association of American Colleges & Universities.

Lisa Garner Santa, DMA, is a professor of flute in the School of Music at Texas Tech University.

Dan Gianoutsos, PhD, is associate dean of the Academic Success Center at the University of Nevada, Las Vegas.

Sunny Gittens, MS, is executive director of the Office of Student Engagement and Diversity at the University of Nevada, Las Vegas.

Ellen Haight is a PhD candidate in the Department of Educational Psychology and Counseling at the University of Tennessee, Knoxville.

Steven Hansen, PhD, is associate director for faculty development in the Center for Teaching Excellence at Duquesne University.

Sally Heilstedt, MA, is dean of instruction at Lake Washington Institute of Technology in Kirkland, Washington.

Katie Humphreys, PhD, is a consultant and former registrar at the University of Nevada, Las Vegas.

Pat Hutchings, PhD, is a senior scholar with the National Institute for Learning Outcomes Assessment and also with the Bay View Alliance.

Kathy E. Johnson, PhD, is executive vice chancellor and chief academic officer as well as a professor of psychology at Indiana University–Purdue University Indianapolis.

Gayle Juneau-Butler, PhD, is a coach consultant at Studer Education and served as assistant vice provost for retention, progression, completion at the University of Nevada, Las Vegas.

Jillian Kinzie, PhD, is a senior scholar with the National Institute for Learning Outcomes Assessment and associate director of Indiana University's Center for Postsecondary Research and the National Survey of Student Engagement (NSSE) Institute.

Deandra Little, PhD, is director of the Center for the Advancement of Teaching and Learning and associate professor of English at Elon University.

Emily Daniell Magruder, PhD, is director of the Institute for Teaching and Learning in the California State University Office of the Chancellor.

Anne Mendenhall, PhD, is principal learning producer at The Church of Jesus Christ of Latter-day Saints and served as director of online education at the University of Nevada, Las Vegas.

Sara Nasrollahian Mojarad is a doctoral student in the Department of Educational Psychology and Counseling at the University of Tennessee, Knoxville.

Julie Nelson Couch, PhD, is an associate professor of English at Texas Tech University.

Taimi Olsen, PhD, is the director of the Office of Teaching Effectiveness and Innovation at Clemson University.

Amy Overman, PhD, is associate director of the Center for the Advancement of Teaching and Learning and professor of psychology at Elon University.

Erin Rentschler, PhD, is assistant director for educational development in the Center for Teaching Excellence at Duquesne University.

James Rhem, PhD, is executive editor of the National Teaching & Learning Forum.

Kristina Ruiz-Mesa, PhD, is an assistant professor of communication studies at California State University, Los Angeles.

Whitney Scott, PhD, is a professor in the Department of Child and Adolescent Development at California State University, Northridge.

Gina M. Sully, PhD, is director of the writing center at the University of Nevada, Las Vegas.

Terri A. Tarr, PhD, is director of the Center for Teaching and Learning at Indiana University—Purdue University Indianapolis.

Jennifer Whetham, MFA, is the program administrator of faculty development at the Washington State Board for Community and Technical Colleges.

Michael Willard, PhD, is chair and professor in the Department of Liberal Studies at California State University, Los Angeles.

Laurel Willingham-McLain, PhD, is the director of the Center for Teaching Excellence at Duquesne University.

Ke Yu, MS, is a business intelligence analyst at the University of Nevada, Las Vegas.

(Continued from previous page)

"Middendorf and Shopkow provide an accessible and long-needed volume that speaks to both faculty and professional developers. Drawing on their expansive experiences and research, they articulate a wide range of contexts for applying the decoding methodology to strengthen faculty's epistemological underpinnings, transform teaching and learning, and inform strategies for curricular development. This valuable resource is accessible across disciplinary, institutional, and international contexts." —*Kathy Takayama, Director, Center for Advancing Teaching and Learning Through Research, Northeastern University*

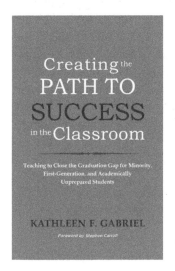

Creating the Path to Success in the Classroom

Teaching to Close the Graduation Gap for Minority, First-Generation, and Academically Unprepared Students

Kathleen F. Gabriel

Foreword by Stephen Carrol

"*Creating the Path to Success in the Classroom* totally delivers. As noted in this book, graduation rates for students in both four-year and two-year educational institutions are depressing. Something has to change, and this book is an important component in bringing about that change by noting how best to help our most vulnerable students. Chapter by chapter, Gabriel dissects and describes fundamental components that impact student success and provides specific strategies for bringing about successful learning outcomes. *Creating the Path to Success in the Classroom* will have a prominent place on my bookcase of essential resources for helping students to succeed in college." — *Todd Zakrajsek, University of North Carolina at Chapel Hill*

22883 Quicksilver Drive
Sterling, VA 20166-2019   Subscribe to our e-mail alerts: www.Styluspub.com

Also available from Stylus

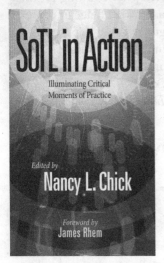

SoTL in Action

Illuminating Critical Moments of Practice

Edited by Nancy L. Chick

Foreword by James Rhem

The aim of this book is to support potential practitioners, inform educational developers who teach new SoTL practitioners, and inspire experienced SoTL scholars to reflect on their own practice. This is a compelling collection for anyone interested in practitioner reflection, intentional design, and advancing the field of SoTL and the quality of teaching and learning.

Overcoming Student Learning Bottlenecks

Decode the Critical Thinking of Your Discipline

Joan Middendorf and Leah Shopkow

Foreword by Dan Bernstein

"Learning can be hard, and one of the beauties of the decoding the disciplines process described in this new volume is its respect for the real difficulties students face as they encounter unfamiliar ideas and mental models. With those difficulties—or bottlenecks—as a starting point, Middendorf and Shopkow lay out an elegant step-by-step structure for improving learning, rethinking classroom practice, and creating a more teaching-positive campus culture."—**Pat Hutchings**, *Senior Scholar, National Institute for Learning Outcomes Assessment and Bay View Alliance*

(Continues on preceding page)